Class in Twentieth-Century
American Sociology

Class in Twentieth-Century American Sociology

An Analysis of Theories and Measurement Strategies

Michael D. Grimes

PRAEGER

New York
Westport, Connecticut
London

Library of Congress Cataloging-in-Publication Data

Grimes, Michael D.
  Class in twentieth-century American sociology : an analysis of
theories and measurement strategies / Michael D. Grimes.
    p.   cm.
  Includes bibliographical references (p.) and index.
  ISBN 0-275-93877-8 (alk. paper)
  1. Social classes—United States. 2. Social classes.
3. Sociology—United States—History. I. Title.
HN90.S6G75 1991
305.5'0973'0904—dc20   90-27840

British Library Cataloguing in Publication Data is available.

Library of Congress Catalog Card Number: 90-27840
ISBN: 0-275-93877-8

First published in 1991

Praeger Publishers, One Madison Avenue, New York, NY 10010
An imprint of Greenwood Publishing Group, Inc.

Printed in the United States of America

The paper used in this book complies with the
Permanent Paper Standard issued by the National
Information Standards Organization (Z39.48–1984).

10 9 8 7 6 5 4 3 2 1

To Michael, Sherry, George, James, and Marci —

my family

CONTENTS

FIGURES AND TABLE

PREFACE

The subject of this book, class inequality, is unavoidably ideological, and, as a consequence, each of us approaches it with certain "taken-for-granteds" that derive from our own unique experiences as incumbents of class positions. My own interest in the subject has its origins in my youth in a Southeast Texas oil "boom" town during the early post–World War II period in American history. In those heady days of American world economic and political hegemony, like most Americans, we were bombarded with a number of key messages that were a part of the conventional wisdom of that period in the nation's history: that America was rapidly becoming a "classless" society; that economic prosperity was within the grasp of all; that success depended upon achievement rather than ascription; and, relatedly, that each of us, regardless of class, race/ethnic, or gender background, had the same opportunity for success. My peers and I, the sons and daughters of (white) working-class families, absorbed these messages like sponges and they quickly became a part of our world views.

However, as we began to move out of our neighborhood environment and encounter the larger world, we began to notice discrepancies between the messages we had internalized and the realities we confronted in our everyday lives. In my own personal experiences within this larger environment, class differences, in particular, seemed to play an increasingly significant role in influencing the life chances of myself and those around me. The effects of class, both subtle and blatant, were apparent to me in a number of different contexts — not only in my family's relative material circumstances, but at church, at school, in politics, and in various social and leisure activities as well. At almost every turn, I found myself and my peers (not to mention our parents) suffering disadvantages relative to our middle- and upper-class counterparts.

In reaction to these relative disadvantages, my peers and I initially simply followed the conventional wisdom and "blamed the victims" (ourselves and our parents) for our personal lack of whatever the key ingredient for success in the particular circumstance happened to be, whether it was "spirituality," "intelligence," "motivation," "manners," "speech," "appearance," "formal education," and so on. In fact, in conformity with the conventional wisdom, many of my former peers (not to mention a large majority of other Americans) have continued to use this approach as a means for understanding their relative successes and failures. For others of us, however, there was sufficient contradictory evidence to suggest that personal attributes alone were not sufficient to explain the many different impacts of class that we observed and experienced. Once stimulated, my own continued awareness of and interest in class inequality eventually led me to seek explanations from within the social sciences in general, and, then, from sociology in particular.

My formal training in the discipline took place during the decade of the 1960s, a time of turmoil and rapid social change within American society as a whole, and a period of growing discontent within the discipline. This training, for the first time, exposed me to ideas critical of our political economy — ideas that seemed better able than the conventional wisdom of my early education to explain the diverse impacts of class that continued to influence the lives of many Americans. Some of the personal consequences of this exposure for me were a move toward the left ideologically and various forms of active participation in efforts to increase society's awareness of the poverty, racism, sexism, and imperialism that are endemic to American society. Professionally, if I had not already (by then) decided to focus my academic interests toward such issues, I certainly did so during this period in my life. Since then, I have spent more than 20 years studying and teaching about inequality, and engaging in various forms of advocacy concerning the melioration of its negative consequences. Within the context of these experiences, it should be clear that I do not, because I cannot, approach the subject matter of this volume without bringing this ideological baggage along with me.

As a part of my efforts to learn more about class, I quite naturally turned to the work of American social scientists. As I have gradually become more familiar with the voluminous literature published in twentieth-century American media on the subject, I have formed several impressions. The first of these is that, during the history of the discipline, there is diversity in the manners in which sociologists have approached the subject. The second is that, for heuristic purposes, the various ways of approaching class inequality can be organized into two basic schools of thought —

"consensus" and "conflict" — according to the nature of the assumptions each makes about human nature and society, and about the
roles that class plays in society. The third impression is that, over
time, the relative popularity of these two perspectives within the
discipline has varied. The fourth is that a fruitful means for understanding this variety is to situate it within the overall sociohistorical,
ideological, disciplinary, and biographical settings within which
each school's perspectives have appeared, prospered, and declined in
relative influence. Thus far in the discipline's history, only a few
studies have attempted to examine theories of class inequality within
American sociology using such a framework, and those that have
done so have been limited substantively or temporally. The purpose of
this book is to fill this important gap in our collective knowledge about
the study of class within American sociology.

One result of my decision to focus attention on the subject of class
inequality in this volume is that little will be said here about other
structural inequalities, such as those based on political, racial/ethnic
identity, or gender. By their omission, I certainly do not intend to
discount or diminish their importance as salient influences on the
lives of American citizens. However, there are both theoretical and
practical justifications for my decision to confine attention here to
issues surrounding class inequality. In terms of the former, I share
with other conflict scholars the belief that, despite the changes that
have taken place since Marx's time, class remains a significant
structural variable affecting the lives of the citizens of advanced
democratic capitalist societies. My personal opinion is that this belief
alone is a sufficient justification for confining attention in this
volume to the issue of class inequality. However, an additional
theoretical rationale for my decision is that, while scholarship within
the discipline has addressed class, political, race/ethnic, and gender
as *separate* dimensions of structural inequality, there has not been
(to date at least), a great deal of progress in dealing with the complex
issue of the *interaction* among these various dimensions. While there
is evidence within contemporary literature (particularly that written
from a "conflict" perspective) that scholars are now beginning to
address this shortcoming, the underdeveloped state of research on
the interrelationships of these various dimensions of inequality offers
a second theoretical justification for confining attention in this
volume more narrowly to the subject of class inequality. From a more
practical standpoint, the complexity of the debates surrounding class
inequality suggests that an adequate exploration of that subject alone
represents a sizable undertaking in its own right. Expanding
coverage to include analysis and commentary on the interaction of
class with the other dimensions of societal inequality would be a
large, unwieldy project. For these reasons, then, I will confine this
inquiry to issues concerning the subject of class inequality.

There are a number of individuals who have had an impact on my perspective. My parents' lifelong struggle to provide for their family and to insure that their children would have a better life than their own has been a very important influence on my life. The efforts of my sister, Sherry, and my brother, George, both to manage their own lives and to contribute to society have also been crucial to my perspective. A lifelong friend and fellow working-class "expatriate," Fred Guarnere, has always been there to provide support and encouragement when I have needed him over the years. Clyde Bullion, my first sociology professor and later friend and colleague, first made me aware of the potential depth and breadth of a "sociological imagination." Chuck Bonjean, who served as major professor for my graduate degrees, provided badly needed guidance and encouragement and helped me to refine and better express my thoughts. Norval Glenn both introduced me to sociological literature on class and served as a positive role model for what it is like to be a professional academic. Joe Lopreato challenged (and was influential in changing) many of my ideas about sociology by exposing me to radical perspectives on the subject. Finally, assisting my son Michael in his efforts to understand and react to the unique influences of class that affect his generation of young Americans has also had a significant influence on the evolution of my own thoughts on the subject.

A number of students and colleagues have contributed to the more limited project reported in this book. Students in my graduate seminars in class inequality over the years have helped me to formulate and better articulate my positions on the various issues within the subject matter area. More immediately, I thank Pam Jenkins, David Maurer, Alice Kemp, John Holmwood, Kevin Smith, Monika Zeehetmayr, Roberta St. Pierre, and Joachim Singelmann for reading and reacting to the manuscript as it has developed during the past few years. My secretary, Julie DeJean, has provided excellent technical assistance in the preparation of the manuscript. In retrospect, I'm sure that the book has profited from their efforts. Any errors, omissions, oversights, or misinterpretations that managed to survive their scrutiny, however, remain my personal responsibility.

Class in Twentieth-Century
American Sociology

1

INTRODUCTION

The subject of class has had a long and controversial career in the history of American sociology. To date, two major studies have explicitly addressed the subject: Charles Page's *Class and American Sociology* (1940), which deals with the period between the late nineteenth century and the 1920s, and Milton Gordon's *Social Class in American Sociology* (1963), which focuses on the period between 1925 and 1955. Together these pioneering efforts provide a comprehensive overview of research on the subject within the discipline during the first half of the twentieth century.

Despite their important contributions, two limitations continue to plague contemporary attempts to understand the career of the subject within the discipline — one temporal, the other substantive/theoretical. The temporal limitation is obvious — the period of coverage for these two books ended almost 40 years ago, and no other study has attempted to update our knowledge about the subject to the present.[1] The second limitation is substantive/theoretical — despite the fact that each of these studies attempted to situate its overview of research within overarching sociohistorical, disciplinary, and theoretical contexts, neither adequately did so from the point of view of contemporary standards within the discipline. The present study takes these limitations as its point of departure. As a result, it seeks to provide a framework within which the changing character of the theories and methodologies employed by scholars in their study of class inequality within American sociology can be interpreted and understood and to employ this framework to describe and analyze the major perspectives on the subject within American sociology since the turn of the century.

This chapter begins with a brief overview of these two pioneering studies that highlights their strengths and weaknesses. Because the shortcomings of these studies point to the need for the construction of

an analytic framework from within which the study of class
inequality within the discipline can be understood, this framework is
developed next. Finally, the framework is applied to twentieth
century American sociology in general as a means for providing a
setting for the analysis of research on the subject of class inequality
by members of the discipline.

OVERVIEW OF EARLY STUDIES OF CLASS
INEQUALITY WITHIN THE DISCIPLINE

Our collective knowledge about the study of class inequality
within American sociology has profited from the work of the two
scholars just mentioned — Charles Page and Milton Gordon. Page's
study, based on his dissertation research at Columbia University,
was conducted during the decade of the 1930s and focuses on the
founding fathers of the discipline — Lester Ward, William Sumner,
Albion Small, Franklin Giddings, Charles Cooley, and Edward Ross
— and the roles played by class in their work. A unique feature of
Page's work is that it devotes particular attention to the rapidly
changing conditions within American society during the post–Civil
War period and examines the influences of these conditions on the
perspectives of these scholars. Within the context of this setting, Page
presents a detailed analysis of the perspective of each of these figures
on the role of class in society, taking special effort to demonstrate the
theoretical ties between these scholars and their predecessors in
Europe.

In Page's presentations of the perspectives of these founding
fathers, he demonstrates both the commonalities and the differences
in the manners in which each treated the subject, showing, for
example, that those whose early lives were spent in the East were
more status quo oriented, while those from the Midwest were more
critical both of society as a whole and of the role of class within society. In spite of his detailed treatment of the ways in which
these scholars used class in their work and his claim that they
were the only social scientists who were even remotely interested in the topic during this important period in the country's
history, Page concludes that these scholars did not elevate class
phenomena to an important position within their work. His
explanation for this fact is that their interests, like those of most of
the American intelligentsia, were "colored" by the "classlessness" of
the American scene (Page 1940:250). He concludes that these
scholars seemed to prefer "the superordination of *community* over all
intra-community groups" (p. 250). However, he does condition this
claim by noting that, toward the end of the period of his study (the late
1920s), sociologists were, indeed, becoming more interested in the
issue of class.

Page's book contains a wealth of information about early figures in the discipline and their treatment of the subject of class inequality. Three aspects of his work deserve particular praise. First, he stresses the role of the sociohistorical context within which the authors were socialized and began their careers and seeks to demonstrate the impact of this context on their work. Second, he also deals with the theoretical ties between these scholars and others within the social sciences, particularly those of European origin. Third, his analysis also focuses on the nature of the discipline during the periods of active scholarship of these authors and speculates on the potential role of these influences on their conceptualizations of class and assessments of its relative importance within society. For these reasons alone, the book clearly deserves Pitirim Sorokin's (1940:662) conclusion that "it is a real contribution to sociological theory."

The second major analysis of class inequality within the discipline is Milton Gordon's *Social Class in American Sociology*, first published in 1950, then updated in 1958. This book deals with the period from 1925 to 1955, and takes up the subject where Page's work left off (D. Smith 1959:371).[2]

Gordon begins his analysis by describing the use of class by human ecologists at Chicago and in Sorokin's classic work *Social Mobility* (1927). He concludes that, while the ecologists dealt only indirectly with class, they nevertheless showed sensitivity to the concept. While he credits Sorokin's important analytical contributions to class theory, he faults him for his lack of attention to empirical issues. Gordon then discusses the research of community scholars. He devotes a chapter each to Robert and Helen Lynd's efforts in "Middletown" (1929 and 1937), to W. Lloyd Warner's research in "Yankee City" (1941) and in "Jonesville" (1949b), and to other studies that were completed later and relied on these earlier efforts for guidance.

Gordon next devotes attention to what he labels "significant problem areas" within the discipline and the "logic of stratification scales." In the "problems" section, he addresses such issues as "functionalism," "the nature of the status order," "class as class consciousness," and "class, occupation, and the mass society." This latter chapter contains a good overview of the issues of concern to class analysts during the period in question. In the "scales" chapter, he reviews and analyzes the earliest scales utilized in class analysis within the discipline, including those by Stuart Chapin, Verner Sims, Alice Leahy, William Sewell, Lloyd Warner, Cecil North and Paul Hatt, and Alba Edwards.

Finally, Gordon offers his own assessment of the place of class within the discipline. He begins by noting the importance of economic factors in class analysis, but then argues that economic factors alone are not sufficient: "The complex and innumerable interweavings of economic factors with politico-community power, with the status structure, with occupational preemption, with cultural attributes, and with group-life divisions constitutes what might be called the social-class system" (Gordon 1963:234). He ends by suggesting that the Weberian trinity of class, status, and power are the most salient variables for use in class analysis.[3]

Reviewers of Gordon's book were impressed with its author's efforts (compare D. Smith 1959; Sjoberg 1959; Chinoy 1959), and the book has served an important role within the discipline — that of updating our knowledge about conceptual and methodological issues in class analysis from the mid-1920s to the mid-1950s. At the same time, it differs from its predecessor (Page's book) in at least one important respect: its relative lack of detailed attention to the settings within which these efforts were developed, and to the influences of disciplinary and biographical factors on the authors' perspectives. Perhaps this can be explained by the author's intended focus on analytical and methodological issues. Yet the omission of these influences detracts from his effort just as the inclusion of them benefitted Page's work. A statement from Sjoberg's (1959:648) review of the book stresses the negative implications of this omission in the book: "Gordon gives all too little attention to the great social forces of our time — wars, a great depression, industrialization-urbanization and even the extension of the democratic process — and fails to adequately deal with the problem of studying social class in process."

Despite their differences, the two books remain landmarks for understanding the use of class within the discipline's early history. *Early* is stressed here because the period of coverage provided by the two books ended with 1955, and no other comparable work covers the period since then. This lack of information on more contemporary research suggests that an update is needed. Such an update should combine the best features of its two predecessors. For example, while Page devotes considerable attention in his work to contextual influences on the theories he discusses, Gordon prefers to discuss these theories in relative isolation. In light of recent scholarship concerning the "sociology of sociology," Page's approach clearly offers greater insights into this important subject. As a result, this study reflects Page's strategy by stressing the roles of such influences as the sociohistorical setting, the dominant ideology, the state of the discipline, and the interaction of these factors with the unique biography of the scholar in influencing the product of his or her labors. While Gordon's book does not stress these particular influences, his effort is more systematic than Page's in its treatment of conceptual and methodological issues. Because this strategy is likewise preferred to the alternative, this study also devotes explicit attention to conceptual and methodological issues when considering the ways in which class was employed by researchers. The period of coverage for this study will overlap with those of the previous authors and extend through to the present (the early 1990s).

TOWARD AN ANALYTIC FRAMEWORK

The last two decades have been significant ones for sociology. During this period the discipline began to turn its own tools inward and to examine the basic philosophical foundations upon which it rests. However, this newly discovered introspection was not a random occurrence; it was instead a response to rapidly changing social conditions and the relative *inability* of established sociological perspectives either to anticipate or to fully explain these changing conditions. In this sense, then, what one major disciplinary analyst (Gouldner 1970) has labeled a "crisis" began within the discipline during the 1960s. One important positive consequence of this crisis period was that the often-unstated assumptions upon which the sociological enterprise had rested for the previous 40 or so years were made public, criticized, and challenged. As a result, this was a period of great intellectual ferment within the discipline — established perspectives were criticized and modified; new, alternative perspectives were put forward, and a great deal of effort was devoted to addressing the various theoretical and methodological concerns that emerged from the debates among scholars. In order to get a perspective on events within the discipline during this period in its history, it is important to develop a frame of reference. This section of the chapter provides an overview of a key study on the growth of the knowledge process and derives from it the frame of reference that will guide the study.

Thomas Kuhn's Model of Scientific "Revolutions"

One of the most insightful (and controversial) "models" of the process by which knowledge develops and changes within science has been offered by the scientific historian Thomas Kuhn (1970). The major focus of Kuhn's work is to demonstrate the inadequacy of the popular view (derived in part from scientific textbooks) that science changes slowly over time as new information is added to existing knowledge in a sort of cumulative, evolutionary manner, and to suggest and defend a radically different explanation based on the role of major discrepancies in the knowledge-accumulation process and that stresses a "revolutionary" model of change.

Kuhn begins with the notion that a science, in any given period, is dominated by a particular *image of its subject matter* (or, to put it another way, a particular way of looking at its world). He labels such

images "paradigms," and characterizes them as "some accepted
examples of actual scientific practice (that) provide models from
which spring coherent traditions of scientific research" (Kuhn
1970:10). This image or paradigm typically emerges from a "pre-
paradigm" (or prescientific) period wherein a number of different
candidates for dominance compete for the allegiances of practitioners
in the field.[4] He argues that the disappearance of this competition
among alternatives "is usually caused by the triumph of one of the
pre-paradigm schools, which, because of its own characteristic
beliefs and preconceptions, emphasizes only some special part of the
too sizable and inchoate pool of information" (Kuhn 1970:17). Once a
paradigm is established as dominant, a period that Kuhn calls
"normal science" begins, during which research is guided by the
paradigm and its preeminence is established. Kuhn (p. 24) shows us
the relationship between a paradigm and the period of normal
science within a discipline as follows:

> the success of a paradigm ... is at the start largely a
> promise of success discoverable in selected and still
> incomplete examples. Normal science consists in the
> actualization of that promise, an actualization achieved by
> extending the knowledge of those facts that the paradigm
> displays as particularly revealing, by increasing the extent of
> match between those facts and the paradigm's predictions,
> and by further articulation of the paradigm itself.

While this period of intensive research is essential for bolstering
the paradigm's position as the dominant perspective within a field,
an inevitable consequence is that it also generates "anomalies," or
facts and events that the paradigm cannot explain. If the amount of
evidence supporting these anomalies grows large, a "crisis" period
ensues within the discipline, wherein the dominant paradigm must
defend itself against other potential explanations for the anomalies
based on alternative perspectives. If the dominant paradigm subsequently is unable to account for these discrepancies, and,
importantly, if a competing paradigm seems better able to do so, a
"scientific revolution" occurs, and the alternative paradigm assumes
dominance. Then follows another normal science period with the
new paradigm providing the perspective within which science is
viewed. Should it, too, prove unable to defend itself against subsequent anomalies (and challenges), the cycle is repeated.

The term "scientific" has been employed thus far to stress the fact
that Kuhn's theory is based on the *natural* sciences, and he, himself,
has questioned whether it can be applied equally well as a model for
describing the growth of knowledge process in other fields. He is
particularly skeptical with regard to the social sciences: "it remains

an open question what parts of social science have yet acquired such paradigms at all. . . . History suggests that the road to a firm research consensus is extraordinarily arduous" (p. 15).[5] He holds this view despite the fact that he derives the idea for his theory from several disciplines that are clearly not within the physical sciences, including psychology, philosophy, and linguistics.

Kuhn's skepticism about the applicability of his scheme to social science has not been shared by a number of the members of the social science community, particularly sociologists. Douglas Eckberg and Lester Hill's (1979) overview of the various applications of his perspective within sociology reviews a total of 12 studies, and there are a number of others as well. One of the most important of their observations concerning these applications is their diversity, in terms of both particular uses of the perspective and findings regarding the paradigmatic status of the discipline. These authors isolate two important issues that have emerged with regard to the application of Kuhn's perspective in any context, but particularly within the social sciences: the ambiguous usage of the term "paradigm" (in both Kuhn's own work as well as those who have attempted to apply his perspective); and the fact that many applications, including his own, have failed to devote sufficient attention to the sociohistorical context within which theories are constructed, tested, and refined. Each of these issues is briefly discussed below.

The Meanings of "Paradigm"

Eckberg and Hill's (1979) explanation for the divergences in both the application of the term and the results of the studies that they reviewed reflects a common complaint about Kuhn's work — the ambiguity in his use of the key concept "paradigm." Analysts of this particular problem conclude that Kuhn used the term in as many as 21 different ways, organized into three different "levels" of meaning: "metaphysical," "disciplinary matrix," and "exemplar" (Masterman 1970).[6] Others claim that these are arranged into a hierarchy within his work, with exemplar embedded within the disciplinary matrix and the disciplinary matrix in turn embedded within the metaphysical (Eckberg and Hill 1979). In addition to this "level of analysis" issue, Eckberg and Hill (p. 926) also note that many sociologists have also misused the concept by failing to realize that two other aspects were central to Kuhn's use of the term: "the *cognitive* nature of paradigms and the *community* structure within which they appear." In terms of this particular issue, they note that many sociologists have made use of only one of these facets of the meaning of the term (generally the former) and that their analyses can be faulted for this omission. Because of such problems, they conclude that sociologists have fundamentally changed the way in which Kuhn meant for paradigms to be defined and offer the following indictment: "When used by sociologists, however, the term comes most often to mean no more than a *general theoretical perspective*" [italics added] (Eckberg and Hill 1979:929).

In short, then, one key impediment to the application of the Kuhnian perspective within the social sciences is the ambiguous nature of his own application of the concept paradigm. This seems to be the case despite his efforts to clarify the original confusion (compare Kuhn 1970, 1974). Because this problem is a crucial one that is also not likely to be resolved to the satisfaction of all, the question becomes: "Given that the most important portion of his perspective is mired in a sea of terminological confusion, what utility does the perspective offer to those seeking to understand the process of the accumulation of knowledge?" I will return to this issue following discussion of Eckberg and Hill's second issue.

The Sociohistorical Context

A second important issue concerning the application of Kuhn's work to the social sciences is its failure to devote explicit attention to the roles of extrascientific influences on the growth-of-knowledge process. It is clear from his own remarks that he was sensitive to both the possibility for and the potential importance of such issues:

> more important, except in occasional brief asides, I have said nothing about the role of technological advances or of external social, economic, and intellectual conditions in the development of the sciences. Explicit consideration of effects like these would not, I think, modify the main thesis developed in this essay, but it would surely add an analytical dimension of first-rate importance for the understanding of scientific advances (Kuhn 1970:x).

While undoubtedly such contextual factors are important influences for any theory's development, the particular nature of social science theories makes them crucial. Additionally, attention to such factors could serve to highlight the most important asset of Kuhn's work — its analysis of the *process of change in scientific knowledge over time*, a subject ignored by most applications of Kuhn's perspective. Many, if not most, of these have taken as their subject the issues of determining just what Kuhn meant by "paradigm," whether or not there are paradigms within the discipline, and, if so, their identification (compare Ritzer 1980; Bryant 1975). Few of these studies have focused on the process by which the growth of knowledge occurs within the discipline. It could be argued that the former issue — the paradigmatic status of the discipline — must be resolved first because of its importance in Kuhn's scheme. However, given the difficulties in resolving that issue, to take that course of action would preclude the exploration of other valuable insights that his framework offers. If, on the other hand, at least a partial resolution to this apparent impasse is possible, then attention can be directed to the other important features of his perspective.

The Analytic Framework of the Study

Any effort to develop a strategy for circumventing some, but certainly not all, of the difficulties inherent in any use of Kuhn's perspective within the social sciences must address Eckberg and Hill's (1979:933) claim that a rigorous application of Kuhn's perspective insists that "paradigmatic status is determined by the workings of a unified group of specialists. If such is the case, one cannot divide a discipline freely into paradigms, but one must be constrained by both *group structure* and *cognitive consensus*." Accepting these rather rigorous requirements, it seems probable that there are no paradigms within sociology at the present time. The reasons for the absence of paradigms are varied and may even lie within the very nature of the discipline itself (Kuhn 1970; Lodahl and Gordon 1972).

While there may be no paradigms within the discipline, this does not mean that distinctive perspectives cannot be identified within the discipline — a number of previous efforts have defined just such perspectives (Friedrichs 1970; Ritzer 1980; Turner 1982).[7] These perspectives have at least three important things in common with paradigms: their implicit assumptions about human nature and society serve to structure scholarly inquiry in diverse ways; they are shared by different groups of scholars within the discipline; and they have tended to vary over time in terms of their relative popularity among practitioners within the discipline. If such reasonably different points of view do, in fact, exist, and yet they are not sufficiently distinctive to meet the requirements noted above for the label paradigm, then what is their nature, and what should they be called? Eckberg and Hill (p 935) seem to prefer the label "general theoretical perspective,"[8] but their own use of this term lacks sufficient specificity. Others have employed labels such as "schools of thought" (Dahrendorf 1958; Tiryakian 1979) or "theory groups" (Mullins 1973) to describe these and other similar points of view. An advantage of these terms is that their use tends to bring into better focus the "community of scholars" dimension of the term that Eckberg and Hill insist is a crucial part of Kuhn's meaning for paradigms. For this reason, the phrase "schools of thought" will be employed here because it seems to capture best the meanings of the various perspectives on class inequality that are the focus of the remainder of the book.

Because the phrase "schools of thought" shares a certain ambiguity with many other alternatives, it is necessary at the outset to specify a number of defining attributes: such "schools" have fundamentally different assumptions about human nature and society; these assumptions result in very different images of the various institutions within society, including those concerning class inequality; these perspectives conceptualize and measure class in fundamentally different ways; the emergence of these "schools" and their relative popularity among the members of the discipline are conditioned by a number of contextual effects, including the overall state of the political economy, the dominant ideology, disciplinary peculiarities, and the unique biographies of the theorists who construct them; and in order to explicitly capture the "community of scholars" aspect of the meaning of the phrase, each of these points of view is identified both with individual scholars as well as with loosely organized groups of scholars.[9]

By means of such a conceptualization, it is possible to make use of Kuhn's insights into the growth of knowledge process within sociology without meeting all of the criteria for the application of his label "paradigm" to the various perspectives that are the focus of this analysis. In particular, the analysis below explores the emergence and subsequent careers of these perspectives within the discipline using insights derived from Kuhn's work and interprets these perspectives from within a framework that more explicitly reflects the sociohistorical and ideological contexts. The following sections provide an overview of the application of this framework to the discipline during the period of concern for this study.

THE CHANGING NATURE OF
SOCIOLOGICAL KNOWLEDGE

A review of the history of the discipline using the ideas developed above suggests that American sociology was, indeed, in what Kuhn would call a "pre-paradigm" ("preschools-of-thought" in my terms) stage in its development from about the turn of the century until the decade of the 1930s. During this period in its development, sociology was heavily indebted to other social science disciplines, particularly anthropology and economics, for both theoretical and methodological strategies (Madge 1962; Oberschall 1972; Bannister 1987). However, the particular indebtedness was general rather than specific, because sociologists were employing bits and pieces from a large variety of different sources in their work (Small 1916). It was in this sense, then, that the discipline was more "pre-" than "paradigmatic" (in Kuhn's terms).

This situation began to change during the decade between the mid-1930s and World War II, as changes began to occur within the discipline — changes that were the result of forces both external to and within the discipline itself (Gouldner 1970). Following on the heels of the first worldwide economic collapse in modern history (an event almost completely unanticipated by classical social scientists such as Adam Smith, David Ricardo, and J. B. Say), the rapid collapse of old regimes in Europe and their replacement by the forces of Nazism and fascism caused great concern among intellectuals about the political and economic stability of the world and about the adequacy of extant theories to predict and explain these events. The fact that these events led to the outbreak of World War II, which further threatened world security, merely added to this climate of uncertainty and insecurity.

These "external" events provided the setting within which sociology was struggling to establish itself as a distinctive scientific discipline within the academic community (Oberschall 1972). The result of the confluence of these external influences and forces internal to the social sciences and to sociology itself was the emergence of a single school of thought — labeled the "consensus" school. Relying heavily upon classical economics, particularly the work of Adam Smith, research on systems from the biologist L. S. Henderson, notions derived from the British social anthropologists B. K. Malinowski and A. R. Radcliffe-Brown, the work of postrevolutionary French social philosophers, particularly that of Emile Durkheim, and the work of Max Weber, Talcott Parsons, along with both colleagues and students, began to organize the previously discordant elements contained within sociology's field of vision into a more rigorously organized, general theoretical perspective labeled "structural-functionalism." By the mid-1940s, within the discipline this perspective had indeed become the single dominant school of thought in the sense that the term is being employed here (Kuklick 1972; Mullins 1973; Ritzer 1983).

By the decade of the 1950s, then, sociology was entering what Kuhn would call a period of normal science with structural-functionalism as the dominant school of thought within the discipline. Recall that, according to Kuhn, such a period is one of intense activity devoted to establishing the promise of the new perspective through both research and application by its supporters. "Consensus" sociology's period of normal science occupied the next 10 to 15 years; a period in world history characterized by the rebuilding of a new world order based on the principles of political stability, economic cooperation and growth, directed primarily by the United States. Peace prevailed both at home and abroad, and it was a period of unrivaled economic growth in both the world as a whole and in America in particular (Cohen and Rogers 1983).

During such a (normal science) period, as Kuhn's perspective suggests, much if not most of the research within the discipline accepts the basic assumptions and theoretical orientations of the dominant school of thought. Yet it should be noted that Kuhn did not contend that the hegemony of the dominant perspective would be total.[10] He simply stressed that it would be the perspective accepted and employed by a majority of the scholars engaged in research within the field. In the case of sociology, there were writers who were both critical of the dominant perspective and who offered alternative perspectives. Perhaps the best example of such a person is C. Wright Mills.[11] In *The Sociological Imagination* (1959), he was not only critical of "established" sociology — taking both the "grand theorists" of the Parsonian variety and the "abstracted empiricists" at Columbia and Chicago, who took as their role model the natural sciences, to task — but he also stressed an alternative form of inquiry, making use of what he called the "sociological imagination" that stressed both the personal (and therefore the "ideological") content of knowledge and the influences of the sociohistorical context on the development of thought (Horowitz 1983). The fact that Mills' work was heavily criticized by consensus-school scholars and its contributions were not fully acknowledged until after his death lends additional support to Kuhn's claim that research considered outside the dominant paradigm is, at best, received unenthusiastically, and, at worst, often ignored by those embracing the dominant perspective (a group that includes, by definition, a majority of the scholars within the discipline).[12] Thus, despite the efforts of scholars like Mills, who was decidedly *outside* of and critical toward the consensus school's perspective, certainly by the end of World War II, this perspective had a sufficiently strong following among sociologists that it was hegemonic within the discipline. This dominance would continue for the next 15 to 20 years.

Events during the 1960s provided a fundamental challenge to establishment sociology, which had, as noted above, only recently emerged from a long period of disciplinary confusion and chaos. In fact, to many scholars within the field, it may have seemed that the discipline and its leading spokespersons had only just begun to receive the long past due credit for its/their unique perspectives on society when the challenges of this new decade began to threaten sociology's newly found status and prestige within the academic community. It is interesting that these challenges were at first, despite the efforts of scholars like Lynd (1940), Mills (1959), and Ralf Dahrendorf (1958, 1959), decidedly extradisciplinary in character. These challenges began early in the decade with the civil rights movement among black Americans who had not been able to assimilate themselves into the mainstream of American society as had so many other ethnic-cultural minorities before them, and on which consensus-school explanations of majority-minority inter-action patterns had modeled the assimilation process. At about this same time, scholars such as Michael Harrington (1962, 1984) were "discovering" widespread poverty in America in a period of unparalleled economic growth and prosperity — again, contrary to consensus-based explanations. Both of these issues were converted into national political issues by the "War on Poverty" of the Kennedy and Johnson administrations in many ways, because they stood in such sharp contrast to the "achievement-based" explanations of neoclassical economic theory, consensus sociology, and other social science perspectives (Lewis 1978). By the middle of the decade, major cities in the United States, including Washington, D.C., were experiencing massive civil disturbances. Subsequent analyses have shown these riots to be a reaction to the disappointments of the poor and blacks with their realization that the aspirations engendered by the War on Poverty and the civil rights movement were not being fulfilled for many because our involvement in Vietnam was draining funds to such an extent that the "war" on poverty came to be seen as a tragic misnomer (*Report of the National Advisory Commission on Civil Disorders* 1968). By the last third of the decade, in reaction to these same stimuli, students at a number of U.S. colleges and universities were demonstrating their anger and frustrations over the U.S. involvement in Southeast Asia and the senseless loss of life there, the draft, ROTC training operations on campuses, and outdated moral and behavioral codes that were also consistent with consensus sociology's theoretical perspective. Finally, by the end of the decade, women were becoming more aware of the social structural and cultural barriers to their full participation in American life. These particular barriers to women's full participation in society were explained by consensus theory as, in part, necessary for the smooth operation of the division of labor in society and in the family (compare Parsons 1951).

In short, the events of the 1960s provided disturbing "anomalies" (to use Kuhn's term) to consensus-inspired sociological explanations, and, in a sense, set the stage for a period of "crisis" (or, again, to use Kuhn's term, "abnormal science") that began late during the decade and continues today within American sociology. As a result, theoretical perspectives based on the consensus model are increasingly being challenged by perspectives based on other models within the discipline in general, as well as within different subject matter areas in particular. These challenges have been particularly widespread in the area of consensus theory's perspective on class inequality.

THE ROLE OF VALUES WITHIN THE SOCIOLOGICAL ENTERPRISE

One of the earliest conclusions to be reached by analysts of sociology's disciplinary crisis (this subject matter area is now called the "sociology of sociology") is the *ideological* character of sociological theories. As discussed above, by the 1960s, events within the larger society had begun to fundamentally challenge the recently emerged theoretical foundation of the discipline's dominant perspective. This theoretical foundation, born during the 1930s, nurtured in the 1940s, and maturing in the 1950s, had explicitly sought to mirror the "value-free" posture of the natural sciences as a means for establishing its legitimacy among the more established disciplines (Gouldner 1970; Kinloch 1981; Bannister 1987).[13] This particular orientation stressed an "objective" approach to both society and social issues. In this context, Gouldner (1970:55) summarizes this orientation as follows:

> it cannot be stressed too strongly that in everyday practice the sociologist believed himself capable of making hundreds of purely rational decisions — the choice of research problems, sites, question formulations, statistical tests, or sampling methods. He thinks of these as free technical decisions and of himself as acting in autonomous conformity with technical standards rather than as a creature molded by social structure and culture.

As the discipline's "crisis" continued, American sociologists began to analyze the dominant perspective and to make efforts to adapt it to these challenges. A major outcome of such efforts was the discovery that the perspective was based on certain *latent* or *implicit* assumptions that had a determinant influence on the explanations that resulted from its application to the description, analysis, and explanation for events within the social milieu. Gouldner (1970:29) was among the first to systematically draw attention to these underlying assumptions:

> deliberately formulated social theories, we might say with deliberate oversimplification, contain at least two distinguishable elements. One element is the explicitly formulated assumptions, which might be called "postulations." But they contain a good deal more. They also contain a second set of assumptions that are unpostulated and unlabeled, and these I will term "background assumptions." I call them background assumptions because, on the one hand, they provide the background out of which the postulations emerge, and, on the other hand, not being expressly formulated, they remain in the background of the theorist's attention.

For sociology in particular, these background assumptions deal with the images of human nature and the social order, as well as their fusion into a composite image reflecting the interaction of the two. And,

importantly, they are not "value-free" but rather, they are, of necessity, "value-laden," since they are derivative from the immersion of
the theorist along with her or his subject matter within a sociohistorical context; they thus reflect *both* this particular setting and the
unique experiences of the theorist within it (Mills 1959; Wallerstein
1976). This is true because such assumptions "provide the inherited
intellectual 'capital' with which a theorist is endowed long before he
becomes a theorist, and which he later invests in his intellectual and
scientific roles, fusing it to his technical training" (Gouldner
1970:34). Gouldner has labeled these summed influences the "world
view" of the theorist. As noted earlier, this world view is unavoidably
"ideological" because it necessarily reflects the theorist's position
within the social order and the "interests" that are derived from that
position. As Kinloch (1981:3) has summarized the situation: "there is
a growing, though still limited, awareness of the extent to which . . .
all 'knowledge' is ideological, in that it represents the vested interests
and viewpoints of particular social groups in specific situations."

The particular world view that emerged from an examination of
the implicit assumptions of functionalism is decidedly conservative,
since it "explains and defends existing institutions, especially those
concerned with government, the economy, and the social structure"
(Carlton 1977:35). As a result, stressing as it does consensus and
equilibrium within the social system, a defense of the existing social
order, and focusing on stability rather than change, this perspective
and its theories had difficulty anticipating or explaining many of the
events common to the period of the 1960s in U.S. society.

In response to this crisis, while some sociologists sought to
modify the dominant perspective to account for these discrepancies,
others began to search for alternative perspectives that could provide
more adequate explanations. A number of scholars began to turn to
the work of other, more radical, scholarly traditions such as
Marxism as an alternative. The world view implicit in the Marxist
tradition is vastly different from that of established sociology in that it
is "revolutionary" in character and, as such, attacks rather than
defends the existing social order (Carlton 1977:35). Marx's perspective also differs from the established viewpoint because it advocates
both "value-guided" research and a theorist's active social intervention to change society. While many established sociologists have
found Marxism unacceptable because of its apparent divergence
from the natural science model, a growing number of scholars have
become increasingly attracted to it.[14]

"SCHOOLS OF THOUGHT" IN MODERN SOCIOLOGY

As suggested above, the debate over the nature of paradigms,
general theoretical perspectives, or schools of thought and their

presence in American sociology is far from being resolved, and, given the relative importance of the issue for the field, debate is likely to continue. As noted in the previous section of the chapter, as a part of this larger effort a number of sociologists have stressed the normative or value-laden character of sociological theories and have argued that, in order to understand their nature, it is necessary to lay bare and to examine the fundamental assumptions that they contain (Horton 1966; Gouldner 1970; Kinloch 1981). Toward this end, some have suggested that a useful framework for organizing the theoretical perspectives at the "macro" level within the discipline involves two perspectives compatible with two major ideologies — a "consensus" perspective that tends to reflect essential elements of conservatism, and a "conflict" perspective that reflects a more liberal/radical viewpoint (compare Dahrendorf 1958, 1959; Horton 1966; Lenski 1966).[15] While there are a number of different ways in which these two schools of thought may be compared, at the most general level they differ fundamentally in their images of human nature and society.[16]

The Consensus Perspective

With regard to the consensus school, John Horton (1966) has noted that scholars from this school are generally skeptical or pessimistic about human nature, holding one of three images: *homo damnatus* — an image that sees humankind as divided into innately superior and inferior groups; *homo duplex* — a Freudian image that sees humans as essentially selfish and in need of restraint by society; and *tabula rasa* — a passive image of human nature derived from behaviorist psychology that views human nature as essentially a rote reflection of the socialization process. As a result of these images, consensus scholars tend to postulate the necessity for a transcendent social order and to hold a positive attitude toward societal stability, social control, and the maintenance of societal institutions (Horton 1966:705).

In short, the consensus theoretical perspective contains implicit (and "value-laden") background assumptions about human nature and society that stress an antisocial image of human nature, the necessary transcendence of society made necessary by this nature, and support for the status quo. That such a perspective is consistent with conservatism is clear when it is compared to Eric Carlton's (1977:35) characterization of that ideology presented earlier in this discussion: "a conservative ideology explains and defends existing institutions, especially those concerned with government, the economy and the social structure." Further support for this linkage comes from Gerhard Lenski's (1966:22) statement: "Historically, conservatives have been distrustful of man's basic nature and have emphasized the need for restraining social institutions."

The Conflict Perspective

The conflict perspective's image of human nature is decidedly more optimistic than that of the consensus perspective. Horton (1966:705) suggests the label *homo laborans* and defines this image of man as "the active creator of himself and society through practical and autonomous social action." Because of this particular image, conflict scholars tend to place human needs first and thus see society as simply an imperfect reflection of human nature. As a result, they argue that "the transcendence of society is tantamount to the alienation of man from his own social nature" (p. 705). Lenski's (1966:22) characterization of the radical image supports this linkage: "radicals have been distrustful of these [society's] restraining institutions and have taken an optimistic view of man's nature." Thus, the conflict theoretical perspective contains implicit background assumptions about human nature and society that stress man's importance relative to society and tends to stress social instability and change as central elements.

To reiterate, analysts of the discipline have identified two fundamentally divergent viewpoints that are candidates for the status of schools of thought within the discipline. These perspectives offer divergent viewpoints on both human nature and the nature of society. Moreover, as will be demonstrated below, because they also provide divergent perspectives on the nature of class inequality in advanced capitalist society (Dahrendorf 1959; Lenski 1966; Grabb 1984; Lipset 1985), they will be employed in the remainder of the study as a framework for my analysis of research on the subject within the discipline.[17]

THE CAREER OF THE CONCEPT "CLASS" WITHIN AMERICAN SOCIOLOGY

Because the conceptual focus of this study — the term "class" — has been defined in a number of different ways, it is necessary to comment briefly on its history as a social science concept and to detail some of the ways in which the term has been used in the past. Dahrendorf (1959:3) reflects its controversial status within the social science literature in his statement: "The concept class has never remained a harmless concept for very long." While the use of the term preceded the industrial revolution, he notes that its history as a tool for social analysis began with the birth of industrial (capitalist) society and the work of Karl Marx (Dahrendorf 1959:4). Marx's use of the term began a tradition of research that conceptualizes class as a unidimensional construct narrowly based on economic criteria. To him, classes are defined as "positions within the productive relations" of the economic structure of capitalist society. His model of the class structure postulates that there are two classes in such societies: one comprised of those individuals who own productive property, the other of those who do not. Each of these classes is said to have different "objective" interests that are antithetical to the other. Marx built a theory of social change around the notion that the exploitation of one class by the other is the primary source for the material inequalities, social conflict, and the recurrent social crises of society. This theory postulates that the conflict between classes will inexorably lead to the revolutionary transformation of capitalist society.

In many respects, scholarship within American sociology on the subject of class inequality can be characterized as reactions to Marx's particular perspective on class. It is important to note here that these scholars were not only reacting to Marx's concept of class, they were also reacting to the entire theoretical edifice that surrounded it.[18] The nature of these reactions reflects the particular ideology of the researcher and, thus, his or her "school of thought" within the discipline. Given their very different perspectives on the nature of society and of social change, the perspectives of consensus scholars differ the most markedly from that of Marx. These scholars often define classes using multidimensional criteria, they visualize the social order as comprised of a large number of different "strata" (they often substitute this term for classes, or add the prefix "social" to it), they tend to minimize the antagonisms between such groups, they adopt an "evolutionary" model of change, and they often employ such phrases as "social stratification" to describe the systems of inequality in society. Scholars from the conflict school of thought, on the other hand, because they share major elements of Marx's image of the nature of capitalist society (class conflict and social change), tend to conceptualize class in a manner more similar to his usage of the term (i.e., as a unidimensional phenomenon that differentiates conflict groups whose antagonisms lead to social change, etc.). These latter theorists can also be further differentiated into subgroups in terms of the similarities between Marx's model of capitalist society and their own.

As these remarks suggest, the term "class" is not an "innocent" concept; instead it has been given a variety of different meanings according to the theoretical orientation of the particular scholar using it. Given that there are a number of different alternatives, my choice is to use "class" and "class inequality" as descriptors of the subject of interest instead of "strata," "social inequality," "social class," or "social stratification."[19] The only exception to this general rule is that I substitute the phrase employed by each scholar when discussing her or his particular theory. Obviously, one of my goals in the remainder of the book is to make the reader particularly cognizant of the terms that theorists concerned with describing and explaining class inequality within American society employ, because these terms provide good clues concerning the nature of their overall orientation toward the subject matter (Alford and Friedland 1985).

A NOTE ON THE SOCIOLOGY OF KNOWLEDGE

Research that seeks to examine the impacts of sociohistorical and ideological contexts on the nature of social theories confronts a major dilemma within the sociology of knowledge: the relative influences of "external" and "intersubjective" factors on the development of theories (Grimes 1988b:344). Theorists at one pole of this dichotomy view "external" influences on thought as virtually "deterministic" and see the theorist merely as a passive "reflector" of these influences. Those at the other pole see theory construction more as the idiosyncratic outcome of a process that is largely "insulated" from environmental contexts. In response to these two extreme perspectives on the theory construction process, Robert Jones (1983:458) takes the position that neither is right. To him, "[s]ocial theories are neither disembodied abstractions nor the mechanical effects of infrastructural causes, but rather themselves 'social actions' performed in response to specific conditions, needs, and purposes." The perspective taken in this study is similar to that of Jones in that it argues that social theories reflect both the contextual environment within which they are constructed and the theorist's "social construction" of that reality based on his or her own unique experiences of it. While such a perspective complicates the assignment of causal priorities, the realities of the theory construction process make this liability unavoidable.[20]

SUMMARY

This chapter began with a review of two major earlier efforts to analyze class inequality in American sociology, Page's *Class and American Sociology* and Gordon's *Social Class in American Sociology*. Since the latter of these works ended its coverage with 1955, it was argued that the time has come to update these classics A strategy was outlined that would combine the broad attention that Page devoted to contextual influences on theorizing with the more analytical focus on conceptual and methodological issues employed by Gordon. An analytic framework was then constructed that began with Kuhn's perspective on the growth of knowledge process in the physical sciences and the controversies that his perspective has generated by sociologists who have attempted to apply it to their discipline. Two major issues in applying his perspective to the social sciences were isolated: the controversy over his meaning for the key concept "paradigm" and his failure to devote adequate attention to the role of the sociohistorical context's influences on theorizing.

The analytic framework proposed for this study stresses the less rigorous label "schools of thought," which still captures both the "cognitive" and the "community" dimensions of the term "paradigm," while also directing attention to the influences of societal and disciplinary settings on the theorizing process. This perspective was then applied to the field for the period between 1900 and the present. The initial years in the discipline's history would be labeled "pre-paradigmatic" by Kuhn because there was no single dominant perspective within the discipline. From about 1930 to 1950, the discipline was increasingly dominated by the consensus perspective that is compatible with conservatism and stresses consensus and order; this domination continued until the decade of the 1960s and research activities during this period reflected its dominance. Its hegemony was increasingly challenged as the events of the 1960s proved difficult to explain with the perspective, and an alternative perspective labeled "conflict" was articulated to better account for these events. An examination of the background assumptions of each of these perspectives revealed that each is ideological and has fundamentally different images of man and society. Each of these perspectives was also shown to have different perspectives on the meaning and role of classes as agents for change within society.

As will be demonstrated in the remainder of the book, for an adequate understanding of American sociologists' "social construction" of theories about class inequality, knowledge about external social conditions, the internal structure of sociology, and a theorist's own unique biography is necessary. Chapter 2 discusses the origins of American sociology in the late nineteenth and early twentieth centuries and the role that the study of class played in the research of its founding fathers. It reveals that the discipline arose during a period of rapid social change as a response to both the inabilities of established social science disciplines to address the problems of the day and a lack of opportunity for new scholars within these more traditional disciplines. The chapter shows that early American sociology was both theoretically and methodologically eclectic, borrowing heavily from older social science disciplines. As a result the discipline's subject matter was loosely organized and no one theoretical perspective was dominant during this period in its history. The chapter notes that treatment of the subject of class by early American sociologists was influenced both by the relative prosperity of the period and by an ideology that stressed individualism, support for the status quo, and the notion that society can (and will be) improved over time through social intervention. As a result, while the founding fathers of the discipline did consider class in their work, the issue did not occupy a central position within the framework of any of them.

Part II of the study focuses on the emergence and eventual theoretical hegemony of the consensus school of thought within the discipline, with its unique perspective on class inequality that was labeled the "functionalist theory of social stratification." The introduction to this section details the variegated societal and ideological contexts that were present during the period in which the theory took shape (the late 1920s through the 1950s), and the efforts of the discipline to establish itself as a legitimate member of the social science community.

Chapter 3 discusses the works of three early researchers who employed elements of a functionalist perspective derived from the work of Emile Durkheim by early twentieth-century British social anthropologists — Robert (and Helen) Lynd, W. Lloyd Warner, and August B. Hollingshead. Materials presented in the chapter reveal that each scholar's use of the perspective varied both in terms of the setting within which he or she worked and their own backgrounds and experiences within the overall societal, ideological, and disciplinary settings.

Chapter 4 examines the formalization of functionalist theory within the discipline, its application to the issue of class inequality, and its eventual theoretical hegemony within American sociology. Materials presented reveal that the theory was a reaction both to the fragmented nature of extant theory within the social sciences and to Marxism's critique of capitalist society. As a result, functionalist theory viewed society as an integrated whole and stressed the positive, integrative, consequences of class inequality. The chapter concludes that the eventual theoretical hegemony of the functionalist perspective within American sociology was due to its compatibility with both the material prosperity and the dominant ideology of the early post–World War II period in the country's history.

Chapter 5 presents an overview of efforts to operationalize class for its application in social science research. According to the materials discussed, these efforts were influenced by several factors, including the rapid urbanization of American society, a shift in focus away from a community or regional setting and toward the national setting, and the growing hegemony of the functionalist perspective within the discipline itself. As a result of these influences, the chapter notes that these scholars conceptualized the class structure of society as a relatively "open" hierarchy of finely graded positions based on attributes of occupations (either prestige or socioeconomic status). The chapter concludes that the indexes developed by these scholars remain important measures of class position within the social sciences today, although they are increasingly challenged by alternative measures.

Part III details the origins and nature of conflict perspectives on class inequality within the discipline. The introduction to this section

notes that the U.S. postwar hegemony over the world political
economy began to deteriorate during the decade of the 1960s
and comments on the important international and domestic
consequences of its declining influence. It also discusses the
"crisis" that developed within American sociology itself as the
functionalist perspective was increasingly attacked for its idealized
image of society and the class structure and for its relative inability to
address the emerging societal issues of the period. Materials
reviewed there reveal that one result of this crisis within the
discipline was the articulation of a conflict alternative to
functionalism.

Chapter 6 presents and analyzes two conflict perspectives on
class inequality that are based on the work of Max Weber — those of
Ralf Dahrendorf and Gerhard Lenski. The chapter reveals that the
authors of these perspectives began by contrasting the assumptions of
the functionalist perspective on class inequality with the more
radical perspective of Karl Marx. Each then blended elements of both
perspectives into alternative theories that stressed a conflict model of
society that featured more antagonistic relationships among classes
and their roles as agents of social change when compared with
functionalist theory. The chapter also reveals that, while these
theories sought to distance themselves from the functionalist
perspective on social inequality, a comparison between their theories
and the "parent" generation of theories (i.e., functionalism and
Marxism) reveals that they remained far more similar to the
functionalist perspective than to the Marxist. The chapter concludes
that the reason for this similarity is that these authors shared with
those of the functionalist perspective faith in the overall vitality of
democratic capitalist society and its institutions.

Chapter 7 discusses the rise of radical scholarship within
American social science and its efforts to develop alternatives to the
functionalist theory of class inequality. As noted there, the major
theoretical antecedent for these scholars is the work of Karl Marx.
The chapter demonstrates that the attempts of these "neo-Marxist"
scholars to update Marxian orthodoxy to the realities of modern
capitalist society had to contend with two issues: the continued heterogeneity and lack of revolutionary consciousness of the working
class, and the proliferation of "middle" classes. The chapter discusses a number of different strategies for dealing with these issues,
particularly those of Erik O. Wright. As noted there, Wright
supplements exploitation based on ownership of the means of
production as a means for defining classes (Marx's single criterion)
with two "secondary" exploitive criteria — organizational and skills/
credentials assets. The application of these three criteria results in a
typology of twelve classes for modern capitalist society. Wright's
latest model is the leading perspective on class inequality today

within radical sociology. The chapter also presents a critique of these various efforts.

Chapter 8, the last chapter in the book, first summarizes the major findings developed in the first seven chapters and then addresses an important substantive issue: are the diverse contemporary theories of class inequality within American sociology "converging" toward some grand "synthesis" or are they "diverging" away from each other? As a means for addressing this issue, the chapter first provides an overview of the trends at important points in the discipline's history, observing that both tendencies are present at different points in time. The chapter concludes that, for the contemporary period, the functionalist perspective on class inequality has fallen out of favor within the discipline, and evidence suggests a growing convergence between "neo-Weberian" and "neo-Marxist" conflict perspectives on the subject.

NOTES

1. Grabb's (1984) book is a partial exception to this statement. However, his goals are different. He provides an overview of both classical and contemporary theorists on the subject and deals with both European and American scholars. Because of this larger focus, his treatment differs from those of both Page and Gordon and the present study. Another exception to this statement is Wright's (1980) article-length treatment of Marxist perspectives on class inequality.

2. Despite this focus, however, it takes a slightly different approach from that of Page in that its attention is directed more to "analytical" and "methodological" issues and less to the contextual influences that Page stressed. This shift in emphasis away from the more theoretical and epistemological concerns of Page can be interpreted as an artifact of changes within the discipline itself. As the discipline entered the decade of the 1930s, sociological research was becoming increasingly empirical. By then, the first major studies of class inequality in American community life were being completed by the Lynds (Lynd and Lynd 1929) and Warner (Warner and Lunt 1941). And, while these studies were certainly guided by theoretical considerations (Grimes 1988a), far greater emphasis was given to more practical issues, such as the conceptualization and measurement of class and a detailed description of its impact on the lives of community residents. This apparent shift in emphasis was widespread within the discipline as a whole, and, in some senses, can be seen as a part of the efforts of sociology to "professionalize" its image within the academic community (Oberschall 1972; Bannister 1987).

3. This disparagement of the economic variable as the single indicator of class position was also typical of scholars during the period in which Gordon wrote. Some have argued that this was a reaction to the Marxist perspective on class (in particular, see Gouldner 1970; Westheus 1976; Horowitz 1983).

4. Kuhn (1970:16–17) explains why this is necessary in the following quote:

> In the absence of a paradigm, or some candidate for a paradigm, all facts that could possibly pertain to the development of a given science are likely to seem equally relevant. . . . No wonder, then, that in the early stages of the development of any science, different men confronting the same range of phenomena, interpret them in different ways.

5. See Lodahl and Gordon (1972) for research that supports the notion that the social sciences in particular are less well developed paradigmatically than the natural sciences.

6. Kuhn (1970, 1974), in response to the controversy over this issue, has reaffirmed that the latter usage (paradigms as exemplars) is the most central meaning in his application of the term in his work.

7. Several of Turner's (1982:13) caveats concerning these perspectives should be kept in mind. First, he states that what we call sociological theory is in reality a much more loosely organized "clustering" of implicit assumptions than is implied in Kuhn's rendering of similar perspectives in science. Second, the perspectives in sociology often "blend into one another" to such an extent that Turner hesitates to call them paradigms in the Kuhnian sense of the term. Note also that Ritzer (1975) explicitly disagrees with Turner's caution on these matters.

8. Eckberg and Hill also offer the term "thematic analyses" in the sense in which Holton (1975) employed the term, but a review of his work suggests that this alternative is too individualistic in its application to be employed in this context.

9. This study will not devote a great deal of attention to this last attribute of schools of thought. However, others such as Mullins (1973) have shown its importance for the development of theories.

10. Even in the normal science period the hegemony of the dominant perspective is never total in Kuhn's opinion. In particular, he makes the point that the socialization process for new scientists is never complete, and that even during such periods some discordant information is transmitted. His point is that the work of younger scholars that typically both questions the dominant perspective and offers alternatives to it should be seen as evidence of the incomplete character of the socialization process and the lack of complete dominance of the hegemonic perspective.

11. For an even earlier critic of the dominant perspective with a slightly different focus of attention, see Robert Lynd's *Knowledge for What?* (1940), a scathing attack on sociology's support for the status quo and its lack of willingness to work for the benefit of subordinate groups.

12. Horowitz's (1983) biography of Mills discusses his personal reaction to his marginality within the discipline and the bitterness that resulted toward the end of his career. Mills' *The Sociological Imagination* (1959) clearly reflects some of this bitterness.

13. This particular "posturing" was, to some extent at least, a reaction against the praxis (activist) orientation of Marx and his followers as well as the "reformist" orientation of early American sociologists and became a hallmark for sociology, particularly during the post–World War II period (Bannister 1987). Under the guise of this orientation, sociologists were not encouraged to even acknowledge, much less to identify and study the influences of, such factors as implicit assumptions and personal value orientations on their research activities, since research decisions were viewed as the rational and objective outcome of a "scientific appraisal of alternatives."

14. As noted above, Kuhn (1970) makes the point that it is generally younger scholars who "challenge" the established viewpoints within a discipline. He notes that this is because they, in a number of senses, are less committed to the established viewpoint than are their older colleagues.

15. As a part of this introspective examination of points of view, a number of schemes for describing the pluralistic character of perspectives within the discipline were articulated (Friedrichs 1970; Gouldner 1970; Turner 1973; Ritzer 1975). While both the number and relative saliency of the criteria employed for organizing the various perspectives that were "discovered" by these scholars was diverse, one of the most central was a division of perspectives into "macro" and

"micro" levels of analysis. Given that most theories of class inequality are couched at the former level, our analysis of schools of thought within the discipline is confined to this level.

16. Lipset's (1985) recent reflective essay on stratification considers this division into theoretical camps to be a fait accompli within the discipline, while Alexander (1988) even goes so far as to trace this division back to the work of Parsons, in contrast to others who see it largely as a reaction to the implicit assumptions contained within Parsons' work (Dahrendorf 1959).

17. It is particularly important that analyses of the class structure of society take into account theoretical perspectives because, as Wright and Martin (1987:5) have observed, "class structure is not an innocent concept. It is impossible to study classes without invoking, if only implicitly, a wide range of broader theoretical commitments."

18. In this context, Alford and Friedland (1985:394) observe that "concepts always contain a theory of causes and consequences of the essential attributes of the phenomenon located and defined by the concept."

19. It should be noted here that this is an "evaluative" choice. I prefer this alternative because I see it as closer to the term's original meaning as an identifier of conflict groups within society based on economic criteria.

20. The theory construction process is viewed here as the result of the "dialectical" interaction of the sociohistorical background, disciplinary influences, and the theorist's own unique biography. In the words of Resnick and Wolff (1987), such a methodology views each of these elements as, at the same time, "overdetermined" by the others and as "overdetermining" the others (in more conventional "positivistic" terminology, a system of mutual feedback is said to exist among the various elements).

I

THE STUDY OF CLASS IN AMERICAN SOCIOLOGY

2

THE ANALYSIS OF CLASS INEQUALITY IN EARLY AMERICAN SOCIOLOGY

Between the last quarter of the nineteenth century and the late 1920s, sociology emerged in the United States and began the process of legitimization as a discipline within the social sciences community. As a part of this process, sociologists were preoccupied with demonstrating the usefulness of their particular viewpoint for the analysis of society. This chapter examines the process by which sociology was institutionalized, its ideological and theoretical nature, and, finally, its treatment of the subject of class inequality in American society during the early days of its history.

THE ESTABLISHMENT OF THE DISCIPLINE

Sociology began to emerge as a distinctive discipline in American academic life during the last quarter of the nineteenth and the first quarter of the twentieth centuries. This section of the chapter first characterizes the sociohistorical and ideological settings of this period in the nation's history and then discusses the origins of the discipline.

The Sociohistorical and Ideological Settings

The post–Civil War period in American history was one of rapid social change. Richard Hofstadter (1955) argues that the changes that occurred during this period were the result of three influences: urbanization, industrialization, and the changing ethnic composition of the population.[1] He stresses that, prior to the period, the focus of life in the United States was centered in the countryside and the small towns that served it. Most of the population was native-born and engaged in agricultural or agriculture-support occupations. Having been born and nurtured in such settings, "the American mind was raised upon a sentimental attachment to rural living and upon a series of notions about rural people and rural life" (Hofstadter 1955:24). These influences included a sense of individuality and self-sufficiency within the setting of the local community. However, rapid urbanization, industrialization, and immigration from Europe following the Civil War brought changes that fundamentally challenged both this style of life and its value system. For example, from about 1860 to the turn of the century

> towns and cities sprouted up with miraculous rapidity all over the United States. Large cities grew into great metropolises, small towns grew into large cities, and new towns sprang into existence on vacant land. While the rural population almost doubled during this half century, the urban population multiplied by almost seven times (Hofstadter 1955:173).

Hofstadter contends that this rapid shift from rural/agricultural to urban/industrial society had dramatic consequences for the mind set of the population:

> the whole cast of American society in this period was deeply affected by the experience of the rural mind confronted with the phenomena of urban life, its crowding, poverty, crime, corruption, impersonality and ethnic chaos. To the rural migrant, raised in respectable quietude and the high-toned moral imperatives of evangelical Protestantism, the city seemed not merely a new social form or way of life, but a strange threat to civilization itself (p. 175).

In Hofstadter's view, one of the most significant consequences of this dramatic shift in the focus of American life was its effect on the relative power and influence of the traditional middle class. Whereas before a person's place in society was defined in terms of his or her role in local community affairs and in traditional economic pursuits, in the new social order the frame of reference suddenly shifted to a national setting. This fact, combined with the growth and increasing influence of large-scale corporate enterprises, caused a fundamental shift in the distribution of power and prestige away from the farmer, the small businessman, the independent professional, and the part-time politician, toward the corporate owner, the big-city banker, the machine politician with his cadre of immigrant voters, and the full-time professional politician. The efforts of these newly deposed traditional groups in society to restore their lost power and prestige gave rise to a reform movement called the Progressive Era whose general theme was the effort to restore a type of economic individualism and political democracy that was widely believed to have existed earlier in America and to have been destroyed by the great corporation and the corrupt political machine; and with that restoration to bring back a kind of morality and civic purity that was also believed to have been lost (Hofstadter 1955:5).

It was within this sociohistorical setting, and, thus, as a part of the growing reaction to rapid social change and the consequent rearrangement of personal and institutional priorities in the early twentieth century, that American sociology was born and nurtured.

For input concerning the prevailing ideology of early twentieth-century America, we must rely on evidence from modern sources.[2] As was noted earlier in the chapter, since sociology was a child of the period in our history labeled by historians as the Progressive Era, it would seem to follow that the ideology dominant in society during the period was liberal. This particular perspective on the world is characterized by two attributes: a tendency to favor change, and a belief that the government should intervene to improve the human condition (Sargent 1981:68). Historians of the period (compare Hofstadter 1955) agree that this was the case. However, commentary by recent sociological analysts about this issue has suggested that the ideology dominating early American society (and thus sociology) was more conservative than liberal (Eisenstadt 1976; Ritzer 1983). Ritzer (1983:33) in particular concludes that conservatism is the more accurate label:

> liberalism, taken to its extreme, comes close to conserva-
> tism. . . . The overriding belief is that the social system
> works or can be reformed to work. There is little criticism of
> the system as a whole. . . . Instead of immanent class
> struggle, the early sociologists saw a future of class har-
> mony and class cooperation. Ultimately, this meant that
> American sociological theory helped to rationalize exploita-
> tion, domestic and international imperialism, and social
> inequality.

This particular characterization is similar to that of Pease, Form, and Rytina (1970) who employ the phrase "evolutionary liberalism" to describe the ideology of the period. Their definition for the phrase also suggests a more status quo orientation than is generally linked to liberalism.

The debate over the ideological character of early American sociology is complicated by the fact that many scholars have often characterized the early periods in the history of the discipline as if they were homogeneous in terms of ideology. In my opinion, such a practice is not justified and is partially the result of a failure to carefully consider the influences of sociohistorical events on these intellectual activities. The period in American history from the turn of the century until the end of the 1920s exhibited an incredible diversity of conditions, which, of necessity, influenced both the ideology of each portion of the total period and the nature of theoretical musings about social phenomena.

With these qualifications in mind, it seems that the characterization "liberal," as that term is commonly used, is an accurate one for the dominant ideology during the years when sociology and the other social sciences were emerging as distinctive disciplines. At that time the society was undergoing a rapid shift from a rural/agricultural to an urban/industrial society, and concern with the negative consequences that accompanied this shift and the government's potential role in dealing with them dominated the intellectual scene. As noted above, the new field was dominated by both Christian and secular reformists during this period, and their major goal was the modification of the old institutional structures of society in light of the changes that were taking place. In this regard, Coser (1978:290) writes: "sociology before 1920 . . . was even more strongly influenced and shaped by the humanitarian, philanthropic, and social reform movements that were actively under way in the country during the nineteenth century." However, as the period continued, the saliency of the shift to urban/industrial society and the problems that resulted from this shift receded from the scene, and the United States entered a period of economic growth and relative prosperity that would last until the eve of the Great Depression. This latter period coincided with the beginning of efforts to professionalize sociology by adopting the natural sciences model and a resulting diminution of the influence of reformism. As Oberschall (1972:205) notes:

> the origin of sociology in reform also serves as a backdrop for the sharp reaction against the preaching, muckraking, and value judgments that set-in in the 1920s when sociology was more firmly established and professionalized, and was trying to thin out of its ranks the reformers and dilettantes who were becoming a source of embarrassment to the discipline.

Thus, beginning during the early 1920s, the ideological posturing of the discipline began to reflect both the changing character of society and its own position as a relatively untried newcomer within the academic scene and, as a result, began to become increasingly conservative and status quo oriented.

Sociology's Emergence

Analysts of the genesis of the discipline agree that sociology's emergence as a distinctive academic discipline was both a part of and a response to the Progressive Movement. Small (1916:828), writing with the advantage of direct personal involvement in the birth of the discipline, captures the linkage between the reformist thrust of the Progressive Movement and the field in this statement:

> in the first place, we must remember that this movement had never been the operation of a single factor . . . it has been the operation of two principal factors, each highly composite; first, an impulse to improve ways of improving the world; second, an impulse to improve ways of interpreting the world.

Hinkle and Hinkle (1954:16) also mirror this linkage: "Arising at a time of industrialization, early sociology concerned itself primarily with the scientific study and amelioration of social problems in urban areas. The founders of sociology . . . were particularly sensitive to these problems which they interpreted as accompaniments of social progress."

While there is consensus that the origins of the field lay within the reformist tradition of turn-of-the-century America, there remain some differences of opinion about the particular twist this reformism took. For example, Hofstadter (1955) stresses that these origins were mostly within the *sacred* version of reformism, citing Christian social reform and gospel movements as salient influences. Ober-schall (1972:204), on the other hand, places more stress on the *secular* roots of these influences: "Even more crucial for the establishment of sociology, its definition, early content, and preoccupations, was its link with the secular reform movement." Evidence supporting these somewhat contradictory opinions is mixed. For example, Coser's (1978:287) explanation for the peculiar nature of the writings of many early sociologists seems to offer support for Hofstadter's position: "The evangelical passion and moralistic rhetoric that informs many of the writings of early American sociologists becomes understandable when it is realized that a very high portion of them were sons of ministers or had themselves been ministers or studied in divinity schools." But the presence of journalists with muckraking credentials such as Robert Park and Franklin Giddings among the founding fathers lends support for Oberschall's position that the secular had a greater influence than the sacred among early American sociologists. While this debate is likely to continue, it should be noted that sociology's efforts during the last 50 or so years to divorce itself from the sacred portion of its heritage might have been an influence that "colored" the perspectives of sociological commentators on the matter.[3] Despite these minor differences of opinion, it seems reasonable to conclude that the discipline emerged as a part of the larger intellectual reaction to a rapidly changing society during the early years of the twentieth century and was largely reformist in nature, at least during the early years of its existence as a member of the social scientific community.

Raison D'être

Simply documenting the emergence of the discipline, however, does not seem to adequately address the question of *why* it emerged. After all, several of the more established social science disciplines were also operating within the same sociohistorical and ideological contexts and thus reacting to these same external stimuli. Therefore, the question of why sociologists sought to differentiate themselves as a group apart from these other orientations still must be addressed. The importance of this question cannot be overestimated since, in effect, the question addresses the raison d'être of sociology as a discipline.

It now seems clear that the emergence of the discipline did not occur randomly in time, but was, instead, a response to the particular sociohistorical circumstances of the period in question and of the attempts of the academic community as a whole to respond to these changes. Within this latter context, evidence points to two distinct, but related, influences on the discipline's emergence: the relative inabilities of more established perspectives to deal with the complex problem of analyzing the rapidly changing society during the early years of the twentieth century, and a comparative lack of opportunities for younger, somewhat less conventional scholars within the older social science disciplines (Oberschall 1972). Each of these influences will be discussed.

For American higher education, the period following the turn of the century was one of tremendous growth and competition. At the same time that state universities were being founded and expanded, wealthy benefactors were establishing such schools as the University of Chicago.[4] For the social sciences in particular, it was also a time for dividing up the academic turf, with new disciplines such as political science and economics being established. As a part of their efforts to legitimize themselves as distinctive perspectives, these new candidates for disciplinary status tended, of necessity, to focus on more narrow, reasonably well-defined, and, therefore, more defensible subject matter areas. However, the task of analyzing the far-reaching changes that were taking place during the period seemed to require more breadth and scope and more flexibility than the frameworks of these recently established social science disciplines were providing at the time. Supporting evidence for such a claim is available from Albion Small's work. In 1904, in an article entitled "The Subject Matter of Sociology," he writes:

> there are important reaches of knowledge about human conditions not provided for in the programs of the older sciences ... [and] the sociologists are attempting to show that the salvation of the social sciences from sterility must be worked out, not by microscopic description and analysis of details alone, but by such correlation and generalization of particulars that the whole social process will be intelligible (p. 282).

It was into this "gap" in the collective social science understanding of the times that sociologists charged with their admittedly eclectic grab bag of perspectives and research techniques (J. Bernard 1929). To quote Small again (1916:831): "More literally, the sociological movement has been spoken of ... as a revolt against unsatisfactory academic conventionalities." Thus, sociology was established and gained its foothold, in part, as a response to the need for an *alternative* perspective to those provided by other social science disciplines in their efforts to explain the rapid changes that were taking place in American society around the turn of the century.

A second influence on the origins of sociology was the comparative lack of opportunity afforded younger scholars within the more established social science disciplines. Oberschall (1972:189) concludes: "the opportunity provided by sociology was exploited not just by intellectually dissatisfied and socially concerned scholars, but by a group of upwardly mobile men who otherwise could not have moved into university positions through the already established disciplines."

In sum, sociology emerged as a response to a particular social and academic climate, with the unique opportunities for growth and expansion that it provided for both older and newer disciplines. With these facts in mind, I next describe the theoretical character of the discipline during these early years and then, with this information in hand, examine the discipline's treatment of the issue of class inequality.

THE THEORETICAL CHARACTER OF
EARLY AMERICAN SOCIOLOGY

The theoretical structure of a discipline must be understood, at least in part, to be the result of the context within which it develops and, thus, to reflect the dominant intellectual currents of that particular setting. Chapter 1 presented an overview of Kuhn's (1970) scheme for explaining the origins and development of science and argued that, with proper consideration of the unique problems in applying his perspective to the social sciences, it offered important insights into the growth of knowledge process within sociology. Recall that Kuhn argues that a science develops by adopting, applying, testing, then rejecting successive images of its subject matter. He labels these images paradigms and believes that they are essential for the development of a discipline because,

> in the absence of a paradigm . . . all facts that could possibly pertain to the development of a given science are likely to seem equally relevant. . . . No natural history can be interpreted in the absence of at least some implicit body of intertwined theoretical and methodological belief that permits selection, evaluation, and criticism (Kuhn 1970:16–17).

Importantly, once such an image is accepted by practitioners in a given field of inquiry, the discipline enters what Kuhn calls a period of "normal science" that he characterizes as one in which there is a rapid expansion in both the content and integration of the information base upon which the discipline depends. If this view is an accurate description of the process by which disciplines develop, then the paradigmatic status of a discipline should have dramatic consequences for its theoretical structure — that is, for its ability to organize, interpret, and understand its subject matter. With these points in mind, let us now examine the paradigmatic status of early American sociology.

A perusal of early issues of the official journal of the American Sociological Society during the post-1900 period, the *American Journal of Sociology*, reveals several assessments of the theoretical status of the discipline. Vincent (1904:159) establishes that a science must have a theoretical structure upon which to base its predictions and also makes a judgement of sociology's status regarding that requirement in his statement: "If the test of the science be the formation of laws and power to predict, sociology is not far advanced on the road to scientific status." At about that same time, Small (1904:282) proposes (and answers) the following question: "Has sociology a material of its own? Jealous friends of the older disciplines promptly answer 'No!' Friends of the new science as confidently answer 'Yes,' but they have not always been able to justify the answer to each other or even to themselves." H. Ford (1909:101), obviously a "jealous friend of older disciplines," in a scathing review of the status of sociology a few years later, observes that "sociology has not yet established any claim to be accepted as a science. . . . We have here an instance of what is a striking characteristic of sociology. It gives a hospitable reception to notions examined, discredited, and rejected by established science." Small (1916:849) with certainly different motives, seems to have reached the same conclusion in 1916 when he writes:

> before we find ourselves in the ranks of social science, we shall have to make very clear, first to ourselves and then to others, that we have a clue to a particular quest, and we shall meanwhile have called in our juvenile pretensions to be the masters of everything while we are giving proof that we can discover something.

From comments such as these, it seems clear that the early years of the twentieth century were spent as much in defense of the discipline both as a separate entity from the older social sciences and as a viable science as in introspection about theoretical issues. However, by the end of the decade of the 1920s, more overtly theoretical looks at the discipline were appearing. Bain's (1929:114) assessment of "Trends in American Sociological Theory," appearing in an anthology about the discipline published in 1929, concludes that

> it has often been remarked that one of the greatest faults of sociological theory, as of all science in its early stages, is its oversimplification, premature generalization, or . . . particularlism. . . . So far sociological theory and research have been less productive of scientific facts than they have of hypotheses, speculation and wishful thinking.

While some, particularly those outside the discipline such as Ford (1909), go so far as to argue that sociology was virtually devoid of any theoretical status at all during this period in its history, most insiders prefer to see it instead as borrowing heavily from the theoretical perspectives of European sociologists and from other disciplines as well (compare Page 1940). Bain (1929:80) lists some of these influences: "Spencerian-Darwinian evolutionary theory . . . economic determinism, the German philosophers of history and historical economists, the French school of Comte, Tarde, Durkheim, LeBon, the statistical approach of Quetelet."[5]

Hinkle's (1980) treatment of the theoretical content of the early discipline also notes these same influences and the resulting eclectic nature of theory during the period. He coins the phrase "evolutionary naturalism" to describe the broad perspective employed by early American sociologists since they seemed, according to him, "fundamentally preoccupied with the explanation of the genesis of and orderly change within social phenomena" (p. 68). Yet his description of the contents of this perspective suggests that his conceptualization of theory is far broader than contemporary uses of the term. In fact, his phrase is similar to "evolutionary liberalism," the phrase employed by Pease et al. (1970:128) to describe what they called an "intellectual undercurrent" present in the discipline during this period. Oberschall's (1972:213) assessment of the theoretical nature of the discipline during these early days seems to share this opinion: "Small was therefore correct in his opinion that sociology became established in U.S. colleges without a central core of scientific method and theoretic content. The intellectual and 'sociological' content of . . . sociology . . . was not impressive."

In conclusion, the evidence reviewed above suggests that, at least during this early period in its history, American sociology was theoretically eclectic at best (compare Reiss 1967:2), or theoretically barren at worse. Such a state of affairs corresponds closely, in Kuhn's scheme, to a "pre-paradigm" period, wherein there are no dominant theoretical perspectives within a discipline. Based on this evidence, a reasonable conclusion is that sociology was without a dominant theoretical perspective for the period between the late nineteenth century and at least the early 1930s. With this in mind, the next task is to examine the discipline's treatment of the issue of class inequality during this early period in its history.

CONCERN WITH CLASS INEQUALITY

Evidence about concern with the subject of class inequality within the discipline during these early years is available from the two studies discussed in Chapter 1 — Page's *Class and American Sociology* (1940), which focuses its attention on the period between the last quarter of the nineteenth century and the early 1920s, and Gordon's *Social Class in American Sociology* (1963), which extends coverage on the subject from the mid-1920s to the mid 1950s.

Page's (1940:231) major observation is that American sociologists, from the last quarter of the nineteenth through the first quarter of the twentieth century, did not consider class inequality to be a major influence in society. However, he makes two important qualifications to this statement. First, the founding fathers of the discipline — Ward, Sumner, Small, Giddings, Cooley and Ross — were explicitly aware of the importance of the subject, especially when they are contrasted with sociologists after World War I. Second, despite their modest levels of interest in the subject, these sociologists remained far more interested in class inequality than did social scientists from other disciplines.

As noted in Chapter 1, one of Page's most important explanations for the relative lack of interest in the subject among early American sociologists, particularly when they are contrasted with their European colleagues, was the unique setting of turn-of-the-century America. He observes that

> no doubt in Europe, the traditional social hierarchies and
> stronger elements of class consciousness, as well as the rise
> of Marxism, stimulated such studies. Because these same
> conditions were lacking or relatively undeveloped in the
> United States and because here existed the additional factors
> of frontier expansion and vertical mobility on a larger scale,
> the attention of our scholars was seldom drawn to the role of
> stratification in our society (p. 250).

Within this context he observes that the thoughts of intellectuals must be understood as an artifact of the period in which they write. The following quote demonstrates both the saliency of this linkage and the relative concern these scholars devoted to the subject:

> they were all keenly aware of the changes taking place in our
> political, economic, and social institutions, and they all
> hoped that their science would aid in the solution of the
> nation's social problems. The problems provoked by class
> shifts and conflicts gained their earnest attention, which
> resulted . . . in the beginnings of an adequate analysis of
> social classes (p. 22).

Another interesting feature of Page's study is its focus on the association between the social backgrounds of these scholars and their concerns with class inequality. For example, he argues that Lester Ward's interest in class inequality was stimulated by the relative poverty of his youth (Page 1940:31). However, he also notes that this linkage between social background and level of interest in the subject did not hold for those members of the founding fathers who were middle class, since some of them shared Ward's perspective on class inequality while others did not.

Other background variables that Page employs to explain differences in orientations toward class among these early scholars are religion and region. While he remarks that the religious ingredient in the backgrounds of some (in particular, Small) led to greater concern with the negative consequences of inequality and a stronger reformist orientation, he also observes that religious backgrounds of others led in different directions (i.e., Giddings). Additionally, as noted in Chapter 1, Page finds that those scholars who spent their youth in the Midwest were more critical of the overall social order and class inequality, while those from the East were more supportive of the status quo.

Additional information concerning the decade of the 1920s is available from Gordon's (1963) *Social Class in American Sociology*. His first subject of attention is the research conducted by scholars at the University of Chicago during the decade of the 1920s. He begins by noting that many of these scholars were sensitive to the issue of social inequality in their work. He singles out such studies as Harvey Zorbaugh's *The Gold Coast and the Slum* (1929), and Clifford Shaw's *Delinquency Areas* (1929) as indicative of this interest. However, he also observes that the particular perspective employed by these scholars inhibited their treatment of social inequality in their work: "Taking stock ... of the relationship of ecological theory to class analysis, it is clear that a rigid adherence to the principle confining the field of human ecology to 'community' and 'competition,' as the ecologists defined these terms, would severely restrict the research into class phenomena" (Gordon 1963:25).

The second subject that Gordon includes in his overview of research on social inequality during the decade of the 1920s was the work of Pitirim Sorokin, whose *Social Mobility* (1927) is characterized as "an analysis and compendium of materials on various aspects of social stratification" (Gordon 1963:52). Sorokin's major focus was on social stratification, class characteristics, and social mobility. Despite this focus, however, Gordon notes that Sorokin did not devote much attention to the associations between these key variables and other dimensions of the social structure. Yet, as indicated by the title to his book, Sorokin was convinced that social mobility was an important aspect of society, but he was also concerned that such mobility opportunities were often constrained by the class system as well. Gordon concludes that while Sorokin's work did raise important issues, its focus was too wide to provide a major source of stimulus for research applications.

In short, while the amount of overlap between Gordon's (1963) book and this initial period in the discipline's history was small and his attention was far less comprehensive than that of Page, it is clear that both Chicago sociologists and other scholars devoted at least some attention to the subject of class inequality in American society during the decade of the 1920s. It is also clear from his treatment that these efforts were marginal to other concerns of the discipline during this period. This assessment supports Page's position that class inequality was not a dominant subject matter within early American sociology.

CONCLUSIONS

The materials presented in this chapter were selected based on the belief that an adequate understanding of the origins of American sociology and its treatment of the subject of class inequality in

American society requires a careful analysis of the sociohistorical setting within which the field emerged during the last quarter of the nineteenth and the first quarter of the twentieth centuries. In this context, it was stressed that the field emerged during a period of rapid social change brought about by a shift from rural/agricultural to an urban/industrial society and should, thus, at least in part, be seen as a reflection of this new society. The dominant ideology during this early period was liberal and stressed both individualism and government intervention to protect and insure individual opportunities. The resulting theoretical structure of the discipline was eclectic, and while early American sociologists were cognizant of class inequalities in society, their interpretation of the saliency of these inequalities was colored both by a belief in basic equality and by the more dramatic influences of other trends, particularly the effects of urbanization, industrialization, and increasing ethnic heterogeneity on life in society. Following World War I, many of the societal problems generated by these trends began to recede from the scene, and the United States entered a period of sustained economic growth and prosperity. Immigration slowed as well and many of the cultural contrasts between the newly arrived and the natives became more muted. Once more, the notion that the United States was the land of opportunity for all seemed to become more popular, and the society became more conservative than was the case in the earlier period. Within the field of sociology, the reformism of many of the founding fathers became passé as the discipline began to establish itself as a legitimate social science, and the focus of sociological attention shifted even further away from class inequalities. In Page's (1940:250) words,

the close of the World War signaled a period of history of American sociology quite different from the years of the Fathers. Their work, with its broad systematization, historical speculation, and concern with the role of class forces in American life, gave way to detailed empirical research in problem areas somewhat narrow in scope. . . . In the decade and a half following the war . . . problems of class were largely neglected.

Thus, as the United States entered the latter part of the decade of the 1920s, many sociologists seemed to share the viewpoint of many others within society, particularly those in the middle class, that capitalism with a marketplace unregulated by government would result in the greatest good for the most people, that class was less important than other major structural variables (particularly community), and that the positive consequences of class position were of greater saliency for the overall society than any of its negative effects. Events of the next few decades in American history would fundamentally challenge key aspects of this point of view.

NOTES

1. Sociological commentators on this period in the discipline's history mirror Hofstadter's perspective. See Oberschall (1972), Hinkle (1980), Page (1940), Madge (1962), Schwendinger and Schwendinger (1974), and Vidich and Lyman (1985).

2. The notion that science should be "value-free," which dominated the field until the early 1970s, mitigated against inquiry into its underlying ideological context (Gouldner 1970). Thus, sources characterizing the ideological content of early American social science will generally be dated post-1970.

3. Vidich and Lyman's (1985) recent detailed treatment of the impact of religion in general and Protestantism in particular on the nature of sociological theorizing offers additional evidence supporting the former claim. In fact, they share my impression that the "professionalization" of the discipline has served to partially obscure the discipline's linkages to the sacred portion of its heritage. Their excellent book is an effort to make these linkages more explicit.

4. It is important to stress that the founding of the University of Chicago had dramatic consequences for higher education in America. Small (1916:764) writes: "It is doubtful if higher education in the United States has ever received as much stimulus from any single event as came to it from the founding of the University of Chicago."

5. It is interesting to note here that Bain's list of theoretical antecedents of early American sociology does not include reference to one of the most salient of the intellectual traditions of late-nineteenth-century Europe — that of the Marxists. Few early American sociologists explicitly discussed Marx and even fewer appreciated the applicability of his perspective to American society.

II

THE EMERGENCE OF
FUNCTIONALIST
THEORIES OF
CLASS INEQUALITY

As America entered the decade of the 1920s, American sociology became increasingly self-conscious of its marginal status as the newest of the social sciences and began efforts to improve its image. There were two related consequences of this move toward professionalization. First, sociologists increasingly adopted the "scientific" model as the standard for evaluating the adequacy of their perspectives and procedures. This resulted in increased scrutiny to both theoretical and research issues within the discipline. Second, the discipline began to distance itself from its earlier reformist orientation by fostering an attitude of "scientific neutrality" toward its subject matters.

One of the most important results of these efforts was the gradual institutionalization of a single school of thought — functionalism — as the dominant theoretical perspective within the discipline, with its accompanying role model of "sociologist-as-scientist." Following remarks concerning the sociohistorical and disciplinary settings, the chapters in this section of the book examine the emergence and eventual hegemony of the functionalist perspective on class inequality within American sociology between the late 1920s and the decade of the 1950s.

THE SOCIOHISTORICAL SETTING

This section reviews the period between the late 1920s and the early post–World War II period, paying particular attention to the contrast between societal conditions at the beginning and the end of the period and those in the middle (the decade of the 1930s).

The 1920s

In many senses, the nation's involvement in World War I brought an end to the reform-minded progressive emphasis in American society discussed in Chapter 2 (Schlesinger 1957:43). Primarily as a result of national experiences during the war, the collective mood became decidedly more pragmatic and less concerned with larger societal issues such as urbanization, big business, and machine politics, which had occupied the stage during the Progressive Era. Instead, the United States began to devote more concern to personal issues, in particular to the satisfaction of pent-up consumer desires and with material success in general. In many respects, the post–World War I U.S. economy was ideally suited to meet these needs because,

> the war had impoverished Europe and hardly damaged the United States at all; when peace came the Americans found themselves the economic masters of the world. Their young country with enormous resources in materials and in human energy and with a wide domestic market was ready to take advantage of this situation (Allen 1931:177).

As a result of the war, then, the United States became the world's greatest financial and creditor nation — it was already the largest producer of manufactures and foodstuffs (Kennedy 1988:327). What followed for the country and its citizens was a decade of unparalleled prosperity. Along with this prosperity came rapid social change and accompanying value shifts. As Allen (1931:122) has noted, "with the old order of things had gone a set of values that had given richness and meaning to life, and substitute values were not easily found." A variety of different causes for these changes have been isolated:

> the postwar disillusion, the new status of women, the Freudian gospel, the automobile, prohibition, the sex and confession magazines, and the movies — [each] had its part in bringing about the revolution. Each of them, as an influence, was played upon by all the others; none of them could alone have changed to any degree the folkways of America; together their force was irresistible (Allen 1931:103).

The central role that economic prosperity played during this period of transition and change also caused a shift in the public attitude toward business. The greedy and self-interested image that business had acquired around the turn of the century (which, in great part, stimulated the public response that was the Progressive Era) gave way to one more in line with that portrayed by Adam Smith and classical economic theory, which had a rather "moral" image of both business in general and of businessmen in particular (Clarke 1982). Thus, to most Americans during the 1920s, "capitalism had transcended its individualism and materialism, becoming social and spiritual"; a career in business was once again a moral calling worthy of emulation and the more narrow Darwinian conception of character as being forged by competitive struggle came to be modified during the 1920s to include new sentiments of business social responsibility (Schlesinger 1957:71–72). Support for this conclusion is readily available from scholarship during the period in the classic analysis of the modern corporation by Berle and Means (1934) that argued that the rise of the modern joint-stock corporation had caused, among other things, a fundamental shift away from a narrow concern with profits toward a new orientation of social responsibility among businessmen.

In light of these images of the new businessman as a protector of society's interests, it is not too surprising that the leadership vacuum that was created by the departure of Woodrow Wilson's particular brand of idealism from public life during the early 1920s was filled by the pragmatism of the leaders of the business community during the presidencies of Warren Harding, Calvin Coolidge, and Herbert Hoover.

The influences of these dramatic changes in the nature of American society during the late teens and early 1920s were reflected in the ideology of the period. As noted earlier, Pease et al. (1970) coined the phrase "evolutionary liberalism" to describe the intellectual undercurrent that was dominant during this period in our history. This viewpoint visualized the economy as a free market capitalist system with a focus on individual motivation and achievement as major determinants for success within a framework that stresses the evolutionary adjustment of the system to changing circumstances. Such an outlook on society and the economy is consistent with the perspective put forward by classical economic theory during the early nineteenth century (compare Sherman 1983), with one slight modification. The new economic order of the 1920s was different from that of early capitalism in that the corporation and monopoly had come to play increasing roles in its everyday operations. Schwendinger and Schwendinger (1974), in response to their perceptions of the salient role that corporations had begun to play, prefer the term "corporate liberalism" to describe the dominant ideology of the 1920s.

In summary, as America prepared to enter the decade of the 1930s, the economy was growing rapidly, there was high employment, the upper and middle classes in particular were enjoying a level of material comfort unparalleled in world history, business interests were in firm control of government, and, in contrast to the turn-of-the-century pessimism, a spirit of optimism about the present and confidence about the future prevailed.[1]

The Great Depression

Quite suddenly, in 1929–30, the pristine image of the future formed under the influence of the events during the 1920s was shattered by the arrival of the Great Depression, and suddenly, as business began to slow down and unemployment grew, following the stock market indexes, the national mood began the long slide into a deepening pessimism and sense of doubt about the vitality of capitalism (Schlesinger 1957, 1958; Allen 1931; Manchester 1974).

What were the major causes of this depression? Schlesinger (1957) has put forth a number of suggestions: the disposition of management to maintain prices and inflate profits while holding down wages and raw material prices, which resulted in a decline of purchasing power; overbuilt productive capacities whose growth had been stimulated by the war; speculation in the stock market that was influenced by tremendous profit opportunities; and inconsistent government tax and monetary policies. In sum, the Depression seems to have been the result of irresponsibilities in both the private and the public sectors of society, stimulated, in part at least, by the rapid rates of growth and change during the 1920s.

Whatever the causes, the consequences, as the early 1930s continued, were massive: hundreds of banks closed, taking with them the savings of millions of Americans; business failure rates escalated; unemployment rates exceeded 20 percent, and combined un- and underemployment rates were far higher than that; further, the welfare "system," which was hopelessly modest, highly decentralized and local, and almost totally privately funded, proved increasingly unable to cope with the growing needs of the population, leaving thousands homeless and without food or clothing.

Despite these growing problems, however, government intervention was not immediately forthcoming. The failure on the part of the federal government to act is at least partially explained by the fact that policy makers turned to both the social sciences and the business community for advice concerning appropriate responses to this largely unanticipated crisis. The newly emerged economics establishment, following the prescriptions of classical economic theory, could not account for the Depression because, according to that perspective, the economy was supposed to be an essentially self-regulating system. Despite the lack of correspondence between theoretical expectations and the realities of the early 1930s, many economists remained convinced that the theory was sound, and, thus, that the economy would, sooner or later, pull itself out of the Depression. Consistent with classical economic theory, they remained wary of government interference in the natural operation of the market system. As a result, President Hoover was inclined to share the perspective of the business community that saw the problem as not endemic to the economy but as "psychological" — the result of a lack of confidence in the economy (Schlesinger 1957:243). Thus, "no basic attempts were made to tackle the structural diffi- culties in the economy — the fatal imbalance between business and agriculture, or the jerry-built banking system, or the unreliable security exchanges — nor was there sustained effort to increase purchasing power" (Schlesinger 1957:246).

Because things seemed to be growing worse, many began to feel that something must be done. Allen's (1940:65) interpretation was that "the country was losing patience with adversity." In the words of Schlesinger (1958:3), "it was hard to underestimate the need for action. It was a matter of seeing whether a representative democracy could conquer economic collapse. . . . Whether revolution was a real possibility or not, faith in the free system was plainly waning. Capitalism would not rise to economic crisis."

Despite their perceptions of threats to basic institutions, however, most Americans seemed unwilling to discard the belief structure with which they had entered the 1930s and unwilling to insist that changes were necessary. The strength of their commitment to the value system is demonstrated by the fact that while there were riots and other forms of serious unrest during the early 1930s, there were no major organized attempts to make fundamental changes in key social institutions. At the same time, it was also becoming increas- ingly clear that the population preferred a different approach for dealing with the problems facing the nation. This was certainly the case for intellectuals during the period. Pease et al. (1970:129) reported that "for the first time, American sociologists appeared to be disposed to abandon adherence to the liberal *laissez faire* ideology and to be willing to examine the economic and political under- pinnings of [the society]."

One good indicator of society's changing mood was the fact that a Democrat, Franklin Roosevelt, defeated the incumbent Republican, Herbert Hoover, in the presidential election of 1932, based on a platform that stressed concerted governmental action as a strategy for dealing with the deepening economic crisis. One also gets a sense that the platform position was more than campaign rhetoric when, as Schlesinger (1958:98) has written, early during the postelection period, the following conversation took place between Roosevelt and one of his advisors: "[the advisor] 'You realize then, that you're taking an enormous step away from the philosophy of equalitarianism and laissez faire?' Roosevelt, silent for a moment, replied with great earnestness, 'If that philosophy hadn't proved to be bankrupt, Herbert Hoover would be sitting here right now.'"

Yet Roosevelt's position was a delicate one. There were pressures from both sides of the ideological continuum for very different strategies for change. On the right were the still powerful, although certainly chastened, business interests. Their attitudes toward the crisis were consistent with classical economics and ranged from one extreme to the other — from letting the economy alone to recover on its own, to making minimal concessions such as investment credits, and so on. From the left side of the ideological spectrum were those, including communists and socialists, who wanted to solve the economic crisis by making dramatic changes in the nature of the entire political economic system. Between these extremes were a myriad of other opinions about the causes of the crisis and its solution. Schlesinger (1957:204) captured the polarization of opinion of many during this period:

> John Maynard Keynes spoke for the pragmatic reformers in his *Saturday Evening Post* article of 1930. "I predict," he wrote, "that both of the two opposed errors of pessimism which now make so much noise in the world will be proved wrong in our time — the pessimism of the revolutionaries who think that things are so bad that nothing can save us except violent change, and the pessimism of the reactionaries who consider the balance of our economic and social life so precarious that we must risk no experiments."

In spite of the fact that there was great domestic pressure on Roosevelt to develop strategies for dealing with the economic crisis, it should not be forgotten that world events, in spite of the prevailing mood of isolationism in the United States, were also to exercise important conditioning influences on his decisions. While the solutions developed in many other Western countries were similar to those adopted by Roosevelt, in that they sought foremost to preserve capitalism and, to a limited extent, to modify it through government actions within the framework of democratic principles, other countries reacted in very different ways. In particular, Germany, Italy, Spain, and Japan reacted to the crisis of world capitalism in a decidedly antidemocratic manner, creating totalitarian, militaristic, and imperial states.

Roosevelt seemed keenly aware of these events as his policies began to take shape (Schlesinger 1957, 1958). Of course, as subsequent events were to demonstrate, Roosevelt charted a course that was midway between those available to him. While his efforts certainly did not challenge the fundamental nature of capitalism as an economic system (O'Connor 1973), his primary focus for those efforts clearly reflected his basic distrust for business interests because it sought to place the public's interests above those of private individuals (Schlesinger 1958). In other words, Roosevelt seemed convinced that the days of laissez-faire were gone and that the government must assume a greater role in economic planning and regulation if the system was to survive.

The actions taken by Roosevelt and the federal government during the middle years of the 1930s tended to reflect this viewpoint — despite mounting opposition from the business community that became increasingly convinced that the president was driving the country down the road to socialism (Schlesinger 1958). Yet, in many respects, the very latitude the country gave to Roosevelt during this period was a testament to how serious the crisis had become to many and to their growing distrust of the motives of the business community. The Roosevelt solution tended to combine a number of different elements. The New Deal stressed actions to control speculative business and finance, to encourage the formation of labor unions, to use the government as an employer of last resort in the area of public works projects, and to provide a social security net beneath the American worker and his or her family. Also, in sharp contrast to Hoover's insistence that government spending levels remain at or below revenues, Roosevelt, under the influence of Keynes, used deficit spending as a means for financing the recovery. Of course, whether this "Keynesian" strategy would, by itself, have ended the Depression must remain a topic for academic speculation, since growing militarism in the world and the beginning of World War II provided the economic stimulus for an end to the worldwide Depression before the effects of the New Deal policies could be determined. By the late 1930s and early 1940s, most of the world was involved in a worldwide struggle that pitted democratic capitalist and socialist countries against the fascist governments of Germany, Italy, and Japan.

The Early Post-World War II Period

One important outcome of the struggle in Europe was that the American wartime economy gradually began to return to the levels of growth and prosperity that it had enjoyed during the 1920s. This period that began with the end of the war witnessed the most rapid and prolonged economic expansion in world history (Cohen and Rogers 1983; Johnson 1983:660). For a number of reasons (including its geographic isolation from the fields of battle, the tremendous growth in its industrial might that resulted from meeting the wartime material needs of its allies, "pent-up" consumer demand from its own large domestic market, the destruction of the industrial and financial infrastructures of the other potential world leaders, etc.), the United States was in a unique position during this period to assume the role of the leading economic and political power in the world (Kennedy 1988), with all the many benefits (and liabilities) that such a role can offer. As a result, a new world order was organized with the United States playing the major role as both the supplier of the capital and material means for rebuilding Western Europe and Japan and as the guarantor of world peace.

As a result of America's growing prosperity in the world economy, the overall standard of living of most of its citizens rose dramatically, unemployment fell, and opportunities expanded. Within this environment, memories of banking and business failures and long unemployment and welfare lines began to recede from the public consciousness, and concern about the limitations of capitalism were replaced by renewed optimism about the future and the vitality of a new model of capitalism with a greatly expanded role for the federal government in its day-to-day operations. A popular book written by economist John Kenneth Galbraith (*The Affluent Society*, 1958) captured the mood of the times. He argues that the days of shortages were over and that the only problem facing affluent Western societies was simply to equitably distribute the abundant outputs of the economy; and, in keeping with the trend toward a modestly interventionist state that was consistent with Keynesianism (and as operationalized by Roosevelt's New Deal), Galbraith envisages the state as playing the key role in mediating and directing these distributive decisions.

With regard to the general intellectual climate, it has been noted that almost as quickly as the economy made its recovery, the pessimism that had pervaded during the darkest days of the Depression was replaced by a renewed optimism and confidence that the new American system that emerged from the Depression and the war was once again strong and healthy (Pease et al. 1970), and that individualism was once again the major ingredient in the success equation. A second example of scholarship during the immediate post–World War II period that is of particular interest here, given his explicit attention to the issue of class inequality, is the work of Daniel Bell (1960). He asserts that the rapidly expanding economy and the overall lessening of economic inequality within society that resulted from this growth has had one important consequence: that class has lost its saliency as a structural variable in postwar America. An important result of this trend, according to Bell, is that the older polarization between the "left" ideology of the working class and that of the "bourgeois" business class that had historically "framed" political debate within capitalist industrial society had reached the point of exhaustion in postwar America and was rapidly giving way to a new middle-class-dominated politics largely devoid of ideology. Bell's image of life within American society during the

1950s seems to reflect a growing consensus among the intellectuals (including Galbraith) that America was rapidly becoming a middle class society and, as a result, that problems such as economic scarcity and the unequal distribution of economic rewards were essentially (or imminently would be) "solved" and thus were no longer of concern to the vast majority of the members of society.

DISCIPLINARY REACTIONS

By the end of World War I, sociology began to experience what might be labeled a new set of growing pains. As noted in Chapter 2, the discipline's establishment within the American academic community around the turn of the century was facilitated more by the growing demand for research on the myriad of societal problems that accompanied industrialization, urbanization, and immigration and the need for professional training for social workers than by its own theoretical and methodological uniqueness (Small 1916; Oberschall 1972). Not long after the discipline got its foot in the door of American academic institutions (even if as only the "littlest science" [Mazur 1968]), however, it was put under increasing pressure by older disciplines, by university administrators, and by various consumers of its knowledge (such as governmental agencies, private foundations, and the general public) to demonstrate that it deserved its newly acquired status as a member of the social science community. Predictably, these pressures gradually increased as the reformist zeal of the Progressive Era slowly began to give way to the more pragmatic orientation toward society that followed the end of the war (Bannister 1987; Vidich and Lyman 1985).

In response to these challenges, many members of the discipline became more self-conscious about its marginal status within the scientific community. One reaction to this disciplinary "identity" crisis was the initiation of attempts to professionalize the field. As scholars turned their attention to this new task, the more established natural sciences provided readily available role models for the discipline. Bannister's (1987:3) recent assessment of this period in the discipline's history reflects this orientation: "During the 1920s, some American sociologists found new life in the old idea that the natural and the social sciences were (or should be) governed by similar concepts and methods."

It is important to note, however, that these scholars were not (at least at first) in the majority, since, for most members of the discipline during this particular period in its history, the natural sciences provided too sharp a contrast to the then taken-for-granteds of early American sociology, particularly its overtly reformist orientation.[2] One observer of the period has remarked that "the identification of 'sociology' with practical or applied sociology and social reform was the majority view even in academic circles and made the task of scientific and academic legitimacy a very delicate and difficult one for the early academic sociologists" (Oberschall 1972:209).

Despite such obstacles, however, as the discipline entered the 1920s, a growing number of sociologists, particularly those at leading research institutions, began to realize that the only means by which the discipline would be accepted by its diverse constituencies was, in some senses, to adopt the orientation and methods of the natural sciences. Despite the fact that the struggle was largely uphill at first, through the efforts of these scholars the discipline gradually began to distance itself from its reformist past and to adopt a new professional orientation.

This new disciplinary posturing explicitly embraced several key features of the natural science perspective — strict neutrality in matters of ethics and public policy, the separation of the role of scientists from that of citizen and reformer, and greater rigor in theorizing and research (Oberschall 1972:242; Bannister 1987:3).[3] One important result of the discipline's stress on the first of these was that it began to distance itself from its reformist roots:

> the origin of sociology in reform also serves as a backdrop for the sharp reaction against preaching, muckraking, and value judgments that set-in in the 1920s, when sociology was more firmly established and professionalized, and was trying to thin out of its ranks the reformers and dilettantes who were no longer needed and were becoming a source of embarrassment to the discipline (Oberschall 1972:205).

Another important consequence was that, by observing the scientific canon of neutrality toward its subject matter, the discipline's early critical posturing toward society began to be replaced by a new viewpoint that offered (at least implicit) support for the status quo. The results of the discipline's greater attention to such issues became increasingly apparent in its media during the 1920s, as the proportion of articles that were philosophical essays or opinion pieces declined and the proportion that adopted the posturing of a disinterested observer increased.

Greater attention to other ingredients in this new professional orientation — particularly to theoretical and methodological issues — was also increasingly apparent. The leading research department within the discipline — at the University of Chicago — played a key role in redirecting the attention of the members of the discipline toward these issues. Coser (1978:312) has observed that

> it seems no exaggeration to say that for roughly twenty years, from the first world war to the mid-1930s, the history

of sociology in America can largely be written as the history of the Department of Sociology at the University of Chicago. During these years, the department set the general tone of sociological inquiries, published the only major journal of the discipline, and trained most of the sociologists who made a mark on the profession and who assumed the presidency of the American Sociological Society.

Research by Chicago faculty and Chicago-trained faculty at other institutions provided important role models for scholarship within the discipline. Methodologically, Chicago scholars pioneered systematic fieldwork-oriented studies and later statistical investigations as well (Coser 1978:312). Further, despite the fact that Chicago was not known for its theoretical contributions, Coser concludes that the concerns of early members of the Chicago faculty with theoretical issues were less apparent than might otherwise be the case only because they were often subordinated to their specific research requirements.

The ensuing several decades witnessed continued concern among sociologists with the scientific status of the discipline. By the middle of the 1930s, for example, a shift in institutional leadership within the discipline away from the University of Chicago had occurred. During this period in the discipline's history, two other institutions assumed important roles in sociology's continued professionalization as Chicago's leadership within the discipline declined — these were Harvard and Columbia universities.

In reaction to the fragmented and disorganized state of theory within the discipline, attention at Harvard was gradually directed toward the development of an integrated theory of society. As will be shown in Chapter 4, the efforts of Talcott Parsons and several of his colleagues and students at Harvard led to the development of what is now labeled the functionalist theoretical perspective. This particular viewpoint was consistent with the prosperity of post–World War II America and dominated the discipline for the next quarter-century. At Columbia, attention was directed toward issues surrounding the improvement of social science research methods and procedures. A major center for social science research was established there with survey research as its hallmark, and members of Columbia's sociology faculty assumed dominant roles in both setting standards for research within the discipline and in representing the discipline as advisors to business and government.

As a result of the leadership provided by scholars at these and other major research institutions, by the end of World War II sociology was firmly institutionalized within American society, the functionalist theoretical perspective dominated the field, survey research was the dominant form of data gathering, and sociology's practitioners were serving as advisors to policy makers at local, regional, and national levels.

SUMMARY

Sociology emerged in early twentieth-century America as a part of the larger Progressive response to the myriad problems that faced the society during the late nineteenth and early twentieth centuries. Given its early roles in training social workers and in providing data for social reformers, the field was established before it developed its own unique theoretical and methodological perspectives. By the early 1920s, however, the discipline came under increased pressure to defend its status both within the university and within the larger society as well. As a response to these pressures, sociologists began to demonstrate greater concern for the professional status of the discipline. In this context, many sociologists increasingly turned to the natural sciences for role models for the discipline. Using the natural sciences as a benchmark, American sociologists adopted a value-neutral orientation toward society and began to pay greater attention to theoretical and methodological rigor in their research. Two important results of the operation of these influences on the discipline by the end of World War II were the emergence, and eventually the theoretical hegemony, of the functionalist theoretical perspective and the adoption of the social survey as the dominant form of research within the discipline. The chapters in this section of the book discuss these trends within the discipline as they apply to the study of class inequality within American society.

NOTES

1. In retrospect, however, it is clear that other segments of the population, including the working class, the farmers, and the poor, did not share in the prosperity of the period, and that all was not well with the American economy (Schlesinger 1957).

2. Oberschall notes (1972:205) that the discipline has battled with two concerns historically — practical concern and social betterment, and scientific objectivity and professionalism. Bannister (1987:10) observes that the years between the wars within the discipline were filled with a debate between those favoring "objectivity" and those favoring "reform."

3. A leading scholar of the period, Sorokin, expresses this new orientation in the following quote from the preface of his *Social Mobility* (1927:ix): "Speculative sociology is passing over. An objective, factual, behavioristic, and quantitative sociology is successfully superseding it."

3

EARLY FUNCTIONALISM: SOCIAL ANTHROPOLOGICAL ANALYSES OF CLASS INEQUALITY IN AMERICAN COMMUNITY LIFE

Many who have analyzed the development of the functionalist perspective on class inequality begin their discussion with the work of Talcott Parsons and his students, whose works were published during the late 1930s and the early 1940s. It is commonly accepted that Parsons fashioned the general perspective from theoretical raw materials derived from European scholarship, and that he, along with his students Kingsley Davis and Wilbert Moore, then applied the perspective to the issue of class inequality (Ritzer 1983). A review of leading stratification texts reveals the dominance of this viewpoint (Abramson, Mizrucki, and Hornung 1976; Rossides 1976; Kriesberg 1979; Vanfossen 1979; Matras 1975). And, although other scholars are occasionally mentioned in the context of the perspective, rarely are their contributions to its development fully explored.[1]

This chapter examines the works of three social anthropologists who wrote during the inter- and early post–World War II period — Robert Lynd, W. Lloyd Warner, and August Hollingshead — and highlights their contributions to the development of the functionalist perspective on class inequality. It should be noted here that their work either clearly preceded that of Parsons and his students or was contemporary with their work. As noted in the introduction to Part II of this book, the period of time during which these scholars completed their research and published their results was extremely heterogeneous. The Lynds conducted their first study of "Middletown" during the decade of the 1920s, a time of rapid growth and prosperity in America. In contrast, their second study of "Middletown" and Warner's research in "Yankee City" both were completed during the middle of the Great Depression. Then, Warner's study of "Jonestown" and Hollingshead's study of "Elmtown" (the same city) were completed during the early 1940s. Finally, Hollingshead and Redlich's study of New Haven took place in the 1950s.

Despite important differences, these studies are similar in several respects. First, each of them employed some aspect of class inequality as a major organizing dimension of its research. Second, these studies also represent early attempts to forge a coherent theoretical perspective on the subject of class inequality in American community life — a perspective heavily indebted to the functionalism of early twentieth-century British social anthropology. Third, for various reasons, including the state of the art within the field and the theoretical predispositions of these scholars, the setting for each (except for Hollingshead's second study) was a single, often small community, and researchers actually spent intensive periods observing and analyzing life within the community. As a consequence of these studies, this period in the history of the discipline was one of tremendous expansion in our knowledge both about life in American society as a whole and about the role that class inequalities play in organizing the relations among the members of society.

These studies also represent a distinct period in the growth of the discipline. As will be shown later, by the end of the 1950s the focus of attention for American sociologists interested in the issues of class inequality had shifted to the national level, and the conceptualization and measurement of class was becoming increasingly oriented toward instruments that could be used in the interview and questionnaire studies of national samples of respondents. In a sense, then, this earlier period represents a kind of adolescence for the discipline during which research was more unstructured and open. In fact, much of the value of these studies (not to mention many of the liabilities) stems from these attributes. While my choice of studies by the Lynds, Warner, and Hollingshead is to some extent selective and does not include all of the many studies conducted during the period in question, these are acknowledged to be the major studies during the period, and each set the pace for research during some portion of the period (Gordon 1963).

ROBERT AND HELEN LYND'S "MIDDLETOWN" STUDIES

I begin my analysis of the major efforts to conceptualize, measure, and employ the notion of "social class" as a variable in social science research in community settings with the work of Robert and Helen Lynd. Their studies of "Middletown" represent the first use of class as an organizing dimension in a holistic setting within American sociology and served as an important stimulus for subsequent research on the subject (Madge 1962: Chap. 5).

The Lynds' Background

At the time of their first study of "Middletown" (the pseudonym that they gave the city in their research reports), neither of the Lynds had received any formal training as social scientists (Madge 1962:131). They had grown to adulthood in middle-class families during the decade of the 1920s, and Robert's formal educational background was in theology. He had graduated from the Union Theological Seminary immediately prior to the beginning of the "Middletown" fieldwork, and the "Middletown" study was sponsored by the Institute for Social and Religious Research, a leading supporter of social research during the period (Oberschall 1972:202). Robert's Ph.D. in sociology was granted by Columbia University at the time he joined the faculty there *after* his "Middletown" research.

Theoretical Antecedents

Because of their relative lack of experience in the social sciences, their search for theoretical and methodological support was somewhat eclectic. As I have shown in Chapter 2, within sociology itself, extant guidelines during this period in its history were theoretically diffused and scattered (see Small 1916). While scholars at the University of Chicago continued to conduct research in the metropolitan area, none of these studies had tried to deal with a community taken as a whole. This does not mean that the results of the Chicago school efforts would not have been useful to the Lynds, however, for such studies did contain valuable insights that could have been applied. Yet studies of particular relevance to their effort, such as Harvey Zorbaugh's *The Gold Coast and the Slum* (1929), were themselves only being written at this time. While the reasons for the Lynds' failure to make use of those insights that were available from sociology are unclear, they seem likely to have been the result of their lack of previous exposure to studies within the discipline.

The Lynds turned instead to the field of social anthropology for theoretical and methodological assistance.[2] In America, that discipline was still fledgling and heavily dependent upon British social anthropology, which itself had begun a rather important transformation during the first quarter of the twentieth century under the direction of W. H. R. Rivers. Langham (1981:50), in his discussion of the rise of British social anthropology, credits Rivers as follows:

> William Halse Rivers was the man who, more than any other, diverted the attention of British anthropologists from the evolution of religious thought to the *synchronic functionings of single societies* ... [and] Rivers and his

colleagues . . . were decisive in bringing about a change over from nineteenth century style social evolutionism to twentieth century style *structural-functionalism* [italics added].

The Lynds make extensive use of both the field research methods and the functionalist perspective of early British social anthropology in their work in Muncie, Indiana (the real "Middletown"). With regard to the former, Hays (1965:368) characterizes their choice of research strategies in "Middletown" as "a pioneering attempt to study an American community by approaching it as an anthropologist approached a primitive tribe." As a part of their research agenda, the Lynds, along with several assistants, spent a total of eighteen months in Muncie during 1924 and 1925, and Robert subsequently returned there ten years later for a shorter period of time. While on location in the city, they made use of participant observation, documents, available statistics, interviews, and questionnaires. The results of their research efforts are reported in two volumes published in 1929 and 1937.

The Research Setting

As the setting within which to study their subject — the "interwoven trends that are life in a small American city" — the authors selected a "typical" Midwestern, industrial city, Muncie, Indiana, which had, by the time of their first research visit, a population of 38,000 (Lynd and Lynd 1929:3ff). They note that there were two major considerations in the selection of Muncie: that it be as representative as possible of contemporary American life, and that it be reasonably compact and homogeneous. In response to these requirements, they sought an industrial city that was undergoing population growth and that had a large native-born population. Their selection of the pseudonym "Middletown" reflects the fact that they considered it typical of small American cities during this period in its history. Their descriptions of the city throughout the first volume (Lynd and Lynd 1929) indicates that Muncie shared in the overall prosperity of the country during the decade of the 1920s, with economic growth, low unemployment, and growing opportunities for its citizens. They also observe that the same optimism about the future and faith in progress said to be characteristic of this period in American history were also typical of "Middletown" residents during this period in its history.

Conceptualizing and Measuring of Social Inequality

As noted above, the Lynds' theoretical framework is derived from Rivers' (1924) work and generally shares his functionalist

orientation.[3] As a result, they structured their data gathering
around his six "main-trunk" activities that they believed were also
descriptive of life in Muncie: getting a living, making a home,
training the young, using leisure, engaging in religious practices,
and engaging in community activities (Lynd and Lynd 1929:4). In
their initial application of Rivers' perspective, they did not weight the
various groups of activities in terms of relative importance in the
lives of the citizens of "Middletown"; however, very early in the study
(p. 21) they observe that

> not only do those engaged in getting the living of the group
> predominate numerically, but as the study progressed it
> became more and more apparent that the money medium of
> exchange and the cluster of activities associated with its
> acquisition drastically condition the other activities of the
> people.

Because of this conclusion, from this point forward in their study,
they place greater emphasis upon the relative importance of "getting
a living" activities when compared with the other main-trunk
activities contained within the original conceptual framework.

As a part of this emphasis, the Lynds sought some means for
operationalizing the differences among the citizens in terms of their
observations (pp. 21–22):

> at first glance it is difficult to see any semblance of pattern in
> the workaday life of a community exhibiting crazy quilt
> array of nearly four hundred ways of getting its living. . . .
> On closer scrutiny, however, this welter can be resolved into
> two kinds of activities. The people who engage in them will
> be referred to throughout the report as the Working Class
> and the Business Class. Members of the first group, by and
> large, address their activities in getting their living pri-
> marily to *things*, utilizing material tools in the making of
> things and the performance of services, while members of
> the second group address their activities predominantly to
> *people* in the selling or promotion of things, services or
> ideas.

Thus, their application of Rivers' scheme to an analysis of life in
Muncie revealed that "getting a living" as a set of activities had
significant consequences for the lives of the citizens of the city, and
that, in pursuing these activities, the citizens' experiences were
sufficiently different that they could be divided into two relatively
distinctive classes that they labeled business and working classes.[4]
They admit that the classification that results from their observations

is crude and contained a certain amount of ambiguity (p. 23),[5] but they conclude that the significance of the division into these occupational classes is so important that these difficulties have to be tolerated:

> there is naturally . . . a twilight belt in which some members of the two groups overlap or merge. . . . While an effort will be made to make clear at certain points variant behavior within these two groups, it is after all this division into working class and business class that constitutes the outstanding cleavage in Middletown. The mere fact of being born upon one or the other side of the watershed roughly formed by these two groups is the most significant single cultural factor tending to influence what one does all day long throughout one's life (pp. 23–24).

Throughout the remainder of the book they demonstrate the saliency of class by dividing the families in the community into these two classes and comparing their activities in each of the remaining five main-trunk activities. For each of these, the attitudes and behaviors of the classes are shown to differ markedly.

Critique

My critique of the Lynds' work will be organized around three sets of salient issues: theoretical/conceptual, methodological, and value configurational. Regarding the first of these issues, the Lynds were heavily indebted to the British functionalist school of social anthropology; this perspective stresses the integrative roles of social institutions and minimizes the disintegrative effects of such institutions. Thus, despite the fact that the Lynds viewed class as a salient influence on the lives of "Middletowners," they still tended to view the class system as being essentially functionally integrated with the other main-trunk activities in the community (Madge 1962). The fact that the Lynds also viewed class as an important source for social differentiation within the community (despite their initial theoretical orientation) gains importance because their study was conducted during times of relative economic prosperity. Class antagonisms, if indeed they existed at all in "Middletown," should certainly have been less evident during such times when compared to more troublesome economic times.[6] Evidence for the impact of the overall societal setting on levels of class inequality is available when the findings of the first study are compared with those of the follow up that was conducted during the Depression years of the 1930s. There, the Lynds find both the economic situation and the assessments of class by "Middletowners" to be very different, with the result that their second report places even greater stress on the conflictual effects of class: the emergence of an "upper class" that was not found in the first study; the wide variation in the effects of the Depression on families by class; and the long-term intergenerational consequences of the class system. Each of these are telling pieces of evidence for the presence of inequality based on class in "Middletown" (Lynd and Lynd 1937). While the changes within the setting that took place between the two studies are important, it is also true that the Lynds' own efforts to interpret the interrelationships among their variables was also changing. For example, while there is no reference to the work of Marx in *Middletown* (1929), in *Middletown in Transition* (1937) not only is Marx cited, but he is also made a part of their discussion and interpretation. One of their observations in the latter report seems to reflect this shift in their perspective: "And, yet, despite the fact that tradition, inertia, and intent combine to blur any potential class differences, indications of a sharpening of awareness of some class lines continually breaks through tendencies to bury them" (Lynd and Lynd 1937:450). For yet another indicator of this shift in their theoretical orientation, the reader should be reminded that Robert Lynd's highly critical *Knowledge for What?*, which appeared in 1940, took the discipline to task for its uncritical acceptance of dominant institutional arrangements in American society. Such a book is far removed from the functionalism of Rivers and British social anthropology.[7]

In summary, the Lynds' conceptualization of class reflects the interplay among the overall setting, their own developing theoretical orientation, their research procedures, and their findings. Their decision to focus on class cleavages within the community seems to have been based more on the saliency of these activities for the lives of the citizens that they observed during their early fieldwork than on their initial theoretical perspective. They chose to operationalize the differences that they observed using a variable based on occupational position. That this decision resulted in some degree of ambiguity is evidenced by their own remarks (Lynd and Lynd 1929:23–24). In their defense, however, the crudeness of their operationalization seems to have been largely an artifact of the research methods they chose to employ in the study. Because of these decisions, the net result of their research was a study that was full of descriptive detail but that lacked analytical rigor by more contemporary standards.[8]

Despite the manifestly functionalist orientation that the Lynds adopted early during their studies and the support for the status quo that such a perspective entails, their own value orientation was far less compatible with that orientation than might otherwise be expected. Even in the early volume, they were careful to delineate the negative consequences of the class system such as the denial of equal opportunity to all within the community. In the later volume, they consistently pointed out shortcomings with the extant system of class inequality and devoted the final chapter to a detailed examination of the crises created in the fabric of life in "Middletown" by the Depression and its aftermath. In short, the value orientation of the Lynds, as evidenced in their publications, moved consistently to the left ideologically during their careers, causing them to increasingly question the utility of the political economy and the dominant ideology that supported it (Lynd 1940).

The information assembled above supports the position that the Lynds' developing theoretical perspective, research findings, and interpretations concerning life in "Middletown" were the result of the interaction of their own personal biographies with the sociohistorical setting within which they conducted their research, the dominant ideology that reflected that setting, and extant theoretical perspectives available to them. As such, the relative prosperity of the early 1920s, with the resulting atmosphere of optimism and faith in the extant political economy and an ideology that stressed that there were opportunities for all and that access to these was limited only by the drive and the application of native abilities, are compatible with a theoretical perspective that views social institutions as mutually integrative and social inequality as having largely beneficial consequences. The changes in tenor and interpretations that appear in *Middletown in Transition*, based on research conducted in very different sociohistorical circumstances during the economic crisis of the Great Depression and the profound pessimism it generated about the future, tend to support this linkage, since the authors, in this context, moved further away from the functionalist interpretations of the earlier study and openly discussed the negative effects of class on the lives of the citizens. This shift in emphasis should in no way be interpreted as an attempt to demean their work or to diminish its importance for subsequent research on social inequality in American sociology. My goal is simply to show that their work was the product of particular periods in history, and thus was influenced by material, ideological, and theoretical settings, as well as by the Lynds' personal experiences during these periods. Failure to make these linkages explicit would result in a less than complete understanding of their work.

W. LLOYD WARNER'S RESEARCH

The second group of studies in which class plays a major role are those completed under the direction of W. Lloyd Warner. I will focus attention on Warner's treatment of "social class" as it was initially developed during his study of "Yankee City," during the early 1930s, and as it was later refined and modified in his analysis of "Jonesville" during the early 1940s.

Warner's Background

W. Lloyd Warner, the principal investigator for both studies, grew to adulthood in a middle-class family environment in post–World War I America. He received a bachelor's degree from Berkeley and attended Harvard for his graduate education. A social anthropologist by education and training, he spent three years during the mid-1920s studying a "stone age" people in Australia (Warner 1937) before returning to Harvard in 1929 as a faculty member. Upon his return, he immediately became involved with Elton Mayo's Western Electric studies, which were sponsored by the university's Committee on Industrial Physiology. It was within this setting that Warner began his research on life in small-town America.

Theoretical Antecedents

Another important influence on Warner's work was the fund of available social scientific knowledge at his disposal. Warner relied much more heavily on anthropology and European sociology than he did on American scholarship for his perspective.[9] Warner's theoretical perspective is informed by three diverse strands of thought and the key individuals who represented them: first, he was influenced by diffusionism as a student of Lowie, a leading proponent of that perspective, while he was at Berkeley; second, functionalism — here he was influenced by both Malinowski and Radcliffe-Brown, who were colleagues at Chicago and in Australia when he was doing his research on a primitive tribe; finally, Durkheimian sociology — largely through the profound impact that Radcliffe-Brown had on him during their association. Analysts agree that Durkheimian sociology was the greatest of these influences (Kuper 1973; Hays 1965). Given the centrality of his influence on Warner and the focus of our argument — Warner's use of functionalism in his work — a brief quote concerning Radcliffe-Brown's perspective seems appropriate:

> Radcliffe-Brown . . . was interested in using the concept of function to introduce the question of equilibrium and social order. . . . His assumptions were . . . that all living societies are functionally harmonious, and that any operational element within a society *does* contribute to the overall concordance. Such assumptions point to the basic metaphor lying behind Radcliffe-Brown's theoretical position — the analogy of society as an organism (Langham 1981:xiv).

Warner's (Warner and Lunt 1941:14) own introductory remarks in the first volume of the "Yankee City" study reflect Radcliffe-Brown's (and thereby Durkheim's) influence:

Yankee City, we assume, was a "working whole" in which each part had *definite* functions which had to be performed, or substitutes acquired, if the whole society were to maintain itself. . . . The observation that most, if not all societies have a fundamental structure or structures which *integrate* and give characteristic form to the rest of society was a leading idea in our theoretical equipment [italics added].

As is suggested by this quote, Warner's theoretical perspective is functionalist in character, stressing as it does a view of society as a stable set of mutually integrative institutions. It is also ahistorical, static, and emphasizes consensus rather than conflict (De Waal Malefijt 1974; Kuper 1973; Chinoy 1950).

The Research Settings

As a part of the Western Electric studies, Mayo and Warner conclude that in order to understand the worker at her or his job, it is necessary to examine the larger context of the worker's life (Warner and Lunt 1941:4). Warner, who already had a keen interest in applying the techniques that social anthropology used to study primitive peoples to modern society, proposed just such an analysis.

It seemed logical that his study should focus on the communities in and around the Western Electric plant in the Chicago area, since that was where the Mayo group was working. However, for several reasons, including the fact that these suburban communities seemed to be disorganized, Warner felt that the techniques of social anthropology would be less useful there. Thus Warner sought a different setting for his research: "We sought above all a well-integrated community, where the various parts of the society were functioning with comparative ease. We did not want a city where the ordinary daily relations were in confusion and conflict" (Warner and Lunt 1941:38).

The site selected as a setting for the research was a small coastal community in New England — Newburyport, Massachusetts — that was given the pseudonym "Yankee City." The city's population at the time of Warner's study was approximately 17,000. Over half of the city's population was native American, with newer immigrant groups comprising the remainder (Warner and Lunt 1941:77). The city's economy was dominated by shoe and other manufacturing; as a result, the authors report that nearly half of its work force was semiskilled. It is also clear from their description that Warner and Lunt (p. 79) viewed the city as a typical American industrial town, both economically and socially. Finally, in keeping with their selection criteria noted in the previous paragraph, the authors also noted that the community had "maintained a stable population in a stable society" (Warner and Lunt 1941:79).

Employing techniques similar to those of the Lynds, Warner and his research associates intensively analyzed life in the community from 1930 to 1934. In the course of their efforts, they made use of a variety of research strategies and materials, including interviews with informants; participant observation; questionnaires; case histories; biographies, life histories, and autobiographies; genealogies and kinship charts; and documentary and written materials (Warner and Lunt 1941:Chap. 3). The results of this particular research project are reported in five volumes published between 1941 and 1952.

Warner's conceptual approach and research strategies were refined and further elaborated during his study of "Jonesville" during the early 1940s. "Jonesville," a small, ethnically homogeneous community (population 6,200 in 1941), was located in the Midwest. The community's economy was based on a combination of agriculture and diversified industries that ranged from coal mining to manufacturing (Hollingshead 1949:59). Its overall atmosphere was characterized by a fellow researcher as a "typical Middle Western community functionally, structurally, culturally, and historically" (Hollingshead 1949:59). The results of Warner's research in "Jonesville" were published in 1949 (Warner 1949a, 1949b).

As indicated by the dates of Warner's studies, both the national and the local settings of his research were dramatically different during the course of these studies. Data gathering in "Yankee City" occurred during the worst period of the Great Depression of the 1930s, his analysis and publication of these results occurred as America was exiting the Depression, entering World War II, and in the period following the war. Data-gathering in "Jonesville" occurred during the early 1940s, and its analysis and publication were during the late 1940s. Since these were times of great change in both the political economy and in the dominant ideology of the society, they serve as important potential influences on his developing perspective of the role of "social class" in American society.

Conceptualizing and Measuring Social Class

Somewhat in contrast to the Lynds' "discovery" that "getting a living" was a dominant feature of life in "Middletown," Warner and his associates entered the "Yankee City" setting convinced that the economic dimension was salient (Warner and Lunt 1941:81):

it was believed that the fundamental structure of our society, that which ultimately controls and dominates the thinking and actions of our people, is economic, and that the most vital and far-reaching value systems which motivate Americans are to be ultimately traced to an economic order.[10]

Convinced that this initial assumption was correct, the authors then proceeded to systematically examine the nature of life in "Yankee City."

In keeping with the procedures employed by anthropologists in their studies of primitive peoples, Warner and his associates depended heavily upon informants as sources of information about the community, and it was these individuals who provided support for both their initial assumption of the dominance of the economic structure and its later modification. According to the authors (Chap. 5), testimony by informants was filled with reference to the differential ranking of individuals in the community according to economic criteria.[11]

Yet, additional evidence provided by his informants convinced Warner that to visualize relations among the citizens of "Yankee City" solely in economic terms was not sufficient:

> economic factors are significant and important in determining the class position of any family or person, influencing the kind of behavior we find in any class, and contributing their share to the present form of the class system. But, while significant and necessary, the economic factors are not sufficient to predict where a particular family or individual will be or to explain completely the phenomenon of social class. Something more than a large income is necessary for high social position. Money must be translated into socially approved behavior and possessions, and they in turn must be translated into intimate participation with, and acceptance by, members of a superior class (Warner 1949a:21).

In this manner, Warner moves away from a purely objective economic basis for his definition of social classes toward a more subjective approach that stresses an individual's prestige within the status hierarchy of the community as reflected in his or her interaction patterns within the community.[12] His definition of class in the "Yankee City" research reflects this shift: "By class is meant two or more orders of people who are believed to be, and are accordingly ranked by the members of the community, into socially superior and inferior positions" (Warner and Lunt 1941:82). With this definition in mind, I now turn to an examination of the manner by which Warner operationalized the term for his "Yankee City" research.

This task is complicated because his description of the means by which social classes are delineated and measured is not sufficiently specified in the "Yankee City" volumes (Davis 1943:512). In the words of one commentator on his work:

> in the earlier studies of Yankee City and Old City the exact method by which the investigators placed individuals in the social class hierarchy is not recorded. . . . In placing people in the class system, respondents [variously] referred to an individual's place of residence, the kinds of people with whom he is in intimate association, the club and associations he joined, and such characteristics as income, education, and occupation (Kornhauser 1953:226).

This problem is corrected to some limited extent in 1949 with the publication of Warner's *Social Class in America* (1949a), wherein he describes and compares the two methods of class determination that were developed and utilized in the various studies and offers specifications for their uses. Of necessity, my discussion will be based on this ex post facto presentation of the techniques.

Evaluated Participation

The first of Warner's approaches to the measurement of class within a community setting is labeled *Evaluated Participation* (hereafter EP), and its purpose is to "translate the criteria and judgments of informants into explicit, verifiable results which will correspond with the class realities of the community" (Warner 1949a:38). It should be noted here that Warner insists that EP relies on informant judgments, rather than researcher judgments, both to define the class system of the community and to assign individuals and families to particular classes. In his own words, "the analyst does not impose his rankings upon the people of the town. . . . We must try to see the problem from the point of view of the informants, for they are the final authorities about the realities of American social class" (Warner 1949a:38).

Just how does the researcher apply EP? First, according to Warner (1949a:116) the class structure of the community is determined "from a number of interviews with several people."[13] Yet no information is provided concerning the selection of, or attributes for, these judges except that they are persons knowledgeable about the community and tend to view the community in class terms. In "Yankee City," the application of this procedure resulted in the delineation of six social classes, which are labeled upper upper, lower upper, upper middle, lower middle, upper lower, and lower lower. Warner argues that these classes are real, in the sense that the people in the community recognize them as such, and that they can be distinguished from one another by two attributes. First, each class has a distinctive life-style and, second, the classes structure social participation within the community.

Next, the individuals and families of the community are assigned to the various classes by means of six different techniques:

> rating by matched agreement — when several informants agree on the class location of an individual or family;
>
> rating by symbolic placement — when an individual is assigned to a class because he has the reputation for engaging in activities considered to be superior or inferior by informants;
>
> rating by status reputation — when informants make remarks about an individual with status connotations;
>
> rating by comparison — where placement is based on a comparison between an individual and others with *known* class positions;
>
> rating by simple assignment to class — when informants assign an individual to a particular class without delineating the entire class structure; and
>
> rating by institutional membership — when class assignment is based on an individual's membership in certain institutions within the community.

Despite the delineation of these criteria for placement, Warner does not provide other salient information about the use of EP. Gordon's (1963:104–5) analysis of the approach specifies four crucial issues that should be specified in such a scheme and assesses EP with regard to them as follows:

> The composition of raters — How are raters chosen and do they represent the community from which they are drawn? Warner provides little information about either the number of raters or the process by which they were selected. Other analysts (compare Lipset and Bendix 1951) have concluded that upper-middle-class citizens are overrepresented among the raters. This fact, of course, has obvious implications for Warner's results.
>
> The composition of the group of community members who are rated — Does this group represent the community and contain both "easy" and "hard-to-rate" members?[14] Here, too, Warner is vague. He does not provide a list of guidelines for the selection of community members. He also decides that persons about whom the raters disagree as to class position should be eliminated. This

act also has grave implications for his study (compare Pfautz and Duncan 1950).

The amount of agreement necessary for both the numbers of classes in the community and the placement of members within these classes. On this key issue, Warner is also vague; he does not provide any benchmark for the minimal amount of rater agreement necessary for assignment.

How are status remarks of the raters "quantified" into ratings? Once again, there are no firm guidelines in Warner's work. Gordon's (1963:107–8) conclusion is that Warner has not provided sufficient information about these issues in his various publications dealing with EP. Because of such criticisms, a number of analysts have raised important concerns about both the reliability and validity of the technique.

Despite such problems, however, EP forms the backbone for Warner's determination of both the nature of the class structure in the communities he studied and for assigning community members to these classes. It also serves as a source for the derivation and the validation of the second of Warner's techniques for measuring class in community settings, the Index of Status Characteristics.

The Index of Status Characteristics

The second of Warner's techniques for measuring social class within the community setting is labeled the Index of Status Characteristics (ISC). Its development was stimulated by the discovery that social class position, as measured by EP, correlated well with certain other, more objective attributes of the socioeconomic position of individuals/families in the community, and by the fact that this association could be used to construct a shortcut measure. In Warner's (1949a:121) own words:

in many situations ... it may be desirable to have a more simply applied technique for estimating social-class position when the limitations of time, money, and personnel make the more refined Evaluated Participation procedures impractical. It was to fill this need that the Index of Status Characteristics was developed.

The original ISC employs six socioeconomic status indicators: occupation, amount of income, source of income, education, house type, and dwelling area. Each of these variables is operationalized into a seven-point scale and weights for each are derived by regressing the EP scores of a sample of individuals against their scores on the seven variables. The weights, then, are based upon the relative importance of each variable in predicting the EP scores of the sample. Collectively, the six-variable model correlates highly with the EP scores, but a four-variable model excluding education and amount of income does almost as well. As a result, Warner uses the four-variable version to construct the ISC. These variables are weighted as follows: Occupation, 4; Source of Income, 3; House Type, 3; Dwelling Area, 2. By using these weighted scores, an estimate of the social class position of members of the community for which no EP evaluation is available can be determined as follows. First, the EP procedure is used to determine the social class position of a sample of the residents of a community. Next, the ISC weights are derived by comparing the EP scores of the individuals in the sample with their scores on the four ISC variables. Then, these weights are used to derive an ISC score for nonsample members of the community. Finally, these scores are collapsed into classes, although Warner's description of just how this would be accomplished is obscure. While Warner insists that the EP and the ISC measure different aspects of social differentiation within the community, he also concludes that their high intercorrelation makes either a good surrogate for the other.

Despite a number of important conceptual and methodological problems, Warner's ISC represents a second generation in the development of measures of class inequality in American sociology. In this stage, researchers attempted, for the first time, to develop more flexible, less time-consuming, and (perhaps) more objective multivariate indexes of class inequality. These, of course, would become more important as the United States urbanized and industrialized following World War II, and as sociologists began to adapt their techniques of analysis to these trends.

Critique

With the publication of *Social Class in America* in 1949, which detailed his approaches and suggested guidelines for their use, Warner claims to offer a rather sophisticated, reasonably valid, set of procedures that results in quantifiable measures that could be used by social science researchers in their efforts to understand both the meaning and the role of class in American community life. The sheer scope and breadth of the Warner studies, when compared with other efforts during this time period, certainly had a positive influence on the popularity of the approaches he developed. Yet Warner's approaches to the conceptualization and measurement of class in American communities, while pioneering, have such numerous shortcomings that their alleged promise has never been fully realized. Since many of the criticisms of his work have been detailed extensively elsewhere,[15] I will simply summarize them here, attempting to explain them by referring to the setting within which Warner's work was conducted and his own developing theoretical perspective. As was the case with the Lynds' research, for heuristic purposes the criticisms may be loosely organized into three categories: theoretical/conceptual, methodological, and value orientational.

Some of the most vocal of Warner's critics have directed their attention to theoretical/conceptual issues. In fact, much of the criticism has been that a major problem with his work is its lack of attention to such issues. As discussed above, Warner begins his "Yankee City" research with the assumption that the economic structure is dominant in the lives of the town's citizens. Such an assumption is compatible with both the study's background in the Mayo Western Electric study and the fact that the study was conducted during the early years of the Great Depression. Yet Warner quickly abandons this economic basis for the class structure in "Yankee City" in favor of a conceptualization based on status reputation. Such a definition of class based on reputation is more compatible with both his functionalist theoretical perspective and his research approach derived from social anthropology, which depends heavily upon informants for crucial information about the community. This dependence upon functionalist anthropology can also explain why, in his research, Warner fails to distinguish adequately among the variety of different meanings of class and their interrelationships. For example, Warner has been criticized for his lack of attention to the issue of political power in "Yankee City" (compare Mills 1942). Thus his desire to move away from a narrow economic interpretation of class (partially in reaction to Marx [compare Warner 1949a]) leads him to conflate the varied meanings of the term in his work and thereby to obfuscate their influences on the lives of the citizens of "Yankee City" and "Jonesville." Some have argued that a partial explanation for his failure to construct and apply a theoretical scheme adequate to address the complicated problems he faced in his research was the fact that he gave no evidence of an awareness of the sociological theorizing about class inequality that was then available (compare Davis 1943). However, I view the problem as more basic than this. His theoretical and conceptual shortcomings seem more likely to be the result of his narrow functionalist orientation and his use of the fieldwork techniques of social anthropology.

In terms of methodology, a number of criticisms of Warner's work question his choice of a research design. Based on his fieldwork experiences in Australia, he attempted to apply anthropology's research techniques, with few modifications, to the study of community life in America. Several of his problems are related to this decision. For example, typical of reports based on data gathered using anthropological fieldwork methods, Warner's published reports are flawed by a lack of sufficient detail about the specification and measurement of variables. As noted above, it was not until the year of the publication of the "Jonesville" research (1949) that detailed specifications for EP and ISC appeared in print. The volumes of the "Yankee City" series are almost totally devoid of concise information concerning the means by which classes are defined and measured. Given the central role that class plays in his research, this omission seems particularly unfortunate. Of course, even with the greater detail provided in *Social Class in America*, numerous questions remain concerning such issues as the "location" of his informants within the class structure of the community,[16] the procedures by which their various perceptions of the class structure are made mutually compatible, details as to how class placement decisions are made, and so on.

Another decision that Warner made, which is compatible with his choice of research procedures, was his choice of small, stable communities as research sites. In selecting a research site for the initial study, Warner had rejected the communities surrounding the Western Electric plant in the Chicago area as being too large, disorganized, and unstable. Might not, as some critics have suggested, Warner's findings have been an artifact of the rather atypical locales of small-town America within which they were set? Such a choice might tend to meliorate many of the negative effects of class, even during a depression. This, of course, addresses another criticism of his work — the generalizability of his findings to other communities in America. Just how applicable are Warner's findings to the New Yorks and Chicagos of the late 1930s and early 1940s?

Another key feature of Warner's perspective is its lack of attention to the role of history in the development of and changes in the class structures in his communities. In contrast to the Lynds, who explicitly focused on changes over time and studied "Middletown" over a 40-year period, Warner's work is decidedly ahistorical.[17]

Finally, the implicit value orientation of Warner's studies has also drawn criticism. Here, many have accused Warner of adopting an essentially conservative perspective in his research, largely supporting the status quo regarding both the nature and operation of the class systems in the communities he studied. Of course, such an approach is also compatible with the functionalist perspective he employs, since it tends to stress the integrative roles of social institutions and minimizes or ignores their disintegrative effects.

The pioneering work of W. Lloyd Warner in the study of class inequality in American society has formed the foundation for much subsequent research in the discipline on the subject, and his work remains a significant part of the heritage of modern research on class inequality. Yet Warner's findings and conclusions concerning class must be seen, in part, as reflecting American society during the time period within which it was written, the dominant value orientation of the period, his own particular emerging theoretical perspective, and the limitations imposed by various other influences, such as the selection of "Yankee City" and "Jonesville" as research sites and the particular research design he employed. As I have shown, Warner, to a much greater extent than the Lynds, was committed to a functionalist perspective. His perspective stresses the integrative role of class in society and minimizes its disintegrative effects. I believe that the evidence for this claim is clear in both "Yankee City" and "Jonesville" despite the fact that both of these studies were completed during a time wherein many of the tenets of "evolutionary liberalism," as expressed in the overall political economy, were being challenged by events both inside the country and in the larger world arena. Yet his selection and use of this particular framework is compatible with both the value system dominant in the 1920s, as he was growing to adulthood, and with extant social science knowledge, particularly social anthropology, that was available to him as he entered professional life. His tenure at Harvard, a prestigious, private university, might also have influenced his perceptions.[18] In a number of ways, then, Warner was a key early figure in the establishment of the hegemony of the functionalist perspective on class inequality in American social science between the early 1940s and the 1950s.

AUGUST HOLLINGSHEAD'S STUDIES

The final studies analyzing the role of class inequality in American community settings, from which important theoretical, conceptual, and methodological indicators resulted, were conducted by August Hollingshead during the early 1940s and early 1950s.

In many senses, Hollingshead's studies bridge two important periods of research on class inequality in American sociology. His first study, published as *Elmtown's Youth* (1949), shares much in common with the studies of the Lynds and Warner because its focus is on life in a small community. In fact, "Elmtown" and Warner's "Jonesville" are the same community. The "Elmtown" study differs from these earlier studies, however, in that its goal was not to analyze the entire corpus of life in the community. Instead, its focus was limited to the study of the impact of "social class" on the lives of adolescents within the community. This shift in focus is important because it marks the beginning of a narrowing of the focus of research, made possible, in part, by the wealth of descriptive information provided by these earlier studies, and by a shift in attention away from the community as the focus of research to the community as a setting within which particular research problems can be investigated. Yet the "Elmtown" study, in large part, still shared with earlier studies the theoretical perspectives and research methodology of social anthropology. On the other hand, Hollingshead and Redlich's later study in New Haven, Connecticut, published as *Social Class and Mental Illness* (1958) completes the transition. In this study, the city is clearly the setting for the research and its relative size makes it necessary to adopt a research design different from that typically employed by social anthropologists in their early studies of life in American communities. As a result, data gathering centered around survey research and available data in the form of patient records rather than the typical participant observation and informants employed in earlier studies. As I will discuss later, these changes also resulted in the development of procedures for measuring class that differed from earlier research. In fact, one of the results of the New Haven study was the development of the Index of Social Position (ISP), historically one of the most important objective measures of class inequality within the discipline. As noted above, with regard to Warner's ISC, the ISP is also a second-generation measure of class inequality.

Biographical Information

August Hollingshead was born in Wyoming to middle-class parents in 1908 and grew to adulthood during the decade of the 1920s. He was graduated from college during the early 1930s, received his Ph.D. from the University of Nebraska in 1935, and was awarded a postdoctoral research training fellowship by the Social Science Research Council in 1941. As a part of this fellowship, he joined other social scientists in the study of a small Midwestern community, under the auspices of the Committee on Human Development of the University of Chicago. He spent the period between mid-1941 and the end of 1942 in "Elmtown" and, following a period in the U.S. Armed Forces during World War II, published *Elmtown's Youth* in 1949. His research in New Haven was begun about the same time in conjunction with psychiatrist Frederick Redlich, and *Social Class and Mental Illness* was published in 1958. Because his studies are separated both in terms of time and subject matter, I will consider each separately with regard to setting, theoretical antecedents, methods of measurement, and so on.

THEORETICAL ANTECEDENTS FOR "ELMTOWN"

Prior to the beginning of the "Elmtown" research, Hollingshead had completed his dissertation (*Trends in Community Development,*

1935) on Nebraska communities using a human ecological perspective. Evidence for the influence of this perspective on his work in "Elmtown" is reinforced by his credits to both Robert Park and Ernest Burgess in the preface to the study. He also gives credit there, however, to Warner and Robert Redfield, scholars more closely associated with the field of social anthropology. As will be shown later, his methodology in the "Elmtown" study was certainly more similar to that of social anthropology than to that of human ecology. He also acknowledges several scholars known more for their work with adolescents, including E. B. Reuter and Robert Havighurst, who was an important collaborator on the "Elmtown" research. He also cites a number of psychological studies on the subject of adolescence, as well, but concludes that these studies seemed more doctrinal than scientific. In sum, evidence suggests that Hollingshead's theoretical orientation for the "Elmtown" study was influenced by both human ecology and functionalist social anthropology.

"Elmtown" as a Research Setting

"Elmtown" was a small, ethnically homogeneous, Midwestern community at the time of Hollingshead's research. Its size was approximately 6,000 residents, 93 percent of whom were native-born. It was the county seat of a predominantly agricultural area; its economy was thus based around agriculture and agricultural-support activities, with mining and manufacturing present as well. The author characterized the community as a typical Midwestern community in terms of its location, size, economic base, population, and institutions (Hollingshead 1949:65).

Conceptualizing and Measuring
Social Inequality in "Elmtown"

Early in his research in "Elmtown," Hollingshead (1949:74) concludes that "Elmtowners think of themselves as members of classes and that they act toward one another on the basis of their judgments about each other's class position." In a manner similar to Warner, he argues that economic criteria are not sufficient in themselves to define what "Elmtowners" mean when they use the term "social class," and he opts for the prestige dimension as his primary referent for the term.[19]

> literally thousands of different values are shared and used daily by Elmtowners to assign to one another positions in the prestige structure. *The important ones are associated primarily with the economic functions from which a family derives its livelihood, and secondarily with its connections in*

the familial, property, ethnic, religious, political, education-
al, recreational, and welfare systems (Hollingshead 1949:79).

As such a conceptualization of class as reputation implies, his measurement of the term seeks to establish its meaning in the eyes of the residents of the community. Hollingshead begins by lamenting the fact that "no commonly accepted methodological tool has been developed for the stratification of a community's population" (Hollingshead 1949:26). This statement is interesting in light of my earlier discussion about Warner's methodology. Recall that Warner's critics took him to task for his measurement of class in "Yankee City," and the publication of *Social Class in America* was his attempt to detail the procedures that he used in that research. Yet Hollingshead, an associate on the "Jonesville" project *after* Warner's research in "Yankee City" was completed, and who was certainly familiar with Warner's approach, could still make this assessment. This suggests that Warner's EP was still "emergent" as early as the 1940s despite his defense of the approach he took in "Yankee City." Concerning this measurement problem, Hollingshead considers several options: that a single-factor index based on an objective criterion could be developed; that a composite index could be employed; or that a measure could be developed that would enable a researcher to "place persons and families functionally in the social structure . . . with the use of local people long resident in the community as judges of their fellow's prestige, status, or class positions" (Hollingshead 1949:27). He selects the third alternative as his approach in "Elmtown." His initial contacts with the residents in the community, in a manner similar to Warner in "Yankee City," were filled with reference to class. As a result, he sought some means for systematizing these references into a measure of "social class." In reviewing a number of interviews that had been completed, he found that 30 families were placed "in similar, if not identical, positions by different interviewees, and equally important, that they used a more or less common set of criteria to explain why different families were in the same station or position" (Hollingshead 1949:29).[20] The names of the 30 families were typed on 3" x 5" cards and given to 25 residents of the community, who had been previously interviewed, with the instructions that they should tell how representative these families were of the different classes in the community and, then, to place each family into one of these classes. The results of this exercise revealed that over three-fourths of the respondents visualized five classes in "Elmtown" and generally agreed where 20 of the 30 families fell into the class structure.[21] These 20 families, then, became a "control" list, and 12 longtime residents who appeared representative of the 5 strata were asked to classify the 20 names based on the following criteria: the way a family lived, the amount of income and possessions, participation in community affairs, and prestige or standing in the community (Hollingshead 1949:31). Once again, a rather substantial amount of agreement was obtained, at least among 10 of the raters, in terms of both the number of classes mentioned and the assignment of families to the various class positions. With this information at hand, Hollingshead then drew a sample of 53 of the families of the adolescents in the overall sample and asked 8 raters to rank them in the class system, with the control group serving as points of reference. Here 29 families of the total were ranked by all 8 raters with a high amount of agreement.

Then, 37 raters were selected to complete the final class placement. These raters were given a list of the control families, asked to discuss the social class positions of the 535 families in the study, and to select a family from the control group with which the particular family was most similar. The average informant was able to classify about 75 families using this procedure. Then, an average rating was computed for each family, and, using this, the family was placed within the class structure of the community. Families with ambiguous scores were placed by the researcher. Finally, since Warner was also studying the same community at that time, Hollingshead compared the 134 families, which overlapped between the two studies, on his measure and Warner's EP scores. He found substantial agreement between the two, thereby providing a concurrent validity check on his instrument.

Critique of the "Elmtown" Measure of Class

As was the case with the previous measures in this chapter, I will discuss the criticisms of Hollingshead's conceptualization and measurement of class in "Elmtown" according to three criteria: theoretical/conceptual, methodological, and value configurational. Like most other studies of this period, *Elmtown's Youth* contained no explicit discussion of the theoretical perspective that the author used. Despite this, evidence points to the fact that Hollingshead shared elements of the functionalist approach, which I noted with regard to the other studies discussed in the chapter. Yet it also seems clear that Hollingshead's dependence on that perspective was not as complete as it was for Warner, since he dealt more overtly with the negative impacts of class than did Warner. As a part of Hollingshead's perspective, in a manner similar to Warner, the author's conceptualization of class "mixes" the various dimensions of the term by focusing on prestige and is therefore unable to detail the unique contributions that the various components of class make to the outcome (Lynd 1961:5). To substitute prestige for class and to confound the two in application serves to make Hollingshead's study far less informative than might otherwise have been the case.

With regard to measurement, the procedures developed and applied for measuring class in "Elmtown" "may appear to be somewhat more objective than was actually the case" (Faris 1950:93). In particular, Hollingshead's selection of raters and his tendency to drop or to classify families whose class positions were ambiguously located by these raters are problematic. Given that these same criticisms were also noted with regard to Warner's work, it should come as no surprise that the two methods agree on the positions of those families that were rated by both.

Finally, the value orientation implicit in Hollingshead's research in "Elmtown" has also been the subject of commentary. Reser (1949:211) takes the author to task for stretching the data in the direction of exaggerating the impacts of class in his assessment:

> in spite of the statistics and all the supporting proof this reader feels that the case is made a little too strong for class and its consequences. . . . It may be wishful thinking but isn't there greater elasticity in our class system than the author implies — or is there?

Others, including Lynd (1961:5), on the other hand, feel that Hollingshead tends to play down the power relationships among the various classes in a manner consistent with the dominant ideology of the period in which the study was completed. Yet, Lynd also notes that, given the stable nature of this "really American" community, the fact that Hollingshead found clearly demarked classes could be said to be compelling evidence that class is a salient dimension of life in American society, a position inconsistent with the dominant ideology of the period. I conclude simply that Hollingshead's first study is reasonably consistent in its theoretical perspective and its methodological procedures with its predecessors, yet does offer some key differences in focus and intent. In retrospect, these differences served as an important benchmark for his later study of New Haven.

Theoretical Antecedents for the New Haven Study

The theoretical antecedents for Hollingshead's study of New Haven are clearly different in several ways from those of the "Elmtown" study. For the New Haven research, perhaps as a result of the earlier study, Hollingshead was convinced that classes are not only present in society, but that they also are of critical importance in the lives of the members of society. Hollingshead and Redlich (1958:4) summarize the current state of knowledge with regard to class with their statement, "a number of social scientists have published extensive evidence to support the fact that American society is stratified." They provide evidence of their own theoretical orientation in several of the assumptions that they isolate as guiding their inquiry:

> first, the social structure of our society is characterized by a system of stratification. Second, individuals living in a given class are subjected to problems of living that are expressed in emotional and psychological reactions and disorders different in quantity and quality from those expressed by persons in other classes. Third, psychiatrists, who are responsible for diagnosing and treating mental illness, are controlled, as members of society, by its value system (p. 11).

In short, by the time of the New Haven study, Hollingshead's perceptions about the nature and role of class in American society were different from his earlier study. As such, the New Haven study, even more than the "Elmtown" study, focuses its attention on the negative consequences of class membership for the lives of the members of society. By taking this orientation, the study is even less consistent with the functionalist perspective that, by this time, dominated the discipline's efforts to study class inequality.

New Haven as a Research Setting

The research in New Haven was conducted during the early years of the 1950s. According to the information reviewed in the introduction to Part II of this book, during this period the economy was growing rapidly and unemployment was low. These were also times of optimism about American society and its institutions. Despite the fact that the authors' description of the city concentrated more on the interaction among the various ethnic groups in an historical perspective than on these more broad issues, there is no reason to suspect that New Haven did not share in the overall prosperity of the remainder of the country during this period in its history.

Conceptualizing and Measuring
Social Class in New Haven

In order to gain some sort of understanding about life in New Haven, the authors had to approach the subject differently than Hollingshead did in "Elmtown." The city's population at the time of the study was 236,000; this fact alone precluded the use of observers and informants as sources of information about the class structure of the city. Yet Hollingshead remains convinced that the conceptualization of class as it emerged in "Elmtown" based on "socially discriminating comparisons people make of each other in their day-to-day behaviors" is valid for New Haven as well. Thus he and his coauthor built a different measure that would describe the status hierarchy in New Haven. Their measure, labeled the Index of Social Position, "was developed to meet the need for an objective, easily applicable procedure to estimate the positions individuals occupy in the status structure of the community" (p. 387). The ISP is based on three assumptions: that there is a class structure in the community; that positions within this structure are determined, in large part, by a few commonly accepted symbolic characteristics; and that these characteristics can be scaled and combined by the use of statistics to yield a quick, reliable, and meaningful procedure for stratifying the population (Hollingshead and Redlich 1958:387).

The authors made use of previous studies on the city and the results of a survey of 552 households to make the initial decision that there was a five-class hierarchy in New Haven and to place each family within this hierarchy.[22] They claim to have agreed on 96 percent of the class placements in New Haven based on three primary criteria: where a family lived; the way it made its living; and its tastes, its cultural orientation, and the way it spends its leisure time (p. 387). These essentially subjective judgments were operationalized into three dimensions. A "residential" scale was developed based on previous research by Maurice Davie (1937) and Jerome Myers (1954); it divided the residences in the city into six levels. A seven-level occupation scale was developed based on the work of Alba Edwards (1938),[23] and an educational scale was developed that divided respondents into seven different categories based on level of formal educational attainment.[24] The authors did not discuss just why these particular decisions were made except by referring to the sources noted above. Following this, they then constructed a matrix of the scores of their sample on each of these three scales and their score on the class measure that had been determined in advance. The patterns in these scores were then examined, looking for clues as to where the continuum could be broken. They divided the continuum where the greatest amount of variation existed among the four variables. They then regressed the class levels of the respondents against the residence area, occupation, and education scores to obtain weights for the variables. Occupation was thus given a weight of 9; education, 5; and residence area, 6. Then each family's score was computed, and these were compared with the raw scores on the original four variables, and the scale broken at the points of greatest heterogeneity. The authors claim that the procedure employed assumes that scores within the resulting groups would be more homogeneous than the scores between such groups (Hollingshead and Redlich 1958:395), and that such classes operationalize the socially discriminating comparisons that they assume people make of each other.

They provide evidence of the validity of the measure by analyzing patterns of exposure to different media among the different classes and conclude that the differences observed offer support for the distinctiveness of the five classes (Hollingshead and Redlich 1958: Appendix 3). The residential variable was later dropped to facilitate the use of the index in community settings wherein the researcher had no knowledge of ecological areas. This resulted in a "Two-Factor Index of Social Position" with weights of 7 for occupation and 4 for education (Hollingshead and Redlich 1958).

Critique of the Index of Social Position

Once again, my critique of the ISP will focus on theoretical/ conceptual, methodological, and value orientation issues. It seems clear that in this second study, Hollingshead has moved away from the functionalist perspective found in his earlier effort. Yet some ties to Warner-brand functionalism remain in that he continues to share a perspective that equates class with prestige and relies on subjective reputational assessments of prestige as a basis for the classification of families in New Haven.[25] Yet he doesn't conceptualize this key variable with enough precision. By adopting this posture, an interpretation of the role that class plays in his research is difficult, if not impossible, to make. This problem carries over, as well, to his operationalization of the term. Here, while claiming that residence area, occupation, and education are the three criteria by which the term can be operationalized, he provides no compelling evidence to support these linkages. The act of combining these indicators into a single index further complicates the problem of making sense out of just what he intends class to mean (Miller and Mishler 1959:187). This confusion carries forward to his actual application of the scheme as well. First he subjectively places the families of his sample into his class scheme. Then he compares these subjective judgments to the objective indicators and derives weights for the latter. Yet he provides few guidelines for just how these judgments were made, except to say that they are primarily based on the very criteria that would later be their objective indicators. Such a procedure seems even weaker than Warner's use of EP to validate his ISC, since in Hollingshead's case it is the researchers who are making these judgments about class position, while at least Warner claimed that these decisions were made by the respondents of the community themselves. However, neither procedure is defensible. Yet another difficulty is that the breakpoints in the hierarchy are determined more by inspection of the patterns in the scores for the four variables than by more objective means. The use of such procedures creates a "fallacy of misplaced concreteness" for the scale, since its scores appear to be rigorously derived, when, in fact, they are not.

Finally, the value orientation of Hollingshead has also attracted comment. As was noted with regard to the "Elmtown" research, some have seen Hollingshead's desire to demonstrate the negative effects of class as resulting in an exaggeration of the implications of his findings. In the words of one reviewer: "At times, however, the researchers' role of advocacy appears to have overwhelmed their scientific attitudes. It is to the biases, and technical deficits growing out of this tendency that sociological reviewers have responded" (Maney 1960:271).[26]

In brief, the theoretical, conceptual, and methodological roots for Hollingshead's research lie within the same functionalist tradition as those of Warner and the Lynds. His exposure to Warner's perspective during his "Elmtown" research is apparent in his New Haven study as well. What was different about Hollingshead, however, was his willingness to focus on the negative consequences of social class for the lives of his subjects. His work is especially important given the contrast between the relative prosperity of the period in which he conducted his research and his findings concerning class inequality.

SUMMARY AND CONCLUSIONS

In this chapter I have reviewed three key sets of studies that were completed by American social scientists between the middle 1920s and the early 1950s. In my review of these studies, I sought to demonstrate that they share several things in common: overlapping sociohistorical settings, an ideology that stresses individualism and corporate responsibility within an evolutionary liberal framework, and common theoretical and fieldwork antecedents within early twentieth-century British social anthropology.

For the Lynds, my research demonstrated that their perspectives were influenced by their personal lack of formal social science training; their dependence on the work of the British anthropologist Rivers for both theoretical and methodological guidelines; and by the fact that their research was conducted during the Roaring Twenties, a time of economic prosperity and optimism in American society. As a result, their theoretical perspective on class inequality was (at least initially) functionalist, and they used participant observation as a research strategy. Despite these influences, Robert Lynd's background in the area of secular reform and investigative journalism also had an impact on their study, particularly on their interpretations of the negative impacts of class on the lives of the citizens of "Middletown." For the second of their studies, the fact that it was conducted during the Great Depression, the contrast between the community then and a decade earlier, and the fact that their own theoretical perspective had drifted further away from functionalism exercised important influences on their findings. As a result, they stressed the negative impacts of class to an even greater extent in the second study.[27]

With regard to Warner, I highlighted several influences on the development of his theoretical/conceptual, methodological, and ideological orientations: his middle-class background during the first quarter of the twentieth century; his formal training as a social anthropologist during the mid-1920s, including his study of a stone-age people in Australia immediately prior to his involvement in "Yankee City"; his more formal dependence on the functionalism of early twentieth-century British social anthropology; and the fact that, at the time of his research during the Great Depression, he was a faculty member at Harvard University. As a result, Warner conceptualized the class system of "Yankee City" as functionally inter-related with the other institutions; thus, stressing its integrative consequences, he emphasized prestige as his means for defining class and reputation as his means for operationalizing it. The net results of his research, despite the fact that the first of his studies was conducted during the early years of the Great Depression, is a concerted attempt to defend the political economy and the evolutionary/corporate liberal ideology that dominated society during his younger years. This is particularly evident in his *Democracy in Jonesville* (1949b), in which he argues for the necessity of class inequality in modern society and suggests how its dysfunctional outcomes are countered by equal opportunities and its more open class structure.

For Hollingshead, the materials reviewed showed that the major influences on his first study were his middle-class background during the 1920s, his early work in human ecology, his participation in the project with Warner and Redfield, and the fact that the research was conducted during the relative prosperity of the 1940s. As a result, his early conceptualization of social class is functionalist, and he employed the fieldwork techniques of social anthropology. At the same time, Hollingshead, certainly more than Warner, stressed the negative consequences of social class in the lives of adolescents in "Elmtown." These differences between Hollingshead and his predecessors continued in his research in New Haven. There, despite the fact that he still conceptualized class in a manner consistent with the functionalist perspective of Warner, he moved further away from the Warner-inspired approach in both his methodology and his more explicit focus on some important negative consequences of class inequality, even during times of relative prosperity in the overall society.

In conclusion, the perspectives of the Lynds, Warner, and Hollingshead must be seen as products of the interaction between a changing political economy with its dominant ideology and their own unique experiences within this overall system. As a result, each embraced (at least initially) points of view on class inequality that are similar to what would later be formalized as functionalist theory. While the fit between the perspectives of these scholars and this perspective is not perfect, the overlap between them is substantial. It is also interesting that the scholar whose perspective remained closest to the functionalist viewpoint — Warner — is also the one among the three who has, until recently, had the most significant influence on the study of class inequality within American sociology.

NOTES

1. See Grimes (1988a) for both a detailed analysis of the reasons why many of the important influences of these earlier scholars have been neglected and a discussion of their contributions to the perspective.

2. It should be noted here that a potential explanation for this choice is the fact that early twentieth-century anthropology (dominated by British scholars) was heavily involved in the study of religious practices and institutions among primitive peoples and, because of this, Robert was likely to have had some exposure to the area during his training in theology. This explanation, however, is speculative at best.

3. Kuper (1973:31) preferred the label "proto-functionalist" for Rivers' work, suggesting that functionalism was more "emergent" in his work rather than being fully developed there.

4. In light of these findings and their labels, it is interesting to note the similarity between their scheme of classification and that of Marx. In fact, given the obvious similarities, some might conclude that Marx's work might have influenced the Lynds. However, Madge (1962:131) observes that available evidence does not suggest that the Lynds had been exposed to Marx's work prior to their first fieldwork period in Muncie. He does argue, however, that because of the events of the Great Depression, the Lynds did study Marx between the two fieldwork periods in Muncie, and that the influence of this exposure is apparent in the second volume in the series, *Middletown in Transition* (1937).

5. In their defense, it should be remembered that their scientific benchmark was social anthropological research during the mid-1920s, most of which was done on primitive societies. In such research, classification schema were certainly less rigorously constructed and applied than in more contemporary research applications.

6. The Lynds' discovery of class differences even in such comparatively good times supports the perspectives of those scholars who tend to stress that class inequalities are important features of contemporary industrial societies.

7. Gouldner's (1980) effort to demonstrate how Marx's interpretations of the demise of capitalism tended to change during the course of his life and to correlate these changes with the overall economic conditions in Europe stands as a classic example of the argument that theorizing is intimately related to the setting within which it occurs.

8. It should also be remembered that their analysis was hampered by the level of methodological sophistication that was extant at the time of their research. Most analysts acknowledge that their studies were among the most carefully done of those using the anthropological approach (Hunt 1929; Gordon 1963).

9. Davis (1943), in particular, has taken Warner to task for ignoring available American sociological insights in his research.

10. While he would later modify this position, it is interesting to speculate on the origins of this "economic" hypothesis. As noted above, his research was a part of the Western Electric study that centered its attention around the job and the interplay between the job and other aspects of life. Remember also that the study was conducted during the early years of the Depression, a period in which the economic structure of society was subject to increased scrutiny.

11. Because of the similarities between this initial assumption about the nature of society and that of the Marxists, Warner later (1949b:9) attempts to differentiate his perspective from that of the Marxists by making two points. First, in contrast to the Marxist viewpoint, Warner insists that the presence of classes does not necessarily mean that they will be in conflict with one another. Second, he also concludes that the Marxian goal of a classless society is impossible in a complex, modern industrial setting.

12. It should be stressed here that while this definition departs from the classical use of the term "class" as denoting a position within the economic structure of the society, Warner continues to employ the term as his primary referent rather than switching to a more accurate term such as "status group," which other functionalists such as Parsons adopted. This decision marked the beginning of a trend within the discipline to expand the use of class to include a much broader range of meaning than that intended by classical economists such as Smith and Marx (or their critic Weber, for that matter).

13. Despite this claim, in an earlier description of the delineation of the class structure of a community, he remarks that "in what was probably the most important and interesting aspect of the entire research, we worked out empirically, by direct observation of a fairly large sample of the total population, the existence of six stratified social classes" (Warner and Lunt 1941:74). This remark suggests a greater role for the researcher's own observations in defining the nature of the class system of the community than Warner noted in *Social Class in America* a few years later. Such inconsistencies plague Warner's work.

14. In "Yankee City," Warner classifies almost every family within the community. In "Jonesville," he uses a sample of community residents. This particular issue concerns just how that sample was selected and the implications for the generalizability of the results given the fact that he provides insufficient information concerning the sampling procedure and also notes that some families, whose placement within the class structure was "ambiguous," were eliminated from the final scores.

15. The sources for my summary of the criticisms include: Mills (1942), Davis (1943), Chinoy (1950), Goldschmidt (1950), Pfautz and Duncan (1950), Hall (1951), Lipset and Bendix (1951), Kornhauser (1953), and Gordon (1963).

16. In particular, critics have argued that the manner in which Warner operationalized the class structure of "Yankee City" may have biased the outcome of his research. Lipset and Bendix (1951:163) go so far as to claim that Warner's sample of informants within the community was biased in favor of the upper middle class and that it is their perceptions that led him to stress the "relational" dimension of the class structure as the most relevant and important. If their claim is true, what this means is that Warner's scheme, so quickly adopted by many American stratification researchers, may suffer from a fundamental bias that questions the validity of his findings.

17. This particular problem has also been found to be common to functionalist research in general (Chinoy 1950; Ritzer 1983).

18. Gouldner (1970) has made the point that the academic setting within which authors work is also a potential influence on their perceptions. He makes this point

with particular reference to the work of Parsons, but there is no reason why it shouldn't apply to other scholars as well.

19. As noted above, "Elmtown" and "Jonesville" are the same community and Hollingshead was a member of the research team directed by Warner in the community. From this, one should expect Warner to have had a significant influence on Hollingshead's conceptualization of social class.

20. These criteria were grouped into five general headings: the way a family lived — place of residence, type of dwelling, and furnishings; income and material possessions; participation in community affairs; family background, including ancestry, kin, politics, and religion; and reputation or prestige (Hollingshead 1949:29).

21. Similar to Warner, Hollingshead chooses to drop the 10 families upon which there was less agreement, noting that these families were "unstable" in their position in the class structure.

22. While they did not clearly detail just how they made this determination and these assignments, it should be noted that the senior author had found five classes in "Elmtown" a decade earlier.

23. These were: higher executives of larger concerns, proprietors, and major professionals; business managers, proprietors of medium-sized businesses, and lesser professionals; administrative personnel, owners of small businesses, and minor professionals; clerical and sales workers, technicians, and owners of little businesses; skilled manual employees; machine operators and semiskilled employees; and unskilled employees.

24. These were: graduate professional training, standard college or university education, partial college training, high school graduation, partial high school, junior high school, and less than seven years of schooling.

25. Haug and Suchman (1971:550) generalize this criticism to most measures of class in American sociology: "Thus, although Weber clearly differentiated class from status honor, . . . American sociologists have tended to use the two interchangeably or in different combinations, as indicators of a variable known as 'social class.'"

26. It should be noted that, by the time this review was written, the functionalist perspective on class inequality, along with its image of "sociologist as scientist," was dominant within the discipline. Given this fact, it should come as no surprise that Hollingshead was criticized for his exaggeration of the negative impacts of class on the lives of American citizens.

27. As noted earlier, Lynd's *Knowledge for What?* (1940) demonstrates how his own emerging perspective was changing over the course of his career. There, he openly challenged many of the assumptions of the *status quo* within American social science.

4

THE FUNCTIONALIST
PERSPECTIVE ON
CLASS INEQUALITY

It was during the late 1930s and the early 1940s that efforts were begun by Talcott Parsons (and several of his students and colleagues) to organize some of the diverse theoretical notions present in American social science during the first three decades of the twentieth century into a relatively coherent perspective they would later apply to the study of class inequality in American society.[1] This chapter summarizes and analyzes the results of their efforts.

TALCOTT PARSONS AND THE FUNCTIONALIST PERSPECTIVE

The 1930s were a theoretically active period in the history of American sociology as efforts were begun to integrate the diverse theoretical musings of early sociologists into a more coherent framework. As the relative influence of the founding fathers at the University of Chicago began to decline,[2] another center of sociological activity began to compete for dominance in the field. The new location was Harvard University, and the leading figure in efforts there was Talcott Parsons, and together they were to succeed Chicago and its faculty as the dominant institutional and intellectual forces in the field.

Biographical Sketch

Born in 1902, Parsons was the son of middle- to upper-middle-class parents; his father was a minister who later became president of a college. The setting for his childhood and adolescence was the Midwest during the 1920s — a time of unparalleled prosperity. The opinion of one analyst is that "some of the most fundamental aspects of Parsons' personal reality had been shaped by the economic prosperity of the 1920s, during which his own personal position coin-cided with the general success of the American economy" (Gouldner 1970:147). During this period he entered Amherst University, intending initially to follow his brother's footsteps into medicine, but he soon discovered that economics was a more salient interest. Pur-suing this subject, he then studied for a year at the London School of Economics, where he was impressed by the work of Bronislaw Malin-owski, the renowned British functionalist anthropologist. From there he went to the University of Heidelberg in Germany, where he was exposed to the work of Max Weber, who had recently died, and whose influence was at its peak there. This exposure led him to com-plete a dissertation on the concept of capitalism in German litera-ture; he received the Doctor of Philosophy degree in economics from Heidelberg. He returned to the United States, became an instructor in the Department of Economics at Harvard University in 1927, and then moved to the newly created Sociology Department chaired by Pitirim Sorokin. He spent the remainder of his career at Harvard.

Parsons began his professional career as an academic at Harvard during the early years of the Great Depression. In many senses, that particular university offered a rather unique intellectual setting within which to work during these difficult years, since, as a privately endowed university, it remained largely insulated from these trying times. Gouldner's (1970:173) interpretation of this situation is informative: "The setting of an upper class university in a university town, then, provided a relatively sheltering environment, to some extent filtering out the crisis in the larger society and per-mitting a somewhat greater detachment from it." While the extent to which this interpretation is accurate is certainly subject to specula-tion, it does seem likely that being employed at such an institution did provide at least the opportunity for such detachment and therefore might have the potential for influencing the interpretations offered to explain the Depression and its relationship to the economic system and the larger society as a whole.[3]

The Emergence of the Functionalist Perspective

Parsons' work during the first decade or so of his career bears the clear imp.int of both "intra-" and "extradisciplinary" forces. With regard to the former set of influences, Parsons was reacting in his work to his perceptions of the overall nature of social science theory and research as well as to the predominance of particular theoretical perspectives within the social sciences. I summarize some of these influences below.[4]

At the most general level, Parsons was disturbed by the rather crassly empirical character of the social sciences at this time in their histories:

the dominant feature of American sociology between the
wars was its empiricism. . . . There was a very strong
prejudice in favour of empirical research, consisting of a
kind of veneration for "facts," neither distorted nor disguised
by any conceptual framework of theoretical preconceptions.
Theory was often equated with philosophy, with political
ideologies, or what has been scornfully labeled "meta-
physics," and it seemed strangely antithetical to scientific
research (Rocher 1975:12).

Clearly, Parsons sought in his work to redress this concentration on
empiricism to the exclusion (and even disparagement) of theory by
stressing the necessity for theory and for theoretical integration in
the social sciences.[5]

Another issue to which Parsons reacted was the preponderant
emphasis on behaviorism that he perceived to be common to the
social sciences during the post–World War I period in U.S. history
(Parsons 1970a:830). In response to this bias, he sought in his own
work to stress the notion of "voluntarism," or man's relative freedom
to act, at least during the early years of his career (Mullins 1973:53).

A third concern of Parsons was that, for most of American social
science's history, its reformist orientation had often made it difficult
to separate the researcher's personal values from her or his research
activities. He also thought that this "activist" stance had negative
implications for the discipline's status within the academic community. In reaction to this, "Parsons strongly believed that objectivity,
which he sees as a kind of mental distance between the scientist and
what he studies, is an essential condition for the high standing of
science in modern society" (Rocher 1975:24). Because Parsons shared
with many of his colleagues the goal of a scientific sociology, he
stressed objectivity and urged a posture of value-neutrality for
sociologists.[6]

Finally, Parsons was also concerned with the highly fragmented
character of theory in American social science. Through the use of
the works of European theorists, his goal was to provide a single,
integrated analytical social science perspective, based on uniquely
American experiences, which combined inputs from several
different disciplines, particularly sociology, economics, psychology,
and anthropology (Parsons 1970a:828).

In addition to these intradisciplinary forces on the formation of
Parsons' perspective, extradisciplinary influences were also strongly
reflected in his work, particularly his own personal background and
his cognizance of and reactions to the world economic crisis and the
events in its aftermath.[7] Mullins (1973:48) states, with regard to these
latter influences: "Gouldner, certainly not a sympathetic witness,
suggests that Parsons' theory of action was deeper than a simple

focus on isolated parts or processes in society; rather, it was of a complexity commensurate with the profundity of current economic and political crises." Gouldner's own assessment reflects the saliency of the influences of the Depression on Parsons' work as well:

> Parsons' theory emerged in a period when the previous American tradition of the study of isolated social problems was manifestly incompetent to deal with social strains that obviously ramified through all institutions and social strata, and when the only other established large-scale social theory well known to many intellectuals was a Marxism that was being stultified by Stalinism (Gouldner 1970:177).

The first part of this quote seems to share the assessment made above that Parsons was motivated to construct his scheme to counteract the rather fragmented approaches extant in the social sciences at the time. It also suggests that the need to correct this shortcoming was exacerbated in Parsons' mind by the economic and social crises of the 1930s and by his perception that extant perspectives within the social sciences were unable to account sufficiently for them.

The second part of the quote suggests a final issue toward which Parsons was reacting — since his theoretical efforts were mounted *despite* the existence of the Marxist explanation, he, like many other American intellectuals, also rejected Marxism as either an explanation for the problems of the Depression or as a blueprint for a new social order to replace capitalism.[8] Gouldner (1970:177) clearly articulates his belief that Parsons' theory was an *explicit* response to Marxism:

> an understanding of the full cultural significance of Parsons's work must see it as in some part an American response to Marxism. It was an American alternative to Marxism, which through both its intellectual adventuresomeness and its seriousness attracted and held the interest of many young intellectuals who were under pressure to respond to Marxism.

Horowitz (1983:177) shares Gouldner's assessment and suggests that other American intellectuals were also seeking a response to the crisis that was non-Marxist, and therefore were drawn to Parson's framework in the following quote:

> to be a Parsonian became for a long time the only way professionals within American sociology could tolerably deal with big issues without being dismissed to Marxian marginalia. Parsons' own awareness of this undoubtedly accounts

for his profound early animus toward Marxism and socialism. He adopted a cold, analytical stance with respect to any
sociology which came within sniffing distance of a positive
appraisal of "dialectics" or any other aspect of Marxology.

Parsons' theoretical efforts, then, should be seen both as a
response to the fragmented nature of existing American social
science and its subsequent inability to provide an understanding of
the significance of the Depression, and as a rejection of Marxism's
interpretation that capitalism itself was the underlying cause of the
crisis and that dramatic social change was the only possible solution.
What, then, were the results of these diverse influences? Since a
detailed examination of Parsons' work is beyond the scope of this
effort (while the process by which it was formed is central to it), I will
confine my remarks to its general character and tone.

Parsons' Functionalist Perspective

In reaction to the behavioralism dominant within the social
sciences at the time, Parsons' general theory stressed that man's
"social actions" are conditioned, but not determined, by a set of
cultural norms that concern themselves with appropriate behaviors
that are consistent with overall societal goals. These norms are
viewed as shared with other members of society, and it is man's
desire for social approval that serves to motivate his actions. Thus,
men's actions occur within and are structured by social institutions,
which are themselves organized around key tasks necessary for
societal survival. These institutions are collectively integrated, with
each contributing to the ongoing stability and survivability of society.
Ritzer's (1983:44) overview of the orientation of Parsons' theory tends
to focus in particular on the interrelationship of such macro-level
structures:

> Parsons tended to concentrate on the structures of society
> and their relationship to each other. These structures were
> seen as mutually supportive and tending toward a dynamic
> equilibrium. The emphasis was on how order was
> maintained among the various elements in society. Change
> was seen as an orderly process ... his basic view of ...
> intra-systemic relations ... *was* that they were defined by
> cohesion, consensus, and order.

In short, to Parsons, society is an integrated whole comprised of
interacting individuals, each of whom is guided in his behavior by a
desire to be rewarded for conforming to a value system that reflects
the needs of the entire system.

Some have held that such an essentially integrative view of society and the key role played in the scheme by culture were both direct responses to Parsons' perception of the failure of the economy during the Depression to provide sufficient integration for the society — a condition presumed to obtain by classical economic theory (Clarke 1982). Gouldner's (1970:141) characterization of this situation shares this assessment:

> in the 1930s the economic system had broken down. It could no longer produce the massive daily gratifications that helped to hold the middle class society together and foster a commitment to its values. If the society was to be held together and its cultural patterns maintained — as Parsons clearly wished — one was constrained to look for *noneconomic* sources for social integration. . . . Parsons expected that morality might cement the society without change in economic institutions and without redistributions of income and power that might threaten established privileges.

The latter part of this assessment also highlights Parsons' antipathy for the Marxist diagnosis and solution to the problems of the Depression, while the former part demonstrates his bias toward a Durkheimian (1933) approach to the problem of societal integration in complex industrial society.[9]

THE EMERGENCE OF THE FUNCTIONALIST PERSPECTIVE ON CLASS INEQUALITY

The application of this perspective to the analysis of class inequality in American sociology took place over the course of a ten-year period that began during the early 1940s. I will present the theory as it developed chronologically rather than separate the works of Parsons from those of his students. This decision seems justified for at least two reasons. First, this essentially "historical" approach is consistent with my belief that theories are "grounded" within a sociohistorical setting that is dynamic and, thus, that the development of a theory must be "located" within that setting for maximum understanding of the interplay between the two to occur. Second, since it has been argued that the functionalist school of thought was emerging during this period in time, it follows that the work of the master and his students should exhibit a reasonably high degree of consistency. If that were not the case, then my arguments for both the distinctiveness of the perspective from others in the field and (subsequently) for its dominance over the other candidates for theoretical hegemony would certainly be weakened.

Early Statements

During the early years of the decade of the 1940s, both Parsons and his student, Kingsley Davis, published major initial statements concerning the application of the functionalist perspective to the subject of class inequality. While these statements have been superseded in terms of notoriety by later efforts, they do, nonetheless, contain important points of reference for the development of the functionalist approach to the subject. Therefore, I will discuss each of them before turning to later work within this tradition.

In 1940 Parsons published "An Analytical Approach to the Theory of Social Stratification." This was his initial focused statement on the subject, and it provided the foundation for the subsequent development of the functionalists' viewpoint on the subject. In contrast to later efforts of the functionalist school, Parsons' treatment of class inequality in this article was decidedly more broad, in that his goal was to explain the phenomenon within the larger context of the issue of just how social order is possible in society (Tausky 1965; Kerbo 1983).

As indicated by the title of this article, Parsons, like other functionalists, prefers the phrase "social stratification" to others descriptive of the various kinds of inequality in society. This preference is interesting for several reasons. First, the functionalists have not generally used the rubric "class," perhaps in reaction to the fact that the term was made popular by the Marxists.[10] Second, the root word "stratum" means a vertical "layering" of elements within a population. It also implies a number of layers. This choice, too, could be interpreted as an effort to define, describe, or depict a structuring of the population into a larger number of layers than the traditional bipolar scheme of most Marxists. Finally, the prefix "social" points to the fact that their conceptualization of this structuring is that it is multidimensional, rather than being based on a single indicator such as class (traditionally an economic variable) or power.[11]

Parsons begins the article with a definition for this key term: "Social stratification is regarded here as the differential ranking of the human individuals who compose a given social system and their treatment as superior and inferior relative to one another in certain socially important respects" (p. 841). He then claims that stratification is a fundamental dimension of a social system, when viewed from the perspective of his theory of action. Within the context of this theory, he sees stratification as providing an important linkage between the individual actor and the social system as follows. Individual actors, to Parsons, are "goal-directed" entities, with sentiments as to the moral desirability of these goals. Yet the set of moral standards that the actor brings to bear when judging these goals is not simply his own, since "there is a tendency for the basic moral sentiments to be shared by the different actors within a system in the sense that they approve the same basic normative patterns of conduct" (p. 845). This set of shared moral sentiments, then, operates to channel the actor's behavior toward socially approved goals. Thus, the apparently self-interested actions of individual actors are, in fact, actions that reflect the goals and needs of the society as well.[12] The social standing that an individual actor possesses within the community is thus seen by Parsons as a reflection of the extent to which his actions have met the expectations of this shared moral code. In Parsons' own words, "it is a simple corollary of the integration of moral sentiments that recognition, or moral respect on the part of others, is dependent on the actor on the whole living up to the moral expectations of these others" (p. 846). When considered from this perspective, then, an individual actor is motivated to action by the shared moral code's definition of desired goals, he is judged by the extent to which he seeks and achieves these socially approved goals, and he is ranked among his peers according to certain salient criteria that are also a part of the social order.

The potential criteria offered by Parsons as a means by which actors are evaluated and subsequently ranked by society include: membership in a kinship unit, personal qualities, achievements, possessions, authority, and power. As a result, then, "the status of a given individual in the system of stratification in a society may be regarded as a resultant to the common valuations underlying the attribution of status to him in each of these six respects" (p. 849).

In actual application, however, some of the criteria become more important than others. In particular, according to Parsons (p. 857), "broadly speaking there are two fundamental elements in the dominant American scale of stratification. We determine status very largely on the basis of achievements within an occupational system which is in turn organized primarily in terms of performance and status within functionally specialized fields."[13] Thus, to Parsons, status in modern American society is the result of "common valuations" of an individual's "performance and status" based on "universalistic criteria," primarily (but perhaps not exclusively) within the occupational field. It is also clear that Parsons sees status as a "reward" for the adequate performance of socially necessary tasks, motivated by an actor's self-interested (yet, at the same time socially conditioned) pursuit of goals. Further, since these goals are derivative of a "shared moral code" that is universally accepted, the resulting distribution of status (and, hence, rewards and privileges) is thus given legitimacy, thereby making the status system integrative with regard to the overall social system. Parsons also argues that this is particularly true for modern societies because, with the decline of caste systems the role of the family unit in status assignment is diminished, thus making the opportunity for social mobility high. He also notes that the very vagueness of the system of stratification itself provides an additional cushioning mechanism.

As will be demonstrated later, a more detailed version of this general characterization of the nature and role of class inequality in American society, as elaborated by several of Parsons' students, would become the dominant viewpoint on the subject for the next quarter century.[14]

An article by Kingsley Davis, published in 1942, entitled "A Conceptual Analysis of Stratification," offers a more focused discussion of Parsons' more general treatment. While the author does not characterize the article as such, it provides more concrete labels and definitions for some of Parsons' terms. While a complete overview of the article would be redundant both with Parsons' earlier effort and with the article Davis later wrote with Wilbert Moore, there are several interesting points about the article with reference to the developing functionalist perspective that deserve comment. One of the major benefits is the fact that Davis provides definitions for key terms in the functionalist lexicon. For example, he begins with a definition of the term "position" as a place in a given social structure that "is functional and purposive . . . with regard to the rest of the structure," and he defines "station" as a cluster of positions that may be combined in one individual. He then states that the term "status" reflects an individual's "generalized position in the structure" (Davis 1942:309). He further notes that

> we may designate as a Stratum, a mass of persons in a given society enjoying roughly the same station. The term carries the implication of rank in a hierarchy of strata, and presumably cuts across the entire structure of society. It implies like interests and common problems, but not necessarily a pronounced solidarity (p. 310).

This particular statement contains two points that have become identified with the functionalist approach to class inequality. First, Davis stresses the notion of a hierarchy, suggesting the likelihood of a number of different strata rather than the limiting case of a polarized two-class structure. This fact is demonstrated more explicitly in Davis' definition of prestige as *"the invidious value attached to any given status or office, or combination of them. Such evaluation is relative, tending to arrange itself in a scale"* (p. 312). Second, while he does go as far as to say that the term implies similarities of interests and common problems, he stops short of endorsing the idea that class consciousness or solidarity might be a result of stratum memberships, since such solidarity might very well lead to actions on the part of stratum members to alter the extant distribution of rewards and privileges, thus proving dysfunctional for the society as a whole. His position regarding this particular issue is made clear in the following remarks:

> the common values define the major prestige system of the society. Consequently, in a solidaristic stratified order, the relative ranking of the strata is agreed upon, thus insuring cooperation, reciprocity, and peace between the members of different strata. . . . The system of common values and ends, implicit in the key statuses and in the general mores governing devotion to duty, take precedence over the differentiated values and ends and thus perform the function of holding the structure together (p. 315).

Finally, his summary paragraph provides both evidence of his ties to Parsons and an interesting preview of the famous article that he would publish with Wilbert Moore three years later:

> treating *stratification* from the abstract structural point of view, we have used *Position* as the key concept. On the societal side, we have defined *Station* as a recurrent combination of positions inhering in the same person, masses of persons with roughly the same station as *Strata*. The *Strata* have different *Prestige* ranks in accordance with the prestige of the positions making up the station. The prestige of a given position depends upon the function which the activities associated with it perform and upon the scarcity of the means for performing this function (p. 321).

Kingsley Davis and Wilbert Moore's Collaborative Effort

In 1945, Davis, along with Wilbert Moore, published what has become the leading statement of the functionalist perspective on class inequality. Whether it, rather than the articles by Parsons and Davis reviewed above, deserves that status is certainly subject to interpretation, since the earlier statements dealt with most, if not all, of the same issues. Yet the fact that the Davis and Moore article is both more clearly articulated and more concise when compared to the earlier papers (particularly the former of the two) may offer a partial explanation for its stature.[15] The article begins with the following statement: "Starting from the proposition that no society is 'classless,' or unstratified, an effort is made to explain, in functional terms, the universal necessity which calls forth stratification in any social system" (Davis and Moore 1945:242). According to the authors, "the main functional necessity explaining the universal presence of stratification is precisely the requirement faced by any society of placing and motivating individuals in the social structure" (p. 242). The authors contend that the placement/motivation problem would not exist if all positions within society were equally desirable; required the same talents, skills, and training; and were equally important for the society. But, in contrast to this situation, they conclude that in most if not all societies "it makes a great deal of difference who gets into which positions, not only because some positions are inherently more agreeable than others, but also because some require special talents and training and some are functionally more important than others" (p. 243). Because of these requirements, they argue that society must accomplish two tasks. First, it must have some sort of inducements to compel the acquisition and performance of role requirements for the various positions. Second, society must develop some means by which these rewards can be distributed differentially according to the importance of and requirements for the various positions. Concerning the reward problem, their list of possible inducements includes: things that contribute to sustenance and comfort, things that contribute to humor and diversion, and things that contribute to self-respect and ego expansion. To the authors, all three of these rewards can and do serve as important inducements for position acquisition and subsequent role performance.

With regard to the issue of the differential distribution of rewards among the positions according to relative importance, Davis and Moore discuss two key determinants for a position's ranking in society. The first is the functional importance of the position for society. They state that while the issue of relative functional importance is hard to determine, there are two clues: the degree to which the position is functionally unique, and the extent to which other positions are dependent upon the one in question. The second determinant of a position's relative importance is the amount of training or talent required to effectively perform the role obligations of the position. Here, the authors state that while almost all positions in society require some sort of training or skill, some require more than others for effective role performance and that the relative amount required plus the relative scarcity of available talent is also a factor determining a position's relative ranking in society.

Thus, in order to insure that the most important positions are filled by the most talented/trained individuals, the authors postulate that society literally builds into these positions differential rewards according to the criteria outlined in the previous paragraph. As such, then, there will result an unequal distribution of rewards and, hence, a system of stratification in society. Davis and Moore summarize their position as follows:

> social inequality is thus an unconsciously evolved device by
> which societies insure that the most important positions are

conscientiously filled by the most qualified persons. . . .
Hence, every society, no matter how simple or complex,
must differentiate persons in terms of both prestige and
esteem, and must therefore possess a certain amount of
institutional inequality (p. 243).

Thus, the theory stresses the role of differential achievement
within a competitive social order as the major means for status
placement and, implicitly, the role of the stratification system in
satisfying a major functional requirement of the social order.

Before I turn to an overview of the various criticisms that have
been made of the functionalist theory since its appearance in the
literature of the discipline, I should, following the chronological
sequence of presentation that I have adopted, amend the theory in
light of Davis' (1948) reaction to the claim noted above, "that it fits a
competitive order but does not fit a noncompetitive one," since it
stresses achievement to the apparent exclusion of ascription. In his
efforts to adjust the theory, Davis contrasts the two polar types of
society and then states that, even in competitive societies, the role of
the two means of status placement would be mixed. He then explains
this fact by noting that the "functional necessities responsible for
stratification do not operate to the exclusion of all other functions"
(Davis 1948:370), and he singles out the family and its role in the
socialization of children as an example of the role that ascription
plays in competitive societies. With this slight modification, then, the
theory places primary, but not total, responsibility for status
placement on *achievement* within the occupational realm in modern
society.

Tumin (1953:387–88) summarizes the major points of the Davis-
Moore theory, and his summary will facilitate a critique of the
theory:

1.   Certain positions in any society are functionally more
     important than others, and require special skills for
     their performance.

2.   Only a limited number of individuals in any society have
     the talents which can be trained into the skills appro-
     priate to these positions.

3.   The conversion of talents into skills involves a training
     period during which sacrifices of one kind or another
     are made by those undergoing the training.

4.   In order to induce the talented persons to undergo these
     sacrifices and acquire the training, their future posi-
     tions must carry an inducement value in the form
     of differential, that is, privileged and disproportionate

access to the scarce and desired rewards which the society has to offer.

5. These scarce and desired goods consist of the rights and perquisites attached to, or built into the positions, and can be classified into those things which contribute to: (a) sustenance and comfort, (b) humor and diversion, and (c) self-respect and ego expansion.

6. This differential access to the basic rewards of the society has as a consequence the differentiation of the prestige and esteem which various strata acquire. This may be said, along with the rights and perquisites, to constitute institutionalized social inequality, that is, stratification.

7. Therefore, social inequality among different strata in the amounts of scarce and desired goods, and the amounts of prestige and esteem which they receive, is both positively functional and inevitable in any society.

I turn now to an overview of the major criticism of the theory.

A Critique of the Functionalist Perspective

If the magnitude of reaction to a theory (however measured) is a reflection of the theory's importance, then the Davis-Moore specification of the functionalist perspective on class inequality is one of the most important, if not *the* most important, statement on the subject within American sociology. Although published over 40 years ago, debate and commentary on the theory continue today. Because of the magnitude of the debate, both in terms of the number of scholars involved, the lengthy time period over which it occurred, as well as its redundant nature, I will not attempt here to follow it chronologically. I will, instead, group the various commentaries by the particular focus of their remarks into a set of major criticisms of the theory.[16] In a manner similar to the overviews of the major criticisms of the earlier theories in the book, these will include theoretical/conceptual and ideological criticisms. However, since none of these authors operationalized the theory in research, methodological criticisms will not be offered (efforts to operationalize the theory are the subject of Chapter 5).

There have been a number of theoretical/conceptual criticisms of the theory. One of the most consistent criticisms of the Davis-Moore formulation is their notion of the differential functional importance of positions in society.[17] Tumin (1953:388) has characterized this particular problem as follows: "The functionalist theory of social organization is by no means clear and explicit about this term. The minimal common referent is something known as the 'survival value' of a social structure." As Davis (1948) reminds us, the original article (Davis and Moore 1945) acknowledged the difficulty in precisely defining and measuring occupations with regard to their functional utility and suggested two "clues" for determining functional importance: the functional uniqueness of the position, and the degree to which other positions depend on the position. Stinchcombe (1963) offers an additional criterion: the degree to which occupations are interchangeable — that is, how easy it is for incumbents of one to assume the duties of another occupation. Most analysts of the theory approach this issue from the standpoint of the difficulties in operationalizing the notion of functional importance: "To test functional importance there must be an independent definition of societal survival, and also there must be criteria that allow measurement of the degree of contribution to societal survival of one role vis-à-vis any other role" (Huaco 1963:804). After reviewing the evidence concerning this issue, Huaco (1966:236) concludes that this basic concept of the theory is a fallacy primarily because its usefulness as a guide to hypothesis formulation has yet to be demonstrated. Others agree with this assessment (compare Reissman 1959; Tausky 1965), and some efforts to assess functional importance have not shown it to be a particularly good predictive criterion (Lopreato and Lewis 1963; Grandjean and Bean 1975).

A second major criticism of the Davis-Moore formulation of the functionalist perspective concerns the process of the discovery and use of talent outlined by the theory. The theory argues that competition for the differential rewards allocated to positions facilitates the discovery and use of scarcely available talent for more functionally important positions. Critics have responded that stratification systems themselves tend to discourage the discovery of talent, particularly among the lower segments of the population (Tumin 1953; Gordon 1963; Huaco 1963, 1966). Vanfossen (1979:29) summarizes this complaint about the theory as follows:

> the more rigidly stratified a society is, the less chance does that society have of discovering any new facts about the talents of its members or of motivating the children of the underprivileged classes. In American society, for example, opportunities to exercise one's abilities are frequently denied to black, poor, and female children.

In response to this criticism, the functionalists (compare Davis 1948) have argued that the major focus for the theory is the differential rewards of positions, not the recruitment of individuals to these positions. Yet they have also admitted the importance of ascription in recruitment to positions, particularly the role of the family in facilitating or inhibiting differentiated opportunities for particular individuals within the system. In sum, it does appear that the theory's implicit assumption of "equality of opportunity" regarding the discovery and use of talent is certainly subject to question.[18]

A third major area of criticism of the theory is its reasoning that, since unequal rewards are necessary as a motivating force, inequality in society is inevitable. Critics have reacted to this issue in several ways. Some have tended to focus on the implicit assumptions about human nature contained within the theory. In the words of Wesolowski (1966:66): "According to Davis and Moore, human nature is characterized, on the one hand, by a drive towards personal advantages, and on the other hand by laziness." He goes on to note that such a view of human nature is not compatible with modern social psychology. A second, related point that critics of this issue have made concerns the position of the theory that differential levels of goods and services are necessary to induce performance. Tumin (1953:291) makes the following observation: "There is still the basic problem as to whether the allocation of differential rewards in scarce and desired goods and services is the only or the most efficient way of recruiting the appropriate talent to these positions." His response to this issue is that there are a number of alternative motivational schemes (functional equivalents) that are available and should be investigated. He mentions explicitly joy in work and intrinsic work satisfaction as possibilities. To Huaco (1966:220), the existence of such equivalents tends to destroy the theory's predictive power. Wesolowski (1966), in this light, has made the point that, for societies in which incomes are less variable (i.e., socialist societies), authority over others becomes highly valued, even more than material advantage or prestige, thereby also questioning the universal applicability of the theory to all societies. Abrahamson et al. (1976: 106) observe that, in response to such criticisms, Davis and Moore did later confine the theory's applicability to competitive, achievement-oriented societies. However, if the points made by Tumin and Wesolowski are valid, the inevitability of inequality in the sense in which Davis and Moore have used the term is certainly questionable.

Others have focused on the theory's neglect of the role of differential power within society in influencing access to positions and rewards and in modifying the distribution of rewards themselves (Wrong 1959; Cohen 1968; Lopreato and Lewis 1963).[19] Kerbo (1983: 132) summarizes this point as follows: "the greater the rewards received by individuals or groups, the greater their ability to make sure they continue to receive such rewards, and even more rewards, no matter what function they serve in society."

Finally, the theory has been criticized for its argument that inequality is functional for society. Tumin (1953:393) has summarized the dysfunctions of social inequality in society. To him, stratification systems:

1. function to limit the possibility of discovery of the full range of talent available in a society;
2. function to set limits upon the possibility of expanding the productive resources of society;
3. function to provide the elite with the political power necessary to procure acceptance and dominance of an ideology which rationalizes the status quo;
4. function to distribute favorable self-images unequally throughout a population;
5. [to the extent that acceptance of inequalities is not accepted] function to encourage hostility, suspicion and distrust;
6. [to the extent that significant membership depends upon one's place in prestige systems] function to distribute unequally the sense of significant memberships in the population;
7. [to the extent that loyalty depends on the above] function to distribute loyalty unequally in the population;
8. [to the extent that participation and apathy depend on significant memberships] function to distribute the motivation to participate unequally in the population.

With regard to its implicit ideology, the theory has also been criticized for its support for the status quo in society (Tumin 1953; Simpson 1956; Dahrendorf 1958). In Vanfossen's (1979:30) words, "functional theories are basically supportive of the status quo because they imply that any scheme of stratification is somehow the best that could be had and that the prevailing distribution of rewards is functionally necessary and therefore desirable." In other words, because the theory takes the position that, at any point in time, the differential distribution of rewards enables the society to fill functionally important positions with the most talented individuals and, thus, to meet its functional imperatives, it tends to support the current system as most adaptive to the environment. Further, since the value system of the society tends to legitimate the current system of inequality, the theory tends to be conservative and supportive of the status quo.

In 1953, Parsons published "A Revised Analytical Approach to the Theory of Social Stratification," wherein he attempts to incorporate some of the earlier criticisms of the theory. In particular, in this revision, Parsons stresses the role of the family system in lessening equality of opportunity in society, and he also addresses there some of the disintegrative aspects of stratification in society and offers some tentative solutions to that problem. He also devotes greater attention there to the role of power in systems of inequality, but it still, for him at least, remains of secondary importance in influencing the distribution of rewards and prestige within society.[20]

Thus, despite numerous criticisms, the functionalist theory of class inequality, as generally outlined by Parsons and more specifically detailed by Davis and Moore, was the leading explanation for social inequality in complex industrial society during the 1950s and the early 1960s.[21]

SUMMARY AND CONCLUSIONS

The major goal of this chapter was to chronicle the development of the functionalist explanation for class inequality in American society, stressing the interrelationship between the theory and the setting within which it developed. The theory took shape during the late 1930s and early 1940s, a period in our history in which there were many challenges to the vitality of our political economy. I have presented evidence that the theory should be seen, at least in part, as a response on the part of its author to the political and economic crises brought about by the Great Depression and World War II and the contrast between this period in our history and the decade of the 1920s, a period of relative world peace and economic prosperity during which he grew to adulthood. I have also stated that the theory was an attempt to provide an alternative macro-structural explanation to that of Marxist theory, whose diagnosis of the crises of the 1930s was that they were the result of "contradictions" inherent within capitalism itself, and that the only viable solution was the transformation of the economy to socialism.

As shown above, the functionalist theory relied heavily on a combination of classical economic theory's assumptions of an equal-opportunity, free-market economy, and Durkheim's notion of functional interdependence in modern society. Because of this, the theory was certainly consistent with middle-class America's image of an ideal society that was influenced by the prosperity that it enjoyed during the decade of the 1920s. Further, given the fact that the immediate post–World War II environment in American society was similar in many ways to that of the 1920s in that there was world peace, a growing economy, and renewed faith in our political system, it should come as no surprise that the theory seemed consistent with events during this period as well. Thus, I believe that both the rise of the functionalist perspective during the pre–World War II period and its subsequent theoretical hegemony during the 1950s in particular are consistent with the thrust of my argument concerning the salient role of the sociohistorical setting in influencing the nature of theoretical perspectives about society. Chapter 5 demonstrates the growing influence of this perspective on the ways in which sociologists measured class inequality in American sociology for the period from about the late 1940s to the late 1960s.

NOTES

1. As will be noted later, Parsons' efforts should be construed as attempting to do what extant research in the United States had not done — to build a theoretically integrated perspective that could better explain social phenomena. To accomplish this end, he returned to the same European sources that many of the earlier American scholars had used, and reinterpreted them in a manner consistent with his own developing perspective (Parkin 1978; Turner 1982).

2. Ritzer (1983) states that the influence of Chicago reached a peak in the 1920s, but began to decline by the 1930s because of the death of George Mead and the departure of Robert Park. He cites Matthews (1977) as offering two key reasons for the decline of Chicago: the preoccupation of the discipline with becoming more scientific, and the resentment of many sociologists outside of Chicago about the dominance of that institution in the affairs of the discipline.

3. This biographical sketch was gleaned from Parsons' lengthy essay entitled "On Building Social Systems Theory: A Personal History" (1970a), which is an autobiographical essay dealing with his perceptions of the various influences on his work.

4. A caveat is in order. It is not my intention to detail the complete theoretical wealth of Parsons' analytical scheme here. Others who are far more skilled and inclined in this direction have begun this task. However, I do believe that, in order to grasp Parsons' treatment of the subject of my inquiry — class inequality in American society — some rudimentary understanding of both his motives and results is necessary. Hence, my modest efforts in this direction.

5. Some, notably Mills (1959), would claim that Parsons overreacted to this empiricism by erecting a theoretical scheme that literally did not articulate at all with the empirically observed world.

6. Parsons' orientation with regard to this issue was the result of several influences. First, Parsons was a student of Weber's work. Weber, in his own efforts to gain the respect of the German academic community, explicitly rejected the more activist Marxist orientation and advocated a more objective mode of inquiry. Second, it should also be remembered that sociology during Parsons' younger years was still striving to be accepted as a legitimate member of the academic community and adopted the natural sciences as a role model as a means to this end.

7. Parsons, himself, retrospectively stressed the importance of these extradisciplinary influences on his work during this period:

> the state of Western society, which might be designated as either capitalism or free enterprise — on the political side as democracy — was clearly in some kind of state of crisis. The Russian Revolution and the emergence of the first socialist state as controlled by the Communist Party had been crucial to my thinking since Undergraduate days. The Fascist movements affected friendships in Germany. Less than two years after the publication of the book, *The Structure of Social Action*, the second World War was to begin, and, finally, came the Great Depression with its ramifications throughout the world (Parsons 1970a:831).

8. Gouldner's explanation for Parsons' rejection of Marxism as a way of understanding the crisis of the Depression stressed his (Parsons') ideological conservatism, which had been formed and reinforced by his middle-class background, his coming to adulthood during the prosperity of the 1920s, and the subsequent isolation and detachment created by the atmosphere at Harvard.

9. A number of critics have attacked both the explicit and the implicit assumptions of the theory. Some of the most important criticisms that have been made include: that the theory is politically conservative because it stresses the maintenance of the status quo; that because the theory's focus is on social structures, it is unable to deal effectively with social change; and that the theory's focus on order and integration precludes its analysis of social conflict as an ongoing activity in society (Dahrendorf 1959; Ritzer 1983:49). Both Parsons (1966, 1970b) and others, including Rocher (1975), Savage (1980), Bourricaud (1981), and Alexander (1987) have reacted to these criticisms and have offered alternative interpretations for each. The debate over these issues is certainly one of the longest-running controversies within the discipline. The reader is directed to these sources for additional information.

10. Earlier scholars, who used pieces of the functionalist perspective, such as Warner and Hollingshead, chose to use the label "class," although both often used the prefix "social" to differentiate it from its more narrow economic roots. Despite their use of class, however, each conceptualized and measured it as status.

11. Of course, the well-known linkages between Parsons and Weber, one of Marx's earliest critics, should also be mentioned here. In particular, Weber argued that Marx's treatment of inequality within capitalist society was too narrowly centered around the economic variable. Weber suggested the famous trinity of class, status, and power as a more realistic conceptualization of social inequality in modern industrial society. Yet, it should also be mentioned that Weber, despite this modification, still believed that economic class was the most salient of the three. Modern day interpreters of Weber, particularly Parsons, seem to have forgotten this fact. See Giddens (1981) and Parkin (1978) for further discussion on this point.

12. The parallel should be noted here between Parsons' image of the relationship between the actor's goals and the needs of the overall society and classic economic theory's notion of the interrelationship between the private acts of men in the marketplace and overall good for the entire system. See Clarke (1982) for a discussion of this linkage.

13. It is interesting that Parsons engaged in a lengthy discussion on the relative influences of the various factors. In particular, he relegated authority to a secondary role, arguing that authority is an artifact of positions that are achieved; he also considered power to be a residual category, and he argued that wealth also played a secondary role in society, noting that it is simply a by product of achievement as well. To some commentators, these defenses demonstrate his ideological conservatism (compare Gouldner 1970). Also, these positions are consistent with Parsons' background in classical economic theory, with its image of the economic structure of early capitalistic society.

14. The reader should be reminded once again about the sociohistorical setting within which this theory was developing and its consistency with this environment. As the 1930s came to a close, whether by Roosevelt's application of the Keynesian "demand stimulation" solutions or the increased role that American industry began to play as the war in Europe escalated, the American economy was beginning to recover its pre-Depression posture. There was full employment, and, as is the case when an economy is growing, there was more opportunity for individual mobility. Because of this, there was also restored confidence in the vitality of capitalism as an economic structure. At the same time, the country's

diverse groups were beginning to unite as a result of the growing commitment to the war effort. As such, the dominant sentiment tended to stress cooperation rather than competition. In short, the setting was certainly compatible with a theory that stressed the role of achievement over ascription as a means for class placement, that emphasized the integrative rather than the disintegrative effects of social differentiation, that stressed the opportunities provided for social mobility, and that minimized the role of unearned wealth as a criterion for class placement.

15. Interestingly, as Abrahamson et al. (1976) have noted, its brevity and clarity not only helped to make it the most visible of the functionalist perspectives on social inequality, but also made it the target of the most vituperative reaction on the part of its critics. It should also be noted that the focus of this article was more narrow than Parsons' earlier effort, since its goal was limited to explaining why social inequality is necessary to insure the functioning of society (Kerbo 1983:129).

16. This grouping strategy was informed by a number of sources, including Tumin (1953; 1960), Huaco (1966), Abrahamson et al. (1976), Vanfossen (1979), and Kerbo (1983).

17. A number of sources have noted this problem with the theory. Some of them include: Tumin (1953), Simpson (1956), Reissman (1959), Tausky (1965), and Huaco (1966).

18. Wesolowski (1966:64) offers additional evidence that indicates that the authors themselves have backed away from this claim for the theory.

19. With regard to this particular issue, it should be added that the various functionalist perspectives on class inequality visualize the dimensions of structural inequality in society, such as class, race/ethnic, power, and gender, to be relatively independent of each other. This, too, is consistent with the perspective's stress on the integrative consequences of class and with its overall image of society as a relatively stable, harmonious system of interacting parts.

20. There remain two articles written by Parsons devoted to the subject that I have not discussed. The first, published in 1949, was both an attack on Marxian theory and a defense of the functionalist theory. Because it adds nothing to what I've outlined above, I will not discuss it here. The second is the third revision of the original article (Parsons 1940), published in 1970 (1970b). It, too, contains limited additional information and will not be discussed here, except to note that Parsons continued there to defend his perspective from attacks by both Marxists and others.

21. Huaco (1966:237) isolates several fragments of the theory that he feels still hold promise:

> unequal rewards attached to different positions are the cause of the mobility of individuals into positions. The existence and operation of the family is the cause of status ascription ... differential scarcity of qualified personnel is the cause of *the range* of unequal rewards attached to different positions.

5

APPLYING THE FUNCTIONALIST PERSPECTIVE ON CLASS INEQUALITY IN SOCIAL SCIENCE RESEARCH

Within the setting of immediate postwar American society, there were two trends within the discipline that would have major consequences for the analysis of class inequality by American sociologists. In retrospect, both seem to have been related to the discipline's increased concern with its status within the scientific community. First, as discussed in Chapter 4, through the efforts of Talcott Parsons and his students, the functionalist perspective became the dominant theoretical perspective within the discipline. One result of the theory's hegemony was that scholars began to apply it in their efforts to address the salient societal concerns of the period, particularly the issue of class inequality. With the publication of "Some Principles of Stratification" (Davis and Moore 1945), the functionalists offered a strong defense for both the integrative consequences of "social stratification" and its inevitability in complex industrial society. Despite the negative reaction that ensued in some quarters, the general hegemony of their perspective within the discipline insured its support as an explanation for the role of class inequality within American society, at least for the next decade or so.

The second trend concerns changes that were taking place in American society as a whole and sociology's efforts to adjust its perspective to meet these changes. By the late 1940s, American society was becoming increasingly urbanized and, as an important consequence of this trend, the Great Depression, and our involvement in World War II, a shift in the focus of attention away from local and regional issues toward those at the national level was occurring. As a result, sociologists began to face the necessity of adapting their viewpoints, theories, and methods, which had been developed and refined in small-town and rural settings, to larger cities and to the entire country as units of analysis. Given both the magnitude and the rapid pace of these societal transformations, it should not be too surprising that sociologists quickly discovered that rather substantial changes would be necessary to adapt their perspectives to these new units of analysis and the unique problems they presented.

Both of these trends would have important consequences for the conceptualization and measurement of class inequality by sociologists during the next two decades. The goal of this chapter is to examine the ways in which sociologists conceptualized and measured class inequality during the early post-World War II period, defined here as between the late 1940s and the late 1960s. After a brief discussion of sociology's changing focus, I present and discuss two major approaches to the measurement of social inequality that appeared during the period — studies stressing the subjective ranking of occupations in terms of relative prestige, and those focusing on the objective ranking of occupations based on socioeconomic criteria.

THE CHANGING DISCIPLINE

In many ways, American sociology had reached a kind of intellectual maturity during the decade of the 1940s. Not only was the discipline becoming increasingly organized as a body of thought, but also the discipline's legitimacy was being affirmed through its increasingly central role in the newly emerging administrative society (Vidich and Lyman 1985).

As discussed in Chapter 4, beginning with this decade the functionalist perspective was developing through the efforts of Parsons and his students and, by the early 1950s, had become the dominant theoretical perspective within the discipline (Kuklick 1972; Ritzer 1983; Turner 1982; Huaco 1986). This particular perspective, a product of Parsons' reaction to the events both within the larger society and the social sciences, sought to provide an alternative to classical economic theory's explanation for the source of integration in modern capitalist society. Parsons, borrowing heavily from Durkheim, located this new source of integration within a shared value system. What emerged from his attempt to provide a theoretical linkage between the personality and the social order was a view of society as a hierarchical system of interrelated parts, seen as functionally interrelated with each other in a dynamic equilibrium. This particular conceptualization of society and its operation yielded a model of change that stressed the gradual evolutionary adaptation of modern industrial society to its environment and postulated the continued existence of capitalism as a form of economic organization. This stood in sharp contrast to the inevitable decline and eventual revolutionary transformation of capitalist society to socialism predicted by the only other macro-level theory of societal organization, that of Marx.

There are two things about the growing hegemony of Parsons' work that are important for our purposes. First, the presence of a single paradigm had a facilitative impact upon research within the discipline. Kuhn's (1970) analysis of the development of science asserts that, following convergence around a single paradigm, research within a discipline will flourish as more and more scholars begin to accept and apply the perspective in their research efforts. This occurs partially because efforts that had formerly been diverted to discussion and debate over the relative merits of different candidates for hegemony could then be devoted to the application of the dominant perspective in research. Such convergence of opinion and increased research activity within a discipline could also serve as evidence to potential clients that the discipline had answers to offer for contemporary problems in society. One indicator that this was occurring for sociology was the fact that, during World War II and the postwar period, increasing numbers of scholars were recruited by business, philanthropic, and governmental institutions (Vidich and Lyman 1985).

Yet it should also be noted that the mere presence of a dominant theoretical perspective and an active research agenda, while perhaps necessary for the recruitment of sociologists by other sectors for practical research applications, are by no means sufficient. It is also necessary that the perspective in question be reasonably compatible with the interests of those contracting for the services of sociologists. Thus, another important reason why sociologists were invited to provide inputs into business and government was the fact that the functionalist perspective offered a model that was both supportive of the status quo and offered a model of change that was evolutionary and gradual. Vidich and Lyman (1985:291–92) reflect this opinion in their characterization of the role for social scientists during these years:

> social science was to harness its technical know-how to the practical programs and institutional reforms that might be realized between the poles of permanent welfare benefits, capitalist and Keynesian economic practices, and a politics of contest among a more-or-less set number of recognized competing interest groups who tacitly agreed not to violate the rules of democracy.

In sum, then, both the presence of relative theoretical consensus and a model of society that was compatible with dominant institutional arrangements facilitated sociology's integration into a service role within the developing administrative state of the 1950s in American society.

In many ways, this drive toward theoretical maturity was merely a part of sociology's efforts to be accepted as a member of the scientific community. This goal required a transformation not only in the ways sociology interpreted and explained societal concerns (its theories), but also in the ways in which sociology studied those issues (its methodologies).[1] Increasingly, then, during these early post-Depression years, sociologists' collective concern with the scientific status of their discipline encouraged them to attempt to emulate the methods, procedures, and outlook of the natural sciences in their work.

It should be remembered as well that from the period of the discipline's infancy in the late nineteenth century until the end of the decade of the 1950s, American society was undergoing a rapid transformation from a sparsely populated, largely rural, agricultural society with, at best, the regional trading community as the norm, to a more densely populated, more heavily industrialized society with more and more of the population living in urban areas. Not only this, but the vast improvement in mass communications during this same period dramatically decreased the sense of isolation and more and more Americans began to think of themselves as members of a nation rather than as merely residents of a particular area. These changes meant that the research problems with which sociologists came increasingly to deal were radically different from the early days of the Lynds' case study of "Middletown." Participant observation simply was not adaptable to larger communities and to the study of national issues. New techniques and procedures were necessary, and sociologists began to adapt their research procedures to these new problems. This shift in the scale of research, then, was occurring at the same time that sociologists were increasingly concerned with becoming more scientific in their research. In particular, during the war years, as sociologists joined in government efforts to understand more about soldiers and the effects of the war on the civilian population, sociologists began increasingly to rely on social surveys of attitudes and census materials as tools for research. These trends would have dramatic consequences for the discipline in the years to come, and are particularly apparent in the immediate postwar research in class inequality that is the subject of this chapter.

THE NATIONAL STUDIES OF OCCUPATIONAL PRESTIGE

One group of early postwar sociological analyses of class inequality provides a good example of the impact of the changes detailed above on research within the discipline. These are the national studies of occupational prestige that were completed during the period between the late 1940s and the early 1960s. They remain important today because they form the basis for one of the most popular contemporary methods for conceptualizing and measuring class inequality in American sociology, the Duncan Socioeconomic Index.

The NORC-North-Hatt Study

In 1947 the first national study of the relative prestige of occupations was completed by the National Opinion Research Center (NORC) under the direction of two sociologists, Cecil North and Paul Hatt.[2] The study grew out of their interest in the role that occupation plays as a dimension of stratification in modern industrial society.

The theoretical antecedents that guided their work must be surmised since they provided little detailed information concerning their assumptions. Reiss' (1961:4) summary of their perspective based on a chapter draft completed by North suggests the presence of a conceptual framework, but it provided little additional information concerning its nature: "North and Hatt, in connection with a larger study of the theory of social stratification, were interested in 'the role of occupation as one distinctive mark of social class distinction.'" Despite this problem, evidence about their perspective can be gleaned from their research itself. Their focus on occupation as a significant indicator of class is not in itself unequivocally linked to any particular theoretical perspective on class, since several use occupation as a key variable. Yet their decision to focus on the relative statuses of these occupations and their conceptualization of the status order as a finely graded hierarchical order based on relative prestige differences among occupations are certainly more consistent with the functionalist explanation for social inequality based on the work of Parsons (1940, 1953), Davis and Moore (1945), Warner (1949a) and Duncan (1961) than they are with the polarized, property-based model of more radical class theorists such as Marx. These decisions were also similar to a conceptualization of class inequality shared by other sociologists of the period. A popular text by Caplow (1950:30) reflects this viewpoint:

occupational position is an important factor in the determination of individual prestige and in the allocation of social privileges. There appears to be a consistent tendency for occupational identification to displace such other status-fixing attributes as ancestry, religious office, political affiliation, and personal character.

In short, both their conceptual framework and their indicators were consistent with the growing theoretical hegemony of the functionalist perspective noted earlier in this section of the book.

Many of their initial ideas were derived from earlier studies on the subject. Counts (1925) completed the first major study to measure the prestige of occupations in the 1920s (Reiss 1961:1; Nam and Powers 1983:3). He asked six groups of raters (composed of students and teachers) to rank-order 45 occupations in terms of relative social standing. He found that the intercorrelations among the different groups of raters averaged .90 and that the social backgrounds of raters had little effect on their rankings. While his findings offered support for the notion that the general public did think of occupations in hierarchical terms, his research was flawed because his sample was small and local and his list of occupations was limited.

Mapheus Smith's (1943) study incorporated several key improvements when compared to Counts' effort. First, his list of 100 occupations was the most comprehensive to date. Second, he asked his respondents to rank each occupation on a discrete scale of 100 in terms of their perceptions of its status in the United States. He then compared the standard errors of different occupations and found that there was more rater agreement for those occupations ranking higher or lower when compared to those in the middle. He also placed each occupation into one of ten major occupational groups in an attempt to derive social strata consisting of occupations with similar prestige. However, his study was also limited by sampling inadequacies since he used groups of high school and college students in only one state, and by the representativeness of his list of occupations.

North and Hatt sought to correct two key limitations of the efforts reviewed above — the fact that earlier research had employed lists of occupations that did not adequately represent the distribution of occupations in society, and the use of limited samples. One goal of their research design was to develop a list of occupations that was representative of all occupations in the United States (Reiss 1961:4-5). Yet they were limited in the total number of occupational titles they could include in their survey. They began with Smith's (1943) list and made additions and deletions consistent with the 1940 Census Report on Occupations. Their original list contained 100 occupations, but this was pared down to 78 by eliminating duplicates and occupations clearly identified with women. To this list, sponsors of the study then added 12, resulting in a total of 90 occupational titles in the final list. These were randomly divided into four "blocks" for use in the survey.[3]

Respondents were asked to judge the "general standing" of each of the occupations according to the following categories (North and Hatt 1947:3):

1. Excellent standing
2. Good standing
3. Average standing

4. Somewhat below average standing
5. Poor standing
X. I don't know where to place that one

Data for the study consisted of the results of 2,920 personal interviews conducted by the NORC field staff. Respondents were selected by means of a quota sample designed to be representative of the adult American population, organized according to the following elements: geography, size of city, age, sex, socioeconomic status, and race (Reiss 1961:6).

Following data collection, a prestige score for each occupational title was derived as follows: after eliminating the "don't knows," the percentage responding to each of the other categories was obtained; each response category was assigned an arbitrary weight, a "5" for "excellent standing" through a "1" for "poor standing"; and the percentages were multiplied by the weights and the total divided by 5 to derive a score with a theoretical range of from 20 to 100. Then each of the occupations was placed along the prestige continuum according to its score. Actual scores ranged from a high of 96 for a supreme court justice to a low of 33 for a shoe shiner.

The NORC-North-Hatt study quickly became a major empirical tool for students of social inequality in American sociology. Reiss (1961:7) summarizes the impact of the study as follows: "few empirical studies have achieved a place in the scientific literature of sociology comparable to that of the NORC-North-Hatt investigation." There are two potential explanations for why the study became so popular among social scientists. The first concerns its methodology. The study had several technical advantages over previous research efforts on the subject. Its overall research design, which included such key features as its categorization of occupations and its use of a national quota sample of respondents, was an important innovation. Such a design was also consistent with trends within the discipline since, during the early postwar period, sociologists increasingly adopted survey research as a data-gathering strategy and began to focus on national attitudes as a key subject of interest (Oberschall 1972). As a result, one potential explanation for the study's popularity was its technically superior application of the survey design to the study of societal inequality. However, before this explanation is accepted as valid, a more careful examination of specific details of their methodology is necessary.

Most analysts of their work have drawn attention to several critical conceptual, methodological, and data analysis problems, two of which will be presented here.[4] Perhaps the most questionable of their design decisions was their list of occupational categories. As noted above, they eventually submitted 90 occupations for respondent judgment. A key question influencing the validity of their study as a description of the status structure of American society is the extent to which this sample of occupations represents all occupations in the society. Reiss (1961:42) makes the following observation following his examination of their list of occupations: "The occupations included in the NORC list do not comprise a set of mutually exclusive categories, which exhaust the logical possibilities of a classification scheme." He concludes that not only were certain segments of the occupational structure overrepresented by North and Hatt (i.e., professionals and governmental occupations), but also that the occupations varied in terms of their levels of specificity. These problems certainly raise doubts about the extent to which their scale can be said to represent the status structure of occupations in American society as a whole.

A second issue that has been questioned is the criteria that respondents employed in making judgments about the various occupations (Reiss 1961; Kriesberg 1962; Gusfield and Schwartz 1963). The evaluation portion of the interview was preceded by a series of questions that attempted to determine the criteria respondents used in making the assessments. These questions asked respondents to pick an occupation appropriate for "an outstanding young man" and to specify why they had made that particular choice. Based on their analysis of these responses, North and Hatt singled out prestige as the most important determinant of respondent decisions. However, others have reviewed their evidence and reached very different conclusions. Reiss (1961:37) observes that

> the respondents in the NORC study, when asked to rate the "general standing" of occupations, do not appear to have made their evaluations in terms of a conscious awareness of the social prestige attached to the occupation. They are more likely, in fact, to emphasize the relevance of indicators sociologists use to measure socioeconomic status, primarily the *income* of the occupational position and the *education and training needed*.

He adds that respondents were not likely to mention prestige as a salient criterion unless given a stimulus to do so. That such a different conclusion could result from examining the original data raises serious doubts about the conclusion reached by North and Hatt that prestige was the major criterion employed by raters.

While there are numerous other points of criticism about their research design that could be added, these seem sufficient to support the position that, in retrospect, despite its innovative approach, their study contained serious methodological flaws. Limitations such as these make an explanation for the study's popularity based on its methodological innovations a less attractive alternative.

A second potential explanation for the popularity of the study is theoretical. As noted above, the authors' perspective on class inequality, their conceptualization of the status structure of modern society, and their results are most compatible with functionalism — the dominant theoretical perspective in American social science at the time — and its viewpoint on class inequality in modern industrial society. Reiss' (1961:7) remarks reflected this alternative explanation: "Given the predilections of American social scientists for social-status scales, the North-Hatt ranking of occupations has been widely accepted as affirming a rank-structure of the prestige status of occupations as a skeletal prestige structure." In other words, given the methodological flaws in their study, a more likely explanation for the study's popularity is that it offered both an image of the social structure of American society as based primarily on status differences and an explanation for the role of occupational status in society that was consistent with the theoretical perspective that dominated the sociological enterprise at the time.[5]

Thus, despite its shortcomings, the NORC-North-Hatt study helped to direct the interests of sociologists toward a view of the social structure of American society that stressed the status dimension of class instead of other alternatives. Such a focus limits scholarly interest in other salient dimensions of class within the discipline.

Subsequent research on the prestige dimension of status by sociologists addressed two major issues: the stability of the occupational status scores over time; and the extension of prestige rankings to a wider range of occupations. In an effort to address the first, Hodge et al. (1964) replicated the 1947 study in 1963. They used identical questions, the same 90 occupational titles, and identical quota sampling procedures (except that they reduced the size of the sample to 651). Their results revealed that the correlation between the 1947 and the 1963 prestige scores for the 90 occupations was virtually perfect (r = .99). They also constructed comparisons with other studies that enabled them to compare prestige scores for some of the occupations for the period from 1925 to 1963. Based on their analysis of these data, they concluded that the occupational prestige structure had undergone no substantial changes between 1925 and 1963. Such findings provided important reinforcement for the relative reliability of the approach but did not address the validity issue.

The second issue that occupied subsequent scholarship was related to the fact that status scores were available from the North-Hatt study for fewer than 100 occupations, a number far short of the several hundred occupations found within society. Efforts continued to seek a way to expand the scale to encompass a larger proportion of the total occupational positions in society. One important outcome of these efforts was the development of Duncan's Socioeconomic Index

(SEI), an approach to measuring occupational status that still remains popular within the discipline today.

Otis Duncan's Socioeconomic Index (SEI)

Between 1947 and the late 1950s, a number of studies made use of the NORC-North-Hatt prestige scores in research applications. Duncan (1961:113) notes two major problems with these studies: none had included all the occupations omitted by the NORC study; and none had corrected the errors in weighting and sampling biases that the original study contained. Duncan's goal was to correct these imperfections. Duncan's work was also influenced by the functionalist perspective on social inequality. Crowder's (1974:19) assessment of his work reflects both the significance of Duncan's work and its theoretical orientation: "Duncan's work has become a major force in present-day American sociological thought on the process of stratification and its theoretical context is that of the *functionalist* theories of stratification" [emphasis added]. Crowder (1974) also summarizes the implicit assumptions of Duncan's perspective: a view of society as a benign system composed of a static hierarchical structure of positions; with individual rewards based on achieved contribution to society's needs; and legitimized by a system of universally shared values.

Within the parameters prescribed by this theoretical perspective, Duncan's goal was to build an index that could serve as an acceptable substitute for the NORC prestige score when no such score was available for an occupation. His solution to this problem focuses on the association between the NORC prestige scores and socioeconomic characteristics of the various occupations, specifically education and income. Duncan (1961:116–17) summarizes the linkage between prestige and his socioeconomic indicators as follows:

> we have, therefore, the following sequence: a man qualifies himself for an occupational life by obtaining an education; as a consequence of pursuing his occupation, he obtains income. Occupation, therefore, is the intervening activity linking income to education. If we characterize an occupation according to prevailing levels of education and income of its incumbents, we are not only estimating its "social status" and its "economic status," we are also describing one of its major "causes" and one of its major "effects." It would not be surprising if an occupation's "prestige" turned out to be closely related to one or both of these factors.

With this linkage established, Duncan then operationalized his indicators. For *prestige*, he criticized the original NORC study's decision to employ all five of the assessment categories (i.e., "excellent," "good," "average," "somewhat below average," and "poor" [standing]) in their measure, noting that the use of these caused "ambiguities." His procedure was to use only the first two categories (i.e., "excellent" and "good" [standing]) as his indicator of occupational prestige. His justification for this modification is that it better differentiated among occupations, particularly those in the middle of the distribution (Duncan 1961:119).

For *income* and *education*, he also rejected a strategy based on average levels, arguing that median levels are insensitive to extreme values; he decided instead to use a measure that reflected the proportion of the members of a given occupation that fell toward the top of the income and education distributions. For income, he used the percentage of the members of an occupation with (1949) incomes of $3,500 or more; for education, the percentage of the incumbents with a high school education or more. For each of these variables Duncan adjusted his data for age, although he later noted that this step proved less necessary than he had originally supposed.

Concerning the *occupation* variable, Duncan found that only one-half of the 90 occupations in the NORC-North-Hatt study matched his list of 1950 census occupations well enough to be a part of his study. Thus, he used only 45 of the original list in his sample of occupations. Prestige scores were then derived from the NORC-North-Hatt study and data for income and education were obtained from the 1950 U.S. Census. Duncan confined his sample to males, arguing that males outnumbered females in the labor force and thus that family status was more likely to reflect the position of the male head of household.

These data were then analyzed using regression analysis after scattergram inspection revealed that the three variables were essentially linear in their interrelationships. The two predictor variables (income and education) explained 83 percent of the variation in the prestige scores of the 45 occupations in the sample. The standardized regression coefficients for income and education were .59 and .55, respectively. These regression coefficients were then used as weights to derive predicted values for the 425 census occupations. The resulting index was labeled the Socioeconomic Index (SEI).

Duncan noted a number of qualifications for the use of the Index. He cautioned that the stratification structure was multivariate and that no single measure could capture its complexity; he suggested that the SEI scores were derived for occupational positions, not for individual incumbents; he noted that the relative stability of SEI scores should be assumed to be valid only in the short term; and he also suggested that, since the scale was constructed using national data, its applicability to local settings was more problematic.

Duncan's SEI and the perspective on "social" inequality that it implied quickly gained popularity and the SEI became the leading measure of class inequality within American sociology. Yet, the SEI, like its predecessor, also suffers from crucial conceptual and operational difficulties. A general critique of stratification research by Haug (1972) offers a number of methodological criticisms of the measure. She begins by noting that measuring class by status confounds the two and makes it impossible to separate and compare the two dimensions (see Mills 1942, for a similar assessment of Warner's earlier conflation of class and reputation).

Next, she criticizes the operationalization of the major variables that Duncan used. Regarding the prestige measure, she notes that, in contrast to NORC procedures that essentially used mean respondent ratings, Duncan elected instead to use only the percent rating the occupation "excellent" or "good" in his adaptation of these scores. This modification caused changes in the rankings of several occupations, particularly some at both the top and the bottom of the hierarchy. Moreover, because the rank-order was viewed by North and Hatt as more important than individual scores, Haug concludes that this decision added error to Duncan's scale. She also observes that, while focusing on "excellent" and "good" rankings could be defended for high-status occupations, it served to give inordinate weight to idiosyncratic opinions for some particular low-status positions from the original list that Duncan included (she mentions specifically shoeshiners, soda fountain clerks, and janitors).

Haug also questions the means by which Duncan operationalized his predictor variables. She observes that using percentages of those above a single point in education and income created some unusual rankings.[6] For example, dentists are ranked above physicians on Duncan's Index, despite the fact that the median income of the latter group is 30 percent higher than the former and both have virtually 100 percent with education above high school. The problem is that internship and residency requirements for physicians lowers the percent with incomes over $3,500. Duncan's rankings of the two occupations stand in contrast to those of the original NORC study in which physicians ranked second and dentists fifteenth (Haug 1972:441).

Duncan's operationalization of the education variable also creates similar anomalies. Since most semi-professions and professions require college or at least some post-high school education, the percents with a high school education or more for these categories are all around 100. This means that, at the upper end of the prestige continuum, income becomes the sole determinant of an occupation's socioeconomic index score. At the bottom of the prestige hierarchy, the opposite problem occurs. There, Haug notes that overeducated occupants elevate the socioeconomic index scores of occupations at this level. Haug also complains that the use of male socioeconomic data to rank predominantly female occupations such as nurses, librarians, and social workers creates anomalies such as student nurses ranking higher in Duncan's Index than professional nurses.[7]

Haug (p. 443) summarizes her assessment of the Duncan SEI as follows: "On the balance, the advantage of the Duncan SEI use of occupation as the sole indicator of social position is outweighed by using prestige as an ordering criterion, calculating prestige scores in a manner that appears to allow for considerable error. . . ."

Thus, in a manner similar to NORC-North-Hatt, Duncan's Socioeconomic Index has been seriously criticized for methodological shortcomings. That these have been obvious for a considerable time makes it difficult to explain the widespread use of the SEI within the discipline by its technical superiority over alternative measures. Its compatibilities with (and the growing hegemony of) the functionalist theoretical perspective seems to be the only other reasonable explanation for its popularity.

Despite the problems with prestige-based status scales noted above, efforts have continued to improve them. For example, Siegel (1971) sought to overcome an important limitation of the SEI in his effort to construct an updated set of socioeconomic status scores for the detailed occupational categories in the 1960 Census labor force. Noting that Duncan's use of prestige scores from only 45 occupations was an important potential source for error, Siegel collected a more comprehensive list of occupational prestige scores from three different sources: the NORC 1963 replication (Hodge, Siegel, and Rossi 1964); a study done in 1964; and a study completed in 1965. Despite the fact that these studies are based on different samples, different lists of occupations, and on different methodologies, he combined them to construct a new index (Nam and Powers 1983).[8]

Summing all the occupations contained within the three studies results in over 600 occupations, 412 of which were distinct, the others overlapping. Siegel used these overlaps to construct his scale through regression analysis. These results were used to provide "prestige scores in uniform metric" for all the occupations in the 1960 Census, including those not rated by the Hodge, Siegel, and Rossi study. Siegel's (1971) index has not proven as popular as the Duncan measure in actual research applications, perhaps because his combination of status scores derived by different means introduced even more margin for error in his transformations (Nam and Powers 1983:14).

Featherman and Stevens (1982) constructed an update of the Duncan SEI using 1970 Census data. Their effort reflects a reaction to several of the problems discussed above. First, they were concerned that Duncan's list of occupations was not representative of all occupations in the U.S. labor force. They made several attempts to substitute other estimates, including those of Siegel. They conclude that none of the substitutes differentiated among the various occupational groups, particularly those at the top and the bottom of the list, as well as Duncan's did. Second, they also made several modifications to the income and education variables in an effort to update these. They observe that the measures that performed best were those most similar in nature to those Duncan had originally employed. It should be noted, however, that in each of these decisions, their desire to approximate the Duncan results as closely as possible was certainly an influence on their conclusions. Finally, in contrast to Duncan and earlier updates of the Index (compare Blau and Duncan 1967; Hauser and Featherman 1977), they attempt to include characteristics of the *total labor force* in their revision.[9] After constructing measures based on both the total labor force and males alone, the authors compared the performance of the two in an effort to examine their comparative utility. Their results demonstrate that the total labor-force-based measure is not an adequate substitute for the more traditional males-only-based index. Their conclusion is that a common index was a desirable goal for researchers within the discipline, but the numerous problems prevented its realization.

Finally, an update of the Duncan measure for 1980 has been constructed by Stevens and Cho (1985). They, too, use both males only and the total labor force as alternative bases for their update. They make an even stronger case for the substitution of the males only by the total labor-force-based measure arguing that the increases in female labor force participation during the past few decades makes an index based on males only much less defensible than in the past.[10]

In conclusion, each of the studies reviewed in this section of the chapter has been criticized for conceptual and methodological shortcomings despite the fact that each improved in various ways upon its predecessors. Yet even if the various technical problems that compromised these studies could somehow be resolved, research would still be plagued by controversies over the meaning and utility of the concept *prestige* and its relationship to other criteria for differentiating occupations.

This problem takes on added meaning when placed within the context of its relationship to theoretical issues within the discipline. As I have indicated above, the very choice of prestige as *the* fundamental dimension of social stratification in modern industrial societies is compatible with the functionalist perspective on class inequality, derived from Weber and Durkheim by Parsons, which dominated the discipline during the period in which these studies were conducted. Despite this compatibility, however, conceptual problems with the term surfaced early and have not been resolved to date. For example, Reiss' (1961:35) interpretation of data from the original NORC-North-Hatt study is that respondents did not appear to have made their rankings of occupations in terms of prestige as claimed by North and Hatt. Instead, their responses to earlier questions that attempted to examine the criteria by which they evaluated occupations indicated that respondents made these judgments based on a variety of different factors, including socioeconomic characteristics such as income and education (Reiss 1961:35). Duncan himself uses the associations between prestige scores and these socioeconomic measures as a means for estimating his SEI scores for the 1950 Census occupations. Yet even his own data reveal that the association between prestige and such indicators is far from perfect.

Given this lack of correspondence, the question of the relative validity of the two as indicators of occupational status becomes important. In response, some have suggested that the use of prestige, a subjective judgment, contains more error than the use of socioeconomic indicators that are objective characteristics of occupations (compare Featherman and Hauser 1976). Combining this with the fact that the use of the prestige variable has been made more difficult, because no single study has gathered prestige scores on all the occupations that are represented in the population, suggests that a more valid procedure would be to use the socioeconomic variables alone to derive an "objective" index to measure occupational status. The next section of the chapter reviews research within the discipline which has taken this approach to measuring class inequality.

SOCIOECONOMIC STATUS MEASURES

Efforts to derive a measure of the relative socioeconomic status of occupations that does not depend upon subjective prestige assessments have a long history in both the United States and in Canada.[11] The research of Alba Edwards, and Charles Nam and his associates summarizes the various issues involved in the task of deriving such a measure. I will therefore confine my attention to their research.

Alba Edwards' Social-Economic Groups

The work of Alba Edwards is the most significant early influence on the development of objective occupational status scales. In his earliest publication on the subject (Edwards 1917), he notes that while the Census Bureau often grouped occupations for purposes of summarization, its grouping strategies were very broad and did not focus on *socioeconomic* attributes of occupations.[12] Edwards argues that the saliency of occupation for the life-styles of Americans and the importance of understanding its correlates and consequences make a more detailed scheme of classification based on these unique attributes of occupations a necessity.

Edwards' theoretical orientation is presented in its most explicit form in 1943. He begins by distinguishing his classification scheme from earlier efforts by noting that, in contrast to those, his social-economic groupings are more than simply large subdivisions of the labor force: "it is evident that each of these groups represents not only a major segment of the Nation's labor force, but, also, a large population group with a somewhat distinct standard of life, economically, and, to a considerable extent, intellectually and socially" (Edwards 1943:179). He also makes it clear that the definitions of these groups involved more than narrowly job-related characteristics:

> as the name states, these are social-economic groups. The workers in each group have been included partly because of their *social* and partly because of their *economic* status. The standard — if it be a standard — is thus a hybrid — partly social and partly economic. And the weight of the social factor varies from one group to another, and from one occupation to another, as does also the weight of the economic factor (Edwards 1943:182) [italics added].

From these remarks it is clear that Edwards employs a multivariate conceptualization of inequality that stresses the importance of a social dimension in addition to an economic dimension. Further, his economic dimension is operationalized in terms of the technical division of labor and tends to minimize other economic attributes such as property ownership or control. This particular conceptualization of class inequality has compatibilities with the functionalist perspective on class inequality in American sociology derived from Weber and Durkheim by Warner and Parsons, since both stress that class is multivariate in origin (although they offer occupation as the best single surrogate for class) and both visualize a social system composed of numerous classes arranged in a hierarchy.[13]

In deriving his scheme, Edwards initially proposes the following nine-category scheme (Edwards 1917:645):

      I. Proprietors, officials, and managers
     II. Clerks and kindred workers
   III. Skilled workers
   IV. Semiskilled workers
     V. Laborers
   VI. Servants
  VII. Public officials
VIII. Semiofficial public employees
   IX. Professional persons

Two observations concerning this early effort are relevant for my purposes. First, since there was no empirical basis for determining either the scheme itself or the assignment of specific occupations to the scheme, Edwards' personal judgment was the only criterion for placement (Nam and Powers 1983:36–37). Second, as inspection reveals, this early scheme, while apparently based on judgments about socioeconomic criteria, did not rank-order the various occupational groups in terms of these criteria.

In 1933 Edwards published a revision of the scheme in which he elaborates more clearly the distinction between "head" and "hand" work that formed the basis for his classification of occupations and presents the occupational groups in a manner more consistent with descending socioeconomic status (Edwards 1933:378):

1. Professional persons
2. Proprietors, managers, and officials
   a. Farmers (owners and tenants)
   b. Wholesale and retail dealers
   c. Other proprietors, managers, and officials
3. Clerks and kindred workers
4. Skilled workers and foremen
5. Semiskilled workers
   a. Semiskilled workers in manufacturing
   b. Other semiskilled workers
6. Unskilled workers
   a. Farm laborers
   b. Factory and building construction laborers
   c. Other laborers
   d. Servant classes

Once again, however, it should be remembered that the Census Bureau in 1933 still did not gather the socioeconomic information necessary to empirically assess the validity of his scheme and its largely implicit assumptions. Edwards later makes these assumptions explicit when he argues not only that the groupings describe distinct social-economic strata, but also that they are arranged in approximate descending order (Edwards 1943:182). The 1940 Census used his scheme for the first time and Edwards was able to validate his rankings empirically using socioeconomic data derived from that census. He was also able to assess the extent to which the groupings constituted a scale. He concludes that they do, but admits that it is only an approximate scale (Edwards 1943:182).

The widespread use of the scale has had both positive and negative consequences for research on class inequality. A positive result is that his scheme provided researchers with a means for objectively classifying occupations into a crude scale and thus for depicting a status structure for American society independent from prestige-based scales, which are believed to be more error-prone estimates of status. One negative result of the scheme's popularity has been a tendency on the part of researchers in American sociology to employ occupation as the sole indicator of status in society, ignoring other key dimensions of inequality. Another negative consequence of the use of the Edwards scale is that it, at best, represents only a crude means for conceptualizing and measuring occupational status. Not only has its integrity as a scale been questioned (Gordon 1963:226–27), but it has also been criticized for attempting to represent the diversity in the entire range of occupations within the labor force by too few categories. Subsequent research would address these issues.

Charles Nam and Associates' Socioeconomic Approach

Growing directly out of the work of Edwards and his predecessors are efforts to construct a more finely graded measure of objective occupational status with more defensible analytical properties. Charles Nam and various associates have been leading proponents of this approach to the status measurement problem within American sociology.[14]

In their most comprehensive publication to date (Nam and Powers 1983), the authors include a theoretical postscript that details their perspective on class inequality in American society. They begin this section by suggesting that its inclusion is motivated by their perception that some readers might think their perspective is atheoretical and lacking in conceptual relevance (Nam and Powers 1983: 123).[15] In defense of their research, they note that their perspective accepts Weber's notion that class, status, and party are the three essential components of social stratification.[16] They insist that, in order to understand the nature of stratification in modern, industrial society, it is necessary to broaden its conceptualization beyond narrowly conceived economic indicators.

The authors also express their belief that while most research in the social sciences has focused on class and status as primary indicators of societal position, much of that research has confused the two dimensions in application. They insist that their perspective makes a clear distinction between class and status and is designed to measure the former.[17] Given their relationship to previous research within this tradition (particularly to Edwards), it is not too surprising that the theoretical underpinnings of this research are similar to those discussed above. As such, they built on a rather narrow aspect of the Weberian conceptualization of class inequality and, as a result, remain compatible with the functionalist perspective on social inequality developed by Parsons' combination of Weber's ideas on social stratification and Durkheim's observations concerning the division of labor in complex industrial societies.[18]

Nam and Powers (1983:43–44) outline four steps that are required to develop a socioeconomic index from Census information: the reporting and coding of occupations, how specific occupations are grouped, what criteria are used to rate occupations, and the procedures for calculating the scores. I will detail how they deal with each of these requirements in their efforts to construct their measure.

As noted with regard to the prestige-based measures discussed earlier in this chapter, a key necessity facing researchers attempting to describe the occupational structure of American society is to employ either the universe of all occupations within the society or some representative sample of them (preferably the former). In their effort to correct the inadequacies of these earlier efforts, the authors employ 19,000 industry and 23,000 occupational titles taken from the *Dictionary of Occupational Titles* (1977), the *Standard Occupational Classification* (1980) and the Census (Nam and Powers 1983:44–45).

Next, the authors face the problem of grouping the 20,000-plus occupations that they include in their study. Like Edwards, one of their goals is to collapse these into a smaller number of reasonably homogeneous categories. Yet they are also critical of Edwards having collapsed the total distribution of occupations into only 12 categories. They note: "An optimum occupational classification system is one on which a parsimonious set of categories is presented without severely reducing the homogeneity of individual categories" (Nam and Powers 1983:47). Their solution to this problem is to employ the scheme used in the 1970 Census, which, while retaining the same number of major groups as did Edwards, also subdivided the labor force into 441 separate occupational categories within the major groups.

The next problem that Nam and Powers face is the selection of criteria for rating occupations. Here they begin by making a distinction between occupational status and occupational prestige, the former referring to objective socioeconomic conditions associated with a particular occupation, the latter to subjective evaluations of an occupation. Then they observe that they conceptualize occupational socioeconomic status in terms of the general life-style associated with holding a given occupation and state that education and income were the two best predictors of that complex. They operationalize these measures by using the median, noting that the mean is more sensitive to skewed distributions. They also note that their choice of an average measure instead of a fixed point of reference used by Duncan in his SEI had the advantage of facilitating subsequent adjustments for changes in the education and income levels of the population (Nam and Powers 1983:47–49).

In their initial application of the scheme, scores were calculated on males 14 years or older in the civilian labor force, because of data availability. The specific means by which scores were calculated included the following steps: arraying occupations according to the median educational level of incumbents; arraying these same occupations according to median income levels of incumbents; by using the number of persons in each occupation, determining the cumulative interval of persons in each occupation for each of the two arrays; and averaging the midpoints of the two cumulative intervals and dividing by the relevant group of experienced labor force participants to get a status score for the occupation. The resulting status score could take on values between 0 and 100 and could be interpreted as the approximate percentage of the relevant group in the experienced labor force who are in occupations below that for a given occupation (Nam and Powers 1983:50).

A number of issues have been raised with regard to their index. First, given the means by which these scores are derived, it is obvious that they are applicable only to the particular group that formed the basis for their calculation — in this case males within the civilian labor force. Subsequent research has noted that increased female participation in the labor force has made this decision more untenable. A number of sources (compare Powers and Holmberg 1978; Boyd and McRoberts 1982) have demonstrated the inaccuracies of employing male-based scales for applications involving females and have suggested that scales based on the entire labor force should be developed. Nam and Powers (1983) have subsequently developed scales for three different data bases: males; females; and the total labor force. Ford and Gehret (n.d.) have also updated these measures using 1980 Census data.

Second, such an index is also time-bound. As the authors note, periodic adjustments are required as the socioeconomic characteristics of the labor force change over time. The authors' decision to employ relative levels of income and education, in contrast to Duncan's use of absolute levels, means that these updates will be easier to accomplish.[19]

Third, scores for several important groups in the general population such as housewives, members of the armed forces, and unemployed workers — are not provided since the technique of index construction required data for these groups that is not generally available. This problem has the effect of limiting the use of the index to employed members of the civilian labor force. Some researchers have attempted to overcome this limitation for some of the groups by assigning scores to these individuals based on other strategies, but these solutions are not without significant difficulties.[20]

These measures have also been criticized for employing occupation alone as an indicator of socioeconomic status. These criticisms typically visualize socioeconomic status as a multidimensional phenomenon and argue that, despite the fact that occupation seems to be the best indicator for the more general phenomenon, the addition of other indicators could improve the accuracy of measurement.

In response, Nam and Powers have also constructed a multidimensional scale that employs occupation, education, and family income scores that are averaged to derive a total score. Such a score, they argue, has the additional advantage of refining the occupational score by accounting for some of the variation in status scores among individuals within the same occupational category (p. 63).

Finally, it should be noted as well that Nam and his associates (as well as the other approaches reviewed in this chapter) generally made no effort to introduce other stratification variables into their measures such as age, race/ethnicity, residence, or religion. These were rejected in part because researchers might want to predict these using the socioeconomic scales (compare Nam and Terrie 1982:38).

These socioeconomic status scales have emerged as a major alternative to Duncan's prestige-based measure (the SEI), and debate continues as to their relative merits (compare Featherman and Stevens 1982; Doyle and Opitz 1985). Together, they have clearly been (and continue to be) the most frequently used measures of class inequality within American sociological inquiry.[21]

SUMMARY AND CONCLUSIONS

I began this chapter by noting that, during the early post–World War II period, sociology responded to the dramatic changes that were occurring in society in a number of ways. The discipline slowly discarded much of its earlier reformist orientation and began a concerted effort to become more scientific in its outlook. One aspect of this trend was the emergence of attempts to examine the diverse approaches of earlier years and to attempt to integrate them into larger theoretical frameworks. A major outgrowth of these efforts was the emergence of what has been labeled the functionalist theoretical perspective, which quickly became the dominant theoretical perspective within the field and consequently began to exert influence on the ways in which sociologists conducted their research. Sociologists also began the process of adjusting their methodological approaches to the changing realities of a dynamic urban/industrial society. One result of the changes that were taking place within the discipline was an expanded role in providing research services to both public and private contractors. In a number of ways, then, this period was shown to have witnessed the emergence of sociology as an accepted disciplinary framework for approaching the multitude of social issues that emerged as a result of the rather dramatic societal changes noted above.

I also demonstrated the various influences of these societal and disciplinary changes in my review of the various approaches to the analysis of class inequality in society. Methodologically, in contrast to their predecessors in the previous chapter, each of the measures reviewed in this chapter was explicitly designed to reflect a national rather than a regional or local system of social differentiation. This shift in emphasis reflects the growing preoccupation of sociologists and the consumers of their advice with the larger frame of reference of postwar American society (not to mention other Western democratic, industrial societies as well).

Theoretically, each of the perspectives reviewed in the chapter was shown to share many of the assumptions of the functionalist perspective on social inequality. As such, often citing Weber, they typically conceptualized social inequality in multivariate terms. Yet, in contrast to Weber, they also tend to diminish the relative importance of strictly economic criteria in determining position within the social structure of society as does the larger functionalist perspective. Their characterizations of the social structure tend to view it as a finely graded hierarchy of positions, each with differing amounts of prestige or socioeconomic status. Each of the studies reviewed in this chapter used occupational position as a surrogate for this multidimensional phenomenon, arguing that it was the single best summary indicator. Access to these (occupational) positions was seen to be through achievement-based criteria such as education and training, and there was at least an implicit assumption of equal opportunity, even though few of these studies concerned themselves with any subject population other than white males. These studies also contained at least an implicit belief in the legitimacy of the distribution of the various rewards that are attached to these positions, be they material or symbolic. A comparison of this overview with the materials in Chapter 4 will demonstrate the strong similarities between the two.

From my point of view, such strong similarities are not accidental. If the linkages between contextual factors and theoretical perspectives presented earlier in the book are accepted as valid, once the functionalist perspective became dominant within sociology during the late 1940s and early 1950s, it is not surprising that empirical scholarship within the discipline would reflect the perspective. In fact, one of the key indicators that has been isolated for the growing hegemony of a particular theoretical perspective is its relative influence over research within a discipline (compare Kuhn 1970; Kuklick 1972). For functionalism in particular, the variety of different circumstances noted earlier insured that its hegemony would be reasonably complete within the discipline for nearly two decades.

NOTES

1. It should also be noted that the process of being accepted as a member of the scientific community required as well a transformation from the explicitly

reformist and critical posturing of early sociologists such as Robert Park toward a more neutral orientation with regard to social issues. This transformation also occurred during the period between 1900 and the decade of the 1940s. That this particular reorientation did not occur without some opposition is demonstrated by the efforts of Robert Lynd (1940) and C. Wright Mills (1959).

2. The study was jointly sponsored by the President's Scientific Advisory Board, the College Study in Intergroup Relations at Wayne State University, the Graduate School of The Ohio State University, and the National Opinion Research Center (Reiss 1961:4).

3. The division of the 90 titles into four blocks was designed to counter the fatigue effects presumed to accompany a request to rank 90 objects by the same criteria (Reiss 1961:6–7).

4. The most comprehensive presentation and critique of their work was completed by Reiss (1961). My discussion will reflect his analysis.

5. Recall that my review of Warner's work noted that it also received wide acclaim within the discipline despite crucial methodological problems. Both these examples provide evidence for the growing influence of the functionalist perspective among students of social inequality in American sociology during the late 1940s and early 1950s in particular, as well as for the significant role that theoretical perspectives play in influencing the direction of scholarship within a discipline in general.

6. Others have questioned Duncan's decision to employ education and income as the sole means for estimating prestige scores. For example, Svalstoga (1965) suggests that prestige evaluations appear to be based on a number of criteria in addition to income and education. North and Hatt's own efforts to understand the basis for prestige rankings in their original study also suggest that prestige rankings are more multivariate (see Reiss 1961).

7. If these problems raise questions about the validity of the occupational ranking scheme itself, Haug notes that they also rendered any effort to divide the scale into a smaller group of occupational categories suspect as well. The first of Duncan's methods divided the hierarchy into deciles on the basis of the occupational distribution of the U.S. population. This action resulted in very different occupations being included within the same category toward the top of the distribution, and similar jobs being split into different categories at the bottom. A second strategy that used the first digit of the SEI score to define ten classes did not improve the situation according to Haug (1972:443).

8. The fact that Siegel combines the results from several studies, despite key differences in methodology, in order to increase the total number of occupations rated, seems to reflect his concern that the NORC-North-Hatt list of occupations was not representative of the occupational structure of American society, which meant that Duncan's subsample was even less so. This problem is exacerbated, according to Siegel (1971:14), by the fact that Duncan used regression analysis, a technique that is particularly sensitive to sample characteristics.

9. Their argument for the need for another update of the Duncan scale is based on two major points. First, even though updates for the 1960 and 1970 Censuses had been completed, they noted that these were tied to Duncan's original relationships among occupational education, income, and prestige. One of their goals was to reexamine these interrelations to determine if changes had taken place during the 30 years since Duncan's effort. Second, the updates had followed Duncan's example and were confined to the male work force only. Given the increased participation of females in the work force and the absence of a measure that could be applied to them, Featherman and Stevens wished to develop a status measure that could be applied to the total work force.

10. I should also mention, in this context, the work of Trieman (1977), which expanded this research tradition to an international arena.

11. See Nam and Powers (1983) for an overview and critique of the various studies in both the United States and Canada.

12. Edwards (1938) notes explicitly the work of another Census Bureau employee, William Hunt, who in 1897 presented a classification of occupations broken into four groups: a proprietor class, a clerical class, skilled workers, and a laboring class. Nam and Powers (1983:35) label this study as a pioneering effort because it "set a precedent for later attempts to attach socioeconomic meaning to census data."

13. Additionally, it should be noted that both schemes focus on the integrative rather than the disintegrative consequences of their scheme of social inequality as a major dimension of the social structure of society.

14. Much of this research has now been published in two volumes: Powers (ed.), *Measures of Socioeconomic Status: Current Issues* (1982) and Nam and Powers, *The Socioeconomic Approach to Status Measurement* (1983).

15. I contend that the failure of several of the analysts presented in this chapter to discuss their theoretical assumptions explicitly was an artifact of the hegemony of the functionalist perspective. However, by the time Nam and Powers wrote this book (1983), many within the discipline began to be more aware of the important role that theoretical perspectives play in stratification research. Their inclusion of this "postscript" could be seen as a response to this increased awareness within the discipline.

16. Elsewhere, Powers (1982) reinforces this linkage, arguing that Weber's influences can be seen in all North American efforts to develop socioeconomic measures.

17. It remains questionable whether or not their operationalization of socioeconomic status preserves this distinction. Certainly when compared to the prestige studies, their measure is less ambiguous. However, their definition of class nonetheless seems to confound class and status. Nam and Terrie (1982:29) have stated:

> the inability of social researchers to develop consensus on the real distinctions between class, status, and party, and further difficulty in specifying the nature of the interrelationships and the variables which are determinants of each aspect, has placed measurement of socioeconomic status in an uncertain position.

This characterization of the situation still seems accurate despite their claims later in the same publication to have resolved the issue satisfactorily.

18. With regard to Parsons' adaptation of Weber, it should be noted that he employed only parts of Weber's perspective on social stratification. For example, Parsons accepted Weber's notion that class was more multivariate than Marx had suggested, but gave far less emphasis than Weber to the continued dominance of the economic dimension and the conflictual nature of status-group interaction in complex industrial society. Here, Parsons was more strongly influenced by Durkheim's vision of the social structure of society and to the means by which the society remains integrated (or perhaps better stated, "regains its integration") through a common value system. See Parkin (1978) for a discussion of Parsons' unusual interpretations of Weber on the issue of social inequality.

19. The magnitude of this problem is demonstrated in Featherman and Stevens' (1982) efforts to construct an update for Duncan's SEI using 1970 Census data. Duncan's use of absolute levels of education and income created a number of transformation problems.

20.   For example, solutions to this problem for housewives have involved one of two strategies. The easiest, and most controversial, is the use of the male head of household's score for the female. There are a number of obvious problems with this strategy. A second approach has been to construct a multivariate index substituting family income for the income of head of household. This solution offers the advantage of better reflecting the socioeconomic status of the entire family. See Nam and Terrie (1982) for discussion on this issue.

21.   It should be noted here that other researchers have criticized one of the most important of the assumptions upon which these scales (and functionalist theory in general) is based — the notion that the American occupational structure is a unidimensional phenomenon that can be accurately depicted as a single hierarchy of finely graded (by whatever criteria) positions (Horan 1978).

III

THE EMERGENCE OF CONFLICT THEORIES OF CLASS INEQUALITY

The decade of the 1960s was a pivotal period for American sociology, as well as for its treatment of the subject of class inequality. As noted in Part II, by the decade of the 1950s, the discipline was, in Kuhn's (1970) terms, in a period of normal science, with the consensus school of thought and its functionalist perspective dominating the landscape and providing theoretical, conceptual, and methodological guidelines for the analysis of American society (Kuklick 1972; Huaco 1986). However, by the end of the decade, evidence that the perspective's hegemony over the discipline would be challenged began to appear in the form of both critical commentary on and the articulation of alternative perspectives to functionalism.

Following a description of the sociohistorical and ideological settings of post-1960 American society, the remainder of this introductory section discusses the rising discontent both with trends within the discipline in general and with the functionalist perspective in particular that began as early as the late 1950s. Following this, the chapters in Part III present and critically analyze two major challenges to functionalism's perspective on social inequality. These challenges argue that key features of this perspective are flawed and seek to modify or replace them. Both of these viewpoints, in contrast to functionalism's consensus model of society that stresses the harmonious consequences of class inequality, adopt a "conflict" model that places far greater stress on its disharmonious consequences. Chapter 6 will focus on those scholars whose perspectives are more indebted to the work of Max Weber, while Chapter 7 will deal with those whose work is more compatible with that of Karl Marx.

THE SOCIOHISTORICAL SETTING

As previously noted, the early post–World War II period (from about 1945 to the early 1960s) witnessed the most rapid and prolonged economic expansion in world history, with the United States assuming the role of the leader of the free world in both economic and political/military terms (Cohen and Rogers 1983; Johnson 1983). Because the relative resources of the United States were so great, no other country, East or West, was in a position to challenge its hegemony (Kennedy 1988). There were several immediate consequences of this newly emerging world order: the rapid reconstruction of Western Europe and Japan; the expansion of capitalism to larger and larger parts of the world; and a period of peace and prosperity, both at home and abroad, that has been labeled "Pax Americana" (Steel 1967). Domestically, as demonstrated by authors such as Galbraith (1958), prosperity appeared to be within the reach of all, and a mood of optimism about the future prevailed. As discussed earlier, this was the setting within which the consensus school's functionalist perspective on class inequality achieved hegemony over other perspectives within the discipline.

It is important to note here that subsequent, retrospective reflection on this period in the nation's history has concluded that much of its optimism was merely an illusory response to the crisis of the Great Depression and the victory over Fascism in Europe, which, in many ways, ignored the important domestic and international problems that faced the country as early as the 1950s (Johnson 1983:613). The evidence presented will support this assessment by demonstrating that America's fate (at least by the decade of the 1960s, if not before) would begin to be decidedly different from that of the early post–World War II years (however idealized by the period's authors).

One of the consequences of the U.S. assumption of the role of world leader following the end of World War II was that it assumed a huge burden of costly defense responsibilities around the world in addition to the responsibilities of a growing postwar welfare state at home. So long as its economy was so predominant (as it was during the early part of the period in question), the benefits derived from this decision far exceeded the costs. Thus, internationally, through such programs as the Marshall Plan, the United States financed the rebuilding of Western Europe and Japan. Domestically, the country began to expand the limited federal role in providing social services, which was established during the Great Depression, into a modern (albeit still limited by West European standards) welfare state. A comment made by one of the major architects of domestic policy during this period, sociologist Daniel Patrick Moynihan, reflects the optimism of the era. In a manner reminiscent of Galbraith's (1958) perspective on the United States of the 1950s, Moynihan remarked in

1965 that the problem facing America was not the question of whether the federal government could discover means for dealing with old problems, but whether it could find new problems to make use of the means at its disposal (Polenberg 1980:175).[1]

The peak post–World War II year for the U.S. economy was 1968; during that year its industrial production reached over one-third of the world's total (Johnson 1983:663). However, at about this same time, evidence began to accumulate that the burden of these broad postwar responsibilities was beginning to weigh more heavily upon the country and its citizens. In addition to the tremendous expense of maintaining "Pax Americana" internationally, the growing U.S. fiscal crisis was exacerbated by several other costly governmental policies/programs/decisions as the decade of the 1960s wore on — the growing expenses of the war in Vietnam, an expanded "War on Poverty," and rapidly growing social services expenditures in other areas, particularly education. As a result, by the late 1960s there was growing evidence that the combined weight of foreign and domestic spending was rapidly becoming too great for the economy to bear (Johnson 1983:663), and these drains on the economy, when combined with increases in the overall size of government as its role in providing services and in regulating business expanded, began to slow dramatically the rate of growth of the economy. At this same time, countries like West Germany and Japan, whose newer, more productive economies were not burdened with huge world system maintenance expenditures, were rapidly gaining on the U.S. economy. The consequences were massive:

> as the United States entered the 1970s, many of the problems that were to plague the decade were already evident: sharpening international competition; relative industrial decline; splits within the business community over appropriate response to these phenomena; declining profits, investment, and productivity at home; increased claims made upon the state; increasing claims by the state upon the economy. All these problems converged in the new economic phenomenon of stagflation that would define U.S. economic performance during the next several years (Cohen and Rogers 1983:114).

Thus, during the decade of the 1970s, the rate of growth in the U.S. economy slowed dramatically (and even was negative for a few years), and it suffered a decline relative to other leading economies (West Germany and Japan in particular). One consequence of this continued decline was that, during the early 1980s, the United States rapidly moved from being the leading creditor nation in the world to being its leading debtor nation (Kennedy 1988:515).[2]

Obviously, there were (and remain) a number of important domestic consequences of the U.S. decline in the world economic arena. One of the most significant of these was that, in contrast to the 1950s, when overall material inequalities were lessening, during the 1970s and the 1980s these inequalities began to grow once again (Blumberg 1980; Polenberg 1980; Wilson 1987; Kennedy 1988).

In short, when the later years of the post–World War II period are contrasted with the earlier years (the 1940s through early 1960s), there appear to be a number of both international and domestic consequences of the U.S. relative decline in political and economic stature in the world community. Perhaps the most significant international consequences resulted from U.S. involvement in the war in Vietnam. Here, for first time, we were was forced to confront the limits of our power in the world (Johnson 1983). As a result of involvement (and subsequent failure) there, the nation's stature in the world community was diminished, and, in a number of ways, the world became a less stable place as a result (Kennedy 1988). Also, the war created numerous schisms at home — between old and young, liberal and conservative, rich and poor, and even between citizen and government.

Domestically, in contrast to the early post–World War II period, as the 1960s wore on there began a long period of reaction to the emerging problems that the nation increasingly faced: the reaction of millions of black Americans to the slow pace of integration; the reaction of the poor to an inadequate social welfare system; the reaction of students against the war in Vietnam and outdated societal norms; the reaction of women to sexism in the operation of the institutions of society; the reaction of consumers to shoddy and dangerous goods and to environmental degradation (both a part of a growing hostility toward business that began during the late 1960s); and, finally, the reaction of citizens to government waste and corruption, expressed in the form of tax revolts, voter apathy, and declining citizen confidence in both government in general and in governmental officials in particular.

Insights into the mood of the post-1950s period in American history are available from scholarly/popular works published then. Beginning as early as the middle 1950s, a number of important books appeared that began to question, in various ways, important features of the conventional wisdom of establishment social science's portrait of American society. This image, which took shape in the early post–World War II period, characterized the country as an affluent middle-class-dominated society, with an economy that was capitalistic, but benignly so, a class system that was open and based on achievement rather than ascription, and a political system that was both participatory and democratic.[3]

The first is C. Wright Mills' *The Power Elite* (1956). Mills' book reacts to the early post–World War II portrait of the American political system as comprised of a myriad of competing, middle-class-based interest groups, each based on a mass constituency, but none of which is sufficiently strong to have its way consistently. Mills argues that, in the postwar period, as society has become more complex, this image of the nature of power in America had become increasingly outdated. In dramatic contrast, Mills claims that decision making in post–World War II America is becoming dominated by a small elite comprised of the leading figures in three key institutional sectors — the military, the business community, and important members of the government — with little or no participation by the majority of the population. This new perspective on power challenged America's image of itself as the world's leading participatory democracy and initiated a debate concerning the reality of power in contemporary advanced capitalist industrial societies that continues today.[4]

A second work reflecting the growing concerns of intellectuals about important problems in America written during the period is Michael Harrington's *The Other America* (1962). Writing at a time when the nation's mood of optimism about the future was still strong (and his contemporaries in American social science were not addressing questions of social inequality/poverty), Harrington seeks to make us aware that, amidst the apparent prosperity of immediate post–World War II America, there were millions of Americans, in cities and in the countryside, young and old, able-bodied and disabled, white, brown, and black, who were not sharing the American dream. Harrington presents both evidence that the problem existed and evidence why, as members of the society, we could not (or would not) see it in our midst. He also offers suggestions as to how we could (and indeed should) address and solve this problem of poverty. Harrington's book has stimulated renewed scholarly attention to the poor and, eventually, concerted social action by the federal government directed at redressing the problem of poverty.

A third piece of scholarship that sought to challenge our conventional wisdom about American society is Baran and Sweezy's *Monopoly Capital* (1966). This book is an ambitious attempt both to criticize extant theories (both neoclassical and classical Marxist) in the field of economics and to offer an alternative perspective, based on the changing realities of contemporary advanced capitalist society. The authors claim that earlier theories (both liberal and radical) about capitalism started with a fundamentally flawed assumption — that contemporary capitalism is competitive. Their alternative stresses the growing monopolization of markets within contemporary capitalism and offers a number of indicators for this trend. This book also demonstrates the growing controversies within the social sciences during the decade of the 1960s generated, at least in part, by the relative inabilities of extant perspectives to satisfactorily explain what was happening in and to America.

There were numerous other books during the period that attacked common academic and societal wisdom about other aspects of society, and these grew in number as the period wore on. For example, Ralph Nader's attack on the safety of an American automobile model, *Unsafe at Any Speed*, published in 1966, reflects a growing skepticism about the social responsibility of business.[5] Rachel Carson's *Silent Spring* (1962) attacks agribusiness and agrochemical companies for their lack of concern for the health of the agricultural work force and the deleterious environmental consequences of pesticides.

Other important books addressed the issues of sexism and racism in American society. Betty Friedan's *The Feminine Mystique* (1963) gives voice to the growing realization that American society was fundamentally sexist, and that, through the operation of both personal and institutional sexism, women were (and are) still being denied equal opportunities within the society. William Wilson's *The Declining Significance of Race* (1978) makes it clear that the optimism of the 1960s and the growth in the U.S. welfare state that was the result did not, in fact, change the fate of the majority of black Americans, who remain at the bottom of society, both materially and socially. His second book, written a decade later, *The Truly Disadvantaged* (1987), paints an even more gloomy picture for those at the very bottom of the American class hierarchy.

As these sources suggest, the last quarter-century has been a difficult one for American society. The rate of economic growth has slowed, U.S. economic dominance is now threatened by other advanced industrial societies, the earlier trend toward a lessening of economic inequalities at home has reversed itself, the promises of equal opportunities for women and blacks remain unfulfilled, and there is a growing awareness that current life-styles within advanced capitalist societies are causing increased strain on the planet's capacity to sustain itself. This portrait stands in sharp contrast to the peace and (apparent) prosperity during both the 1920s and the early post–World War II years; it also raises the question of the extent to which the dominant ideology of those earlier periods in the nation's history (labeled "evolutionary liberalism" by one group of scholars [Pease et al. 1970]) can be said to characterize American society in the post-1960s period. The evidence reviewed above suggests that the dominant ideology during this period, particularly as expressed by a growing segment of the social science intellectual community, was becoming decidedly more critical. In contrast to evolutionary liberalism, Pease et al. (1970:128) also define a second potential intellectual current labeled "structural realism." This alternative viewpoint is far more critical of society; as such, it stresses the role of social structure itself in generating and perpetuating social, economic, and political inequalities. Because of these attributes, it seems to be a more accurate descriptor for the ideology of a growing segment of the American social science community as it entered the late post–World War II period.[6]

It should not be surprising that this rapidly changing societal setting influenced both sociology in general and the relative status of the functionalist theory in particular. The next section examines the changes that took place within the discipline in the later post–World War II period, particularly the growing challenge to the functionalist perspective's hegemony over the field.

DISCIPLINARY REACTIONS

By the late 1950s, a number of scholars, both at home and abroad, stimulated by their perceptions that the discipline and its dominant perspective were not adequately addressing many of the problems facing American society, began to point to numerous shortcomings in both.

Critical Commentary on the Discipline

While certainly not the first (or, for that matter, the last) to be critical of the discipline, C. Wright Mills' analysis is certainly one of the most critical in content and radical in terms of prescription for changes needed.[7] Because it touches on a number of the criticisms that others have made as well, it will provide the framework for the critique of the discipline that began to emerge during the early 1960s.

In his most lengthy and best-articulated analysis of the discipline, *The Sociological Imagination* (1959), Mills criticizes the social sciences (and sociology as the leading discipline within the group), for their (its) failure to live up to their (its) potential role in society — in his view, an activist role that addresses and attempts to offer solutions for society's problems. He characterizes the mood of the late 1950s as follows:

> just now, among social scientists, there is widespread uneasiness, both intellectual and moral, about the direction their chosen studies seem to be taking. This uneasiness, as well as the unfortunate tendencies that contribute to it, are, I suppose, part of a general malaise of contemporary intellectual life. Yet perhaps the uneasiness is more acute among social scientists, if only because of the larger promise that has guided much earlier work in their fields, the nature of the subjects with which they deal, and the urgent need for significant work today (Mills 1959:19).

He suggests three general directions in which work that is sociological has tended to move historically: toward a theory of history, toward a systematic theory of "the nature of man and society," and toward empirical studies of contemporary social facts and problems. To Mills, while each of these directions is necessary for the growth of a discipline, there needs to be a balance among them. He then outlines several ways in which sociology, in particular, had, in his day, become distorted by its relative stress on some of these directions in relation to others. The first is that the work of some of the "grand theorists" of modern (1950s) sociology (i.e., Parsons' functionalist theory in particular), while claiming to set forth a general sociological theory that could facilitate sociology's efforts to address the problems of society, is nonetheless flawed in at least two important ways. Their theories are so abstract and use such a specialized vocabulary that they are difficult to translate into commonly understood language (and therefore to apply in research); and, despite the claim that these theories are general theories of society, they fall short because they exclude important issues from concern (Mills 1959:35). These distortions are judged by Mills to be destructive of, rather than as constructive for, sociology's efforts to address important social issues.

The second distortion is sociology's preoccupation with being scientific and with methodology to the exclusion of theory. According to Mills, in contrast to "grand theorists," who have virtually no concern with empirical research, other sociologists tend to get bogged down in technique to the detriment of advancing the discipline's understanding of society. In a sense, then, these sociologists become technocrats and allow their methods to define the problems they can address (thereby excluding many crucial social issues from their purview). While the grand theorists eschew empirical research, these "abstracted empiricists" tend to eschew theoretical interpretations of their work.[8] To Mills, neither approach is adequate.

The third habitual distortion of Mills' day concerns "types of practicality." By this he means that in all of our research, we, as students of society [unavoidably] "assume and imply moral and political decisions" (Mills 1959:76). Particularly, for the first time in the discipline's history (according to Mills), sociologists are coming into contact (and forming relationships), not with the bottom of society, but with representatives of the very top, with "business executives and with generals having sizable budgets." This has led to a "new practicality" in which social scientists begin to consider the interests of the wealthy and powerful (and the funding agents they control) in their research decisions, thereby potentially ignoring important social issues affecting the bulk of society. This, too, according to Mills, distorts the role that sociologists should be playing in society.

The fourth "habitual" distortion involves what Mills calls the "bureaucratic ethos." Here, research (and therefore sociologists) becomes, like much else in an advanced society, subject to the control of bureaucracy. This distortion is particularly likely to affect the research of abstracted empiricists who tend, like their bureaucratic counterparts, to operate according to sets of firm, rigid rules. In the service of bureaucracy, according to Mills, research is, often subtly, steered away from controversial topics or "bent" to serve the interests of the dominant groups in society.

Finally, Mills' fifth distortion of social science research concerns its preoccupation with "philosophies of science." To Mills, too great a preoccupation with the natural science model serves to constrain the kinds of research social scientists can (and should) do. He refers his readers to the classic scholars in the field, noting that they typically avoided rigid sets of procedures and methods. Too much preoccupation with science and methods, according to Mills, leads to a neglect of substantive problems.

The image of the 1950s American sociologist that emerges from Mills' portrait, although certainly highly polemicized, would be shared, to various degrees, by others within the discipline as society entered the decade of the 1960s and beyond. Certainly his image of the sociologist as a disinterested technocrat, speaking in an almost unintelligible language full of specialized terms, under the control of funding agencies dominated by the wealthy, studying system problems of social disorganization and social control using stilted, formal procedures, would, a generation later, provide a growing body of radical sociologists with a larger-than-life target. As will be discussed later, however, Mills was not alone in his critical posture toward the discipline and its dominant theory; his voice was joined by a number of other, more mainstream scholars as well.

Critical Commentary on the
Functionalist Perspective

In the latter half of the 1950s, scholars also began to critically examine the dominant theory of the period (Parsons' brand of functionalism). In one of the earliest of these efforts, David Lockwood (1956), a British sociologist, calls the discipline's attention to a number of functionalism's most significant shortcomings. He begins his critique by acknowledging that it is necessary for any analysis to "single out relatively stable points of reference, or 'structural' aspects of the system under consideration, and then to study the processes by which such structures are maintained" (Lockwood 1956:135). He then affirms that this is the approach that functionalism takes to social system analysis. However, he also points out that, because function- alism is heavily weighted toward this goal (i.e., the maintenance of social stability) by its stress on normative elements, it literally ignores the other side of the coin — the nonnormative forces present in any society that are "productive of social conflict and instability." Because of its built-in biases, Lockwood insists that, rather than providing a "synthetic" science (a goal of many European sociologists), Parsonian functionalism has instead fashioned sociology into a "special" social science.[9] To Lockwood, this decision fundamentally limits the theory's utility because this focus renders it less able to deal with the critical issue of the dynamics of social change and instability.

Ralf Dahrendorf (1958), another European sociologist, stresses this same limitation by means of a comparison between functionalist theory and utopian theories. He begins by first listing the "structural requisites" of utopian societies: they do not grow out of familiar reality, they are based on universal consensus, utopian stability is due to social harmony, all social processes within utopian societies follow patterns, and utopias are socially isolated from other communities or societies. He then examines functionalist theory for evidence of the presence of these attributes and shows that, indeed, all of them are present there as well. Then, in response to functionalist theory's one-sided characterization of society, Dahrendorf counters that "society has two faces of equal reality: one of stability, harmony, and consensus, and one of change, conflict and constraint" (Dahrendorf 1958:127). He concludes that sociological explanations must include both these realities if such explanations are to be of any value.

Reacting to this issue, Dahrendorf then offers an alternative to functionalism — a theory of social conflict. He begins this task by pointing to a long tradition of concern with social conflict within the discipline, but notes that the work of Parsons has deflected research away from the question of "What drives societies onward?" to "What holds them together?" (p. 170). Dahrendorf is critical of this shift in focus and suggests the need to redirect attention back to the former question.

He postulates that two separate strategies are necessary in explaining social change. The first is the construction of a structural benchmark from which change can be measured. The second is the determination of the direction of change, or, even better still, the moving force that causes the change to occur. According to Dahrendorf, a comprehensive theory of society must adequately deal with both these needs. His contention is that functionalist theory, because of its preoccupation with answering the question "What holds society together?" addressed the former need but not the latter.[10] To demonstrate this shortcoming, he then outlines two "models of society," one for functionalist theory, the other for conflict theory (Dahrendorf 1958:174):

Elements of Functional Theory	*Elements of Conflict Theory*
1. Every society is a relatively persisting configuration of elements.	1. Every society is subjected at every moment to change: social change is ubiquitous.
2. Every society is a well-integrated configuration of elements.	2. Every society experiences at every moment social conflict: social conflict is ubiquitous.
3. Every element in a society contributes to its functioning.	3. Every element in a society contributes to its change.
4. Every society rests on the consensus of its members.	4. Every society rests on constraint of some of its members by others.

His point in this comparison is to demonstrate that both theories are only partial reflections of reality and that neither is a "general" theory of society. He then provides a list of requirements for an alternative theory of social conflict and outlines his own version of the theory.[11]

In contrast to Dahrendorf's treatment of consensus and conflict theories, which tends to highlight their differences, Pierre van den Berghe (1963) offers a comparison of the two perspectives that stresses their similarities. He begins by dissecting the two theories and salvaging both common and unique elements from each. For functionalism, he stresses that its model of dynamic equilibrium (and not its stress on consensus) is really the most important (and useful) part of the theory because it allows the theory to examine change, although only to a limited extent (p. 697). For Marxist theory, he singles out the potential utility of a refined dialectic based on its claim that social change is ubiquitous and is often generated by and within the social system itself, deriving from contradictions between elements of the system (p. 699). Following this, he lists four important points of convergence and overlap between the two theories:

1. Both theories are holistic (i.e., both look at societies as systems of interrelated parts).
2. Both theories deal with conflict and consensus, although the theories differ in terms of the relative emphasis on each.
3. Both theories share an evolutionary notion of social change.

4. Both theories are fundamentally based on an equilibrium model.

Van den Berghe (pp. 704–5) claims that this last similarity between the two theories represents a theoretical convergence and he is hopeful of the possibility of reaching a balanced theoretical synthesis of the two in the future. This synthesis has not, at least to date, occurred.

As these remarks suggest, by the middle of the 1960s, the dominant theoretical perspective in the discipline — functionalism — was under siege from both liberal and radical scholars.[12] An important consequence of this debate was the birth of a new "conflict" alternative to functionalism. And, despite efforts by some scholars to effect a theoretical synthesis between the two (van den Berghe 1963), this schism has led to a growing bifurcation of macro-level sociological perspectives into consensus and conflict schools of thought (T. Bernard 1983).

SUMMARY AND CONCLUSIONS

This introduction to Part III first provided an overview of the sociohistorical setting in the United States since the end of World War II, and then turned to a discussion of activities within the discipline of sociology itself. This period in our history began with the allied victory and the reorganization of a new world order with the United States as the leading economic and military power in the world. The nation's sizable resources were used to assist in the reconstruction of both Western Europe and Japan, and the longest sustained period of world economic growth in history resulted. The domestic result was that we had the highest standard of living in the world, and material and social inequalities among its citizens were decreasing, and the future looked bright.

As the United States entered the decade of the 1960s, because of greater economic competition from Western Europe and Japan, its economic growth began to slow at the same time that its international and domestic obligations either remained high or even accelerated. As a result, budget deficits began to grow, and we moved from the largest creditor nation to its largest debtor during the early 1980s. One important domestic consequence was that material and social inequalities within the society began to grow once more. This decline in the U.S. position in the world community resulted in a growing mood of pessimism in the country, as numerous groups, whose opportunities were blocked, began to react to the stagnant economy and to their continued oppression. During this period, social scientific and popular literature became increasingly critical of American society in general and of the perceived inability of established theoretical perspectives to explain the dramatic events of the period in particular.

Within sociology itself, a number of critics raised concerns about both the state of the discipline and its dominant theory — functionalism. The sociological establishment was accused by one leading critic of being divided into, on the one hand, grand theorists who put forth virtually untestable theories full of technical jargon, and, on the other hand, abstracted empiricists whose concern with technical competency and grantsmanship hamstrung them on the other. The entire establishment was accused of being more concerned with the scientific status of the discipline than with addressing and offering solutions to important social issues.

The leading theoretical perspective of the period — functionalism — an intellectual product of the early post–World War II period, was criticized for its utopian image of society and for its inherent inability to contend with the rapidly changing circumstances of post-1960 American life. The result of this intradisciplinary conflict was the emergence of (or perhaps the rediscovery of) a new theory that was explicitly designed to explain social conflict and the bifurcation of sociology into two competing schools of thought. Chapters 6 and 7 will discuss the application of this "new" conflict perspective to the issue of class inequality in contemporary American life.

NOTES

1. The optimism of the period stands in sharp contrast to the scarcity mentality that would become a reality only a few years later as the U.S. "fiscal crisis" grew (O'Connor 1973).

2. In this context, Kennedy (1988:515) notes that the United States runs the risk of "imperial overstretch," defined as "the fact that the sum total of the United States' global interests and obligations is nowadays far larger than the country's ability to defend them all simultaneously."

3. Since the goal of Part III is to reflect the growing dissension within the social science community that began during the middle to late 1950s, only works critical of this image will be discussed. However, the enduring popularity of these books offers support for their use as indicators for the growing skepticism of intellectuals during this period in American history.

4. In retrospect, it is interesting to note that the perspective of the "pluralist" school of thought (the label given to the perspective on power dominant during the early post–World War II period) has moved closer to the perspective of Mills than vice versa since his critique (see Dahl 1982).

5. This portrayal of corporate America stands in sharp contrast to that provided by Berle and Means' *The Modern Corporation and Private Property* (1934), which reflected the 1920s viewpoint that business was, indeed, becoming more socially responsible as its day-to-day operations came increasingly under the control of professional managers.

6. Their own survey of research revealed that "evolutionary liberalism," because of its compatibility with America's unique history, has dominated the history of American sociology. However, it should be noted that their survey of

research ended with the mid- to late 1960s and thus did not offer insights into the post-1960s period in the discipline's history.

7.   As noted in Chapter 3, one of the earliest systematic critiques of the discipline was Robert Lynd's *Knowledge for What?* (1940). There, he chastised the discipline for its failure to acknowledge and address the myriad of problems facing the members of the society. Instead, he accused sociologists of being too cognizant of the interests of its wealthy and powerful benefactors. This particular criticism has been a recurrent one since then, as attested by the work of others such as Mills (1959) and Lee (1978).

8.   It is important to remember that, at the time Mills was writing this particular book, he was employed at Columbia University, a leading center for social science research during the 1950s. His biographer (Horowitz [1983]) makes the point that, at this time, Mills had alienated many of Columbia's faculty and was very despondent that his work hadn't received the support he thought it deserved from either his colleagues at Columbia or the discipline as a whole. It seems reasonable that some of his negative reaction to empiricism can be traced to his situation there.

9.   Lockwood does concede that Parsons was concerned with the scientific status of the discipline and that, as a part of this concern, making the discipline seem less ambiguous, even at the cost of making it less synthetic, may have seemed worth the cost at the time. It is obvious, however, that Lockwood doesn't agree with this decision.

10.   It is interesting here that he notes that the "residual" categories that a theory leaves behind are often fruitful points of departure for new developments. For functionalist theory, he suggests that what are labeled "dysfunctions" may be a good place to start (Dahrendorf 1958:174). Burawoy (1990) makes this same point for Marxist theory.

11.   In contrast to functionalism's focus on the normative order of society, Dahrendorf's conflict theory is organized around the notion of "structured" social inequalities. It is discussed in detail in Chapter 6.

12.   There are several additional contributions to this debate that should be mentioned here. Horton (1966) applied the consensus-conflict framework in his critical analysis of theories of social problems. He stressed that the two perspectives differed in terms of their images of man and society, their methodologies, their ideologies, and so on (aspects of his perspective were reviewed in Chapter 1). Lenski (1966), in a manner similar to Dahrendorf, used the framework as a starting point in his critique of theories in his analysis of social inequality. Finally, Turner (1973) accuses Parsons' critics of both exaggerating the properties of his theory and of making many of the same mistakes he made in their reformulations. A good summary of many of the issues around which this debate has focused is available in Thomas Bernard (1983).

6

NEO-WEBERIAN THEORIES
OF CLASS INEQUALITY

As American sociology entered the decade of the 1960s, several disparate elements of a fundamentally different perspective on class inequality, with roots within both American and European traditions of thought, began to appear in the discipline's media. Just as the functionalist perspective has been interpreted as a polarized reaction to Marx's viewpoint on both the nature of society and social change, this new perspective sought, in light of the realities of post–World War II Western capitalist society, to offer alternatives to the functionalist perspective that addressed its "overreaction" in the opposite direction. The authors of this new perspective combined elements of functionalism with elements of other, more radical, perspectives to construct new synthetic theories of class inequality that, in contrast to functionalist theory, placed greater emphasis on the conflictual nature of both society as a whole and the interrelationships between or among its classes. This chapter begins with a discussion of the nature of social conflict theories in general and then presents and analyzes two major conflict perspectives on the subject of class inequality that are heavily indebted to the work of Max Weber — those of Ralf Dahrendorf and Gerhard Lenski.

THE NATURE OF CONFLICT THEORIES
OF SOCIAL INEQUALITY

While in many ways all theories are synthetic in the sense that they take bits and pieces of previous work and integrate them into a new perspective, the work of conflict theorists in the American tradition has been particularly so. A few remarks about the origins of these theories will support this assertion.

As demonstrated in Chapter 4, the functionalist perspective reflected, in part, Parsons' concern with the rudimentary nature of social science theory, its preoccupation with empiricism, and its relative inability to adequately address the issues surrounding the Great Depression (Mullins 1973; Rocher 1975). It should also be understood as a uniquely American reaction to the only other general theory of society available at the time — that of Marx (Gouldner 1970; Horowitz 1983).[1] In this regard, then, functionalism sought to counter Marxism's animus toward capitalism by offering a comprehensive theory that, in many key respects, defended it. Its major cornerstone was Parsons' *The Structure of Social Action* (1937). There, the author assembled his theory, taking key elements from several important European and American scholars, including Durkheim, Weber, Alfred Marshall, and Vilfredo Pareto. Subsequent commentary on his use of these theorists (particularly Weber, but Durkheim as well) has concluded that he selectively perceived them in a manner that supported, rather than was critical of, the ultimate vitality of modern advanced capitalist society (Giddens 1981; Parkin 1978; Grabb 1984). The perspective that resulted from Parsons' own synthesis of these selectively sampled ingredients into a coherent whole — functionalist theory — was, in the words of one of its critics, "slanted in that it underrates conflict and disequilibrium, and assumes too much continuity, gradualness and uniformity in the process of change" (van den Berghe 1963:698).

The theory's major critics, then, in reaction to its allegedly utopian image of contemporary capitalist society, sought either to correct its biases by bringing back into the equation elements from other perspectives, particularly those of a de-Parsonianized Weber and Marx, or to reject it entirely. The former group developed perspectives that fell into the middle ground between the extremes of functionalism and Marxism on the issue of class inequality within contemporary capitalist societies. The latter group rejected most, if not all, of functionalism's perspective and typically confined attention more narrowly to the task of adapting orthodox Marxism's perspectives to the realities of class inequality within advanced capitalist society. For purposes of organization, the first group of theorists is labeled "neo-Weberian," while the second is labeled "neo-Marxist." The remainder of this chapter focuses on the former group of theorists, while Chapter 7 will consider the latter.

NEO-WEBERIAN THEORIES OF CLASS INEQUALITY

Two major neo-Weberian conflict perspectives on class inequality have dominated the American scene since they were first presented in work published between the late 1950s and the mid-1960s. Each, while beginning with a careful consideration of the potential contributions that Marxist perspectives might have in correcting or supplementing functionalism's description of class inequality in contemporary capitalist society, eventually rejected most of these in favor of frameworks more compatible with the work of Max Weber. The remainder of this chapter will first consider the perspective set forth by Ralf Dahrendorf and then discuss that offered by Gerhard Lenski.

Ralf Dahrendorf's Perspective on Class Inequality

As a part of his early critique of functionalism and his efforts to direct the discipline toward a conflict perspective on society, Dahrendorf constructed an alternative to functionalism's perspective on class inequality in modern capitalist society. Following a brief overview of his biography, the remainder of this section of the chapter will summarize and critique his theory.

Biographical Sketch

Dahrendorf was born in 1929 to middle-class parents. His father, a Social Democratic Reichstag deputy, was arrested after the Nazis came to power. Dahrendorf himself was arrested in 1944 for anti-Nazi activities and spent time in a concentration camp. Following the war, he earned a Ph.D. in philosophy from the University of Hamburg and a Ph.D. in sociology from the University of London. During the period in his scholarship during which his major efforts on conflict sociology and class inequality were written, he was a university professor in Germany and held visiting positions at several universities in the United States (he later was director of the London School of Economics and is currently a professor at the University of Konstanz in Germany). During the post–World War II period he also held a number of political posts, including membership in the Baden-Wurttemberg state parliament and the Bonn Federal Parliament, Parliamentary State Secretary at the German Foreign Office, and a member of the European Economic Community Commission (Dahrendorf 1967b, 1982).

A "Conflict" Theory of Social Inequality

In the preface to *Class and Class Conflict in an Industrial Society* (1959:viii) Dahrendorf writes a concise statement of the problem he addresses in the book:

> I am concerned with a problem, namely, with the puzzling fact that social structures as distinct from most other structures are capable of producing within themselves the elements of their supersession and change. Social structures not only are subject to change, but create permanently and systematically some of the determinant forces of their change within themselves.

He expresses concern that neither functionalism nor Marxism adequately addresses this problem because each stresses either consensus or conflict to the exclusion of the other. His goal is to combine elements of both perspectives into an alternative framework with which the determinant forces for structural change can be identified and the processes through which they influence structural change specified.

1. *Theoretical Antecedents.* Given the central position occupied by the work of Karl Marx in the study of social change, the first part of Dahrendorf's book is devoted to an exposition and critique of Marx's work. For purposes of discussion, this overview and critique is organized into the following issues: Marx's image of the nature of society and of social change; the role that classes play in social change; the nature and number of classes in capitalist society; the ways in which classes interact; the role of the economic sector vis-à-vis other institutional sectors; and, finally, the sources for, and nature of, social change.

Marx's image of society (and of social change) is especially important for Dahrendorf. He writes:

> for Marx, society is not primarily a smoothly functioning order of the form of a social organism, a social system, or a static social fabric. Its dominant characteristic is, rather, the continuous change of not only its elements, but its very structural form. This change in turn bears witness to the presence of conflicts as an essential feature of every society (Dahrendorf 1959:27).

Dahrendorf observes that not only is Marx's image of society "in clear contradiction" to that of contemporary scholarship, but it is also "considerably more useful" in understanding advanced industrial society.[2]

A second important aspect of Marx's work for Dahrendorf is the fact that Marx saw classes not simply as descriptive labels for different groups in society but as "a tool for the explanation of changes in total societies" (Dahrendorf 1959:19).[3] In other words, Marx believed that it was conflict between classes over scarce societal resources that caused change in the structure of capitalist society. These two key features of Marx's work form the foundation for Dahrendorf's theory of social conflict.

While sharing these points of agreement with Marx, Dahrendorf parts company with him on many other salient features of his theory. His justification for many, if not most, of these departures is that the changes that have taken place within modern "industrial" society since Marx's time have revealed a number of important shortcomings in his theory.[4] While many of these departures are major, to many of Dahrendorf's subsequent critics the most important of his modifications to Marx's theory center around the term "class" itself. For Marx, there are two major, homogeneous classes in capitalist society — the bourgeoisie and the proletariat — and membership in each is determined solely by ownership or nonownership of productive property. Dahrendorf accepts Marx's two-class scheme as conditionally valid, but not without some crucial modifications. His first modification is motivated by his claim that, within modern industrial society, the separation of ownership from effective control over productive resources (i.e., the rise of the joint stock company and the increasing separation of ownership from control over the day-to-day operations of companies) renders Marx's criterion for class placement useless. As a means for correcting this problem, he "replace[s] the possession, or nonpossession, of effective private property by the exercise of, or exclusion from, authority as the criterion of class formation" (Dahrendorf 1959:136). Dahrendorf (p. 137) defends this change by claiming that authority is the more general social relation, and control over the means of production is but a special case of authority.[5] Dahrendorf also questions Marx's claim that labor would become increasingly "deskilled" and homogeneous as capitalism matured, citing evidence of the continued diversity among workers. He even questions whether speaking of the "working class" makes much sense in modern society (p. 51).[6] Finally, he also points to the continued growth of the middle classes as another problem encountered when applying Marx to contemporary society.

Another issue in Dahrendorf's critique of Marx's theory centers around the manners in which classes interact. Marx believed that, because classes have contradictory interests resulting from the ownership/nonownership of productive property, they are generally engaged in overt conflict with each other and their interrelationships are, therefore, normally confrontational and antagonistic. Dahrendorf's (1959:65) assessment of this position is that "Marx displayed a certain sociological naiveté when he expressed his belief that capitalist society would be entirely unable to cope with the class conflict generated by its structure." In contrast, Dahrendorf claims that most societies are able to deal with such conflicts by institutionalizing them through various means. Because of the regulation that results from this process, the particular form that conflicts may take is more varied, and, under certain circumstances, class conflict may even become latent in society for long periods of time (Dahrendorf 1959:135–36).

Dahrendorf also disagrees with Marx concerning the nature of the interaction between the economy and other institutional sectors within society. Marx's heuristic model of society divides it into two strata: a "base" that is the economy and the "superstructure" that contains the other institutions in society (i.e., the political, religious, etc.); the model postulates that causal determination runs from the former to the latter — that is, that changes in the other institutions must be traced to changes in the economy (Wacquant 1985:22).[7] In contrast, Dahrendorf insists that, while the economy remains prominent in modern society, the relationship between it and other institutions is now more complex than during Marx's time. To support this interpretation, he makes a number of points with regard to the political institution in particular that indicate both its independence from the economy and its growing relative importance in modern society.[8]

Finally, Dahrendorf is also critical of Marx's perspective on the sources for and the nature of structural change in society. He observes that Marx insists both that class conflict is the major source for societal change and that the nature of the antipathies between the bourgeoisie and the proletariat insures that change will be revolutionary in nature (i.e., sudden, violent, and massive). Dahrendorf counters that, while class conflict is an important source for change, other, nonclass conflicts, such as religious or ethnic conflicts, contribute to social change as well. He also insists that change within modern industrial society can be, and, indeed, more often is, evolutionary rather than revolutionary (Dahrendorf 1959:130). To support this claim, he posits the following, rather benign, characterization of the nature of conflict within industrial society: "Instead of a battlefield, the scene of group conflict has become a kind of market in which relatively autonomous forces contend according to certain rules of the game, by which nobody is the permanent winner or loser" (p. 67).

Following this critique of Marx's viewpoint on the issues described above, Dahrendorf then provides a selective review of the work of other scholars that supports his positions on these issues. His major sources here include Pareto, Gaetano Mosca, Marshall, Geiger, Joseph Schumpeter, Elton Mayo, and Weber. Then, with this information in hand, Dahrendorf outlines his own perspective.

2. *Dahrendorf's Theory of Class Inequality.* As a first step in assembling this theory, Dahrendorf describes and compares two (meta-) theories of society dominant historically within Western thought — the "integration" image (used by functionalist theorists) and the "coercion" image (used by conflict theorists). He first praises the coercion image as a more accurate reflection of the realities of contemporary industrial society and then selects it as the background for his theory. He likewise rejects the integration image's unit of analysis — the social system — and suggests that the relevant unit of analysis for his theory is Weber's notion of the "imperatively

coordinated association" (ICA). For these associations, he identifies the major focus for his theory as follows: "One of the central theses of this study consists in the assumption that this differential distribution of authority becomes the determining factor of systematic social conflicts of a type that is germane to class conflicts in the traditional (Marxian) sense of this term" (Dahrendorf 1959:165). Within ICAs, he claims that authority is distributed in a zero-sum manner, with some positions possessing authority and others being excluded from its possession.

Based on this differential distribution of authority, he further postulates that the occupants of these two different sets of positions will have interests compatible with whether they possess, or are excluded from, the exercise of authority. He writes: "The occupants of positions of domination and the occupants of positions of subjection hold, by virtue of these positions, certain interests which are contradictory in substance and direction" (p. 174). These different sets of interests are said to be "objective" (in that they are derived from the positions themselves) and either "manifest" or "latent" — that is, a position occupant may or may not be aware of them. Groups of position occupants who share common latent interests are labeled "quasi-groups," while those that share common manifest interests are labeled "interest-groups."[9] These, then, are the basic concepts in his model.

Using these concepts, Dahrendorf next addresses the interrelationships among social classes, class conflict, and structure change. He defines *social classes* as organized or unorganized groups of individuals that share manifest or latent interests that arise from the authority structure of an ICA. *Class conflict* is defined as any group conflict that arises from and is related to the authority structure of an ICA (Dahrendorf 1959:238). His theory predicts that these (class) conflicts can vary in both intensity and violence. With regard to the former, it predicts that less intense class conflict is likely when classes are organized, when different group conflicts within a society are disassociated, and when the distribution of authority within an ICA is disassociated from the distribution of rewards and facilities. For the latter, it predicts that violence in class conflict decreases to the extent that classes are organized, that absolute deprivation of rewards and facilities on the part of a subjected class gives way to relative deprivation, and to the extent that class conflict is regulated (Dahrendorf 1959:239).

His theory predicts that group conflict of the class type effects *structure change* within associations in which it occurs, defining such change as any deviation of the values or institutions within a unit of analysis that involves the incumbents of positions of domination. Structure change is said to vary in terms of two criteria: radicalness (the significance of consequences and ramifications of structure change) and suddenness (the extent to which the incumbents of positions of domination are replaced). The theory postulates that radicalness of structure change co-varies with the intensity of class conflict, while suddenness of structure change co-varies with the level of violence in class conflict. Following the narrative presentation of the theory, Dahrendorf then summarizes it by means of a set of formal propositions. Then, in the remainder of the book, he applies his theory to a number of issues within postcapitalist society, marshalling evidence to support its relative utility.

3. *Critique*. Dahrendorf's ambitious wedding of functionalism and conflict theories in his effort to provide a more adequate perspective for examining the structural sources for social change in modern capitalist society has been subjected to careful analysis and commentary by a number of its critics. The major theoretical/ conceptual, methodological, and ideological criticisms of the theory have been organized into three general issues: its causal imagery, the structure of its propositions, and its substantive implications (Turner 1973). With regard to its causal imagery, in contrast to Marx, whose theory addresses the institutional "substructure" (i.e., Lockwood's [1956] "factual" substructure) of society, by focusing on legitimized authority relations within imperatively coordinated associations, Dahrendorf's theory is accused of confining its attention to the institutional and cultural (i.e., Lockwood's [1956] normative) level of analysis (Turner 1973:239).[10] In other words (using Marx's terms), Dahrendorf's theory focuses its attention on a part of the superstructure of society, and not on its base. This change in focus, according to his critics, effectively precludes a "genuine causal analysis of conflict" whose sources lie at the substructural level (Weingart 1969; Turner 1973).[11]

Dahrendorf's theory has also been criticized for the structure of its propositions. While its author did construct a system of propositions to summarize his theory (Dahrendorf 1959:236–40), according to Turner (1973:240): "there is a conspicuous omission of crucial variables, such as the nature of authority and the type of domination-subjugation, which could make the theoretical scheme more complete." This problem is seen as due, in part, to Dahrendorf's treatment of key concepts in his theory (such as ICAs, legitimacy, authority, etc.) as constants — that is, his failure to treat them as variable phenomena. With regard to one of these key concepts, Turner (1973:240) writes:

> since it is from legitimated authority and relations of domination-subjugation that conflict ultimately springs, it is somewhat surprising that this concept is not viewed as a variable phenomenon varying at a minimum in terms of

such properties as the degree of power differential, intensity, scope, and legitimacy.

Turner concludes that without greater attention to the nature of these concepts and their interrelationships, the theory falls short of its goal of offering an adequate model for structural change.

Finally, the theory's substantive implications have also been questioned. Here Turner (1973) summarizes the conclusions of a number of Dahrendorf's critics (van den Berghe 1963; Weingart 1969; Boskoff 1972) who see his theory as based on the same systems model as Parsons' and thus no better able to explain conflict than is the functionalist model. Turner (1973:243) summarizes this point as follows: "One extreme conclusion to be drawn from these subtle assumptions [about the origins of conflict] is that Dahrendorf has implicitly embraced the very theoretical tenets [those of functionalism] that he has, in a most polemical fashion, openly rejected." This point has led a number of Dahrendorf's critics to observe that his theory, despite his rhetoric to the contrary, is similar to functionalism in its implicit conservatism — its support for both the status quo and its conclusion that class inequalities offer positive consequences for society as a whole are evidence that support this conclusion (Grabb 1984:123).

In light of these criticisms, then, it seems that Dahrendorf has come full circle from a rather caustic critique of functionalism to a theory that shares many of its major limitations. Because its "hidden" assumptions are so similar to those of functionalism, Dahrendorf's theory has proven no better than its predecessor in addressing the subject of class conflict and social change in modern capitalist society.[12] Despite the limitations of his efforts, however, his work has played an important role in both exposing the limitations of functionalism (Turner 1973:236) and reawakening the discipline's interest in the issue of class inequality (Grabb 1984:124).

Gerhard Lenski's Perspective on Class Inequality

A second major theorist who has sought to counter the biases of the functionalist theory on class inequality by integrating elements from both functionalist and conflict traditions into a new synthetic alternative perspective is Gerhard Lenski. This section of the chapter begins with a brief overview of his biography, and then outlines and analyzes his theory.

Biographical Sketch

Gerhard Lenski was born in Washington, D.C., in 1924. His father was a Lutheran minister, had a Ph.D. in history, and later became a seminary professor. Lenski grew to maturity during the

Great Depression and entered Yale University in 1941, majoring in economics. His education was interrupted by World War II, during which he spent time in the U.S. Army as an enlisted man. Upon returning to Yale after the war, he changed his major to sociology and, following graduation, entered graduate school, receiving his Ph.D. in 1950. He first taught at the University of Michigan and then moved to the University of North Carolina, where he remains today.[13]

A Theory of Social Stratification

Lenski begins the major statement of his perspective, *Power and Privilege: A Theory of Social Stratification* (1966:vii), by observing that one of the most difficult tasks facing students of class inequality is organizing the "diverse and often contradictory" materials that have been written on the subject historically into some sort of a framework. He suggests that a promising resolution to this problem is to apply Hegel's notion of the dialectic, which postulates that "ideas generate opposing ideas and that the struggle between them generates a synthesis which incorporates elements of both within a new and distinctive context" (p. viii).

To Lenski, the application of the dialectic to the literature on class inequality suggests two important conclusions. First, that since ancient times, the literature can be organized into two schools of thought, one that takes an essentially conservative ideological position that class inequality is both inevitable and just, and another that takes the opposite, radical position that it is neither. His second conclusion is that the logic of the dialectic also suggests that one means for resolving the impasse between the opposing viewpoints is the construction of a synthesis of the two. To Lenski, this process has already begun in the literature on class inequality; he cites Davis, Parsons, Dahrendorf, van den Berghe, and Mills as contemporary examples of this trend (p. 18). It is clear from his remarks that he sees his work as continuing this project by building on their accomplishments.

1. *Theoretical Antecedents.* Lenski's overview of previous research on class inequality ranges from early pre-Christian viewpoints on the subject through the work of functionalist and conflict scholars of the early post–World War II period. In addition to the examples of the trend toward a synthesis among his contemporaries that were mentioned above, other major figures he discusses are Adam Smith, Marx, Mosca, William Graham Sumner, Pareto, Weber, Sorokin, and Stanislaw Ossowski. From his overview of their, often diverse, perspectives, he identifies *eight basic issues* about the subject of class inequality on which conservative and radical scholars disagree.

The first of these is *the nature of man himself*. According to Lenski, conservatives tend to be distrustful of man's nature and traditionally emphasize the need for restraining institutions. Radicals, on the other hand, tend to distrust these institutions and have greater faith in man's nature (p. 22). The second issue is *the nature of society*. Lenski observes that conservatives traditionally see society as a social system with various needs of its own that must be met if it is to meet the needs of its citizens. Radicals, in contrast, tend to view society as the setting within which struggles among its citizens take place.

The *degree to which systems of inequality are maintained by coercion* is the third issue. Here, Lenski argues that conservatives tend to assign coercion a minor role in the maintenance of society, while radicals have tended to assign it a major role in the maintenance of the status quo. The fourth issue about which conservatives and radicals disagree is the *degree to which inequality in society generates conflict*. Here, the author states that conservatives tend to minimize the relationship between the presence of social inequality and conflict, while radicals tend to see conflict as a chief consequence of social inequality in society. The *means by which rights and privileges are acquired* is the fifth issue of disagreement. With regard to this issue, Lenski writes that conservatives tend to stress hard work, delegation by others, and so on, as avenues to rights and privileges, while radicals tend to stress such means as force, fraud, and inheritance. The sixth issue is *the inevitability of social inequality*. The author states that, historically, conservatives have viewed inequality as inevitable, while radicals see it as a by-product of particular stages in society's development and, thus, eventually unnecessary. *The nature of the state and of law* is issue seven. Here conservatives tend to defend both as organs of the total society that promote the common good, according to Lenski, while radicals argue that both are mere instruments of oppression used by the leading class for its own narrow benefits. The final issue about which conservatives and radicals disagree is *the nature of the concept class*. For conservatives, the author contends that class is only a heuristic device for labeling groups of persons with similar attributes. Radicals, on the other hand, have tended to view classes as social groups with distinctive interests that bring them into conflict with other groups with different interests. Lenski concludes this discussion with the observation that a synthetic perspective on the subject must either take a position with regard to each of these issues or reformulate them in some way (p. 33).

2. *Lenski's Theory of Social Stratification*. Lenski begins the presentation of his theory by summarizing his viewpoints on two key issues — the natures of man and society. His image of man's nature

is a complex one, combining elements from both conservative and radical viewpoints: man is a social animal, man is ultimately self-serving, man lives in an environment of scarcity and therefore must struggle with other men for survival, men are unequally endowed by nature with the abilities necessary for these struggles, and man tends to be a creature of habit (pp. 25–32). His image of society is also an amalgam of the two viewpoints: society is complex and imperfect; both conflict and cooperation are pervasive within it; it, too, is basically self-serving, and its nature reflects both individual and system needs, with these often in conflict with one another (p. 34). These images form the constant elements of his theory of class inequality.

Lenski next turns to the major focus of his theory: the question of how a society's resources are distributed (in his terms, the nature of the distributive system). In his view, man's self-serving nature is tempered by the fact that his interests can only be satisfied by establishing cooperative relationships with others. Therefore, as a first rule, he must share a sufficient amount of the fruits of his labor to insure the survival of the other members of society upon whom his own survival depends (p. 44). Lenski's interest, however, is not on this limiting case but, instead, is on what happens to what's left over when these minimum needs are met (i.e., what is done with the society's surplus?). Given an environment of scarcity and man's basically self-interested nature, Lenski concludes that the existence of a surplus is bound to give rise to conflict over how it should be distributed. To answer this key question, Lenski employs Weber's concept of power (i.e., the probability of persons or groups carrying out their will even when opposed by others [Weber 1947]) and postulates that power will determine the distribution of nearly all of the surplus possessed by a society (not all, because he notes that a limited portion of the total is altruistically distributed). Lenski then introduces two other basic elements in his distributive system — privilege and prestige — and shows how they are related to power. First, he hypothesizes that privilege (defined as the possession or control of a portion of society's surplus) is largely a function of power. Likewise, prestige is said to be largely a function of both power and privilege (p. 45).

Lenski follows this with a discussion of the major sources of variation in the basic relationships posited by his model of the distributive system. The "most important single determinant" of differences in distributive systems is *variation in the level of technological development* of the society (p. 90). This influence is deemed crucial because it determines the level of productivity in the society and, thus, the amount of surplus that is available for distribution. Lenski observes that, in the simplest of societies, there is literally no surplus to distribute; as a result, the goods and services there are distributed based on need, and there is very little social inequality (p. 437). However, as societies become more technologically advanced, their economies generate surpluses, and it is these that become the objects of conflict concerning "who gets what and why." This factor (level and mode of technology) is also important because it influences several other features of the organization of society (basic demographic, political, and productive patterns of organization). Lenski also singles out several other second-order determinants that have potential impacts on distributive systems, including: environmental differences, variations in the military participation ratio, and variations in the degree of constitutionalism (p. 90).[14] Finally, he also notes that, since his model is conceptualized as an open system, there might be other influences as well that might emerge as the theory is applied to actual societies.

With the dynamics of his model of societal distribution systems specified, Lenski turns to the nature of their structure. The structure of these systems is seen as multidimensional and as containing three types of units: individuals, classes, and class systems. He defines classes as "aggregation[s] of persons in society who stand in a similar position with respect to some form of power, privilege, or prestige" (pp. 74-75). His position with regard to these variables is that the central determinant of class is power, and that privilege and prestige are derivative elements. With regard to class membership, he asserts that an individual can be a member of more than one class, and that these multiple memberships don't necessarily overlap with each other (particularly in modern industrial societies). He also indicates that members are not necessarily aware of their common interests with others in a particular class (p. 75). He then introduces the notion of class systems and locates them at a level of organization within his distributive system between single classes and the total distributive system. He views this level in his model as important because

> one of the greatest advantages of a conscious recognition of class systems as a distinct level of organization is that we are led to see that the struggle for power and privilege involves not only struggles between individuals and classes, it also involves *struggles between class systems, and thus between different principles of distribution* (p. 81).

He follows this with a discussion of how class systems vary from each other in terms of their importance and complexity, span and shape, degree of mobility, degree of hostility, and degree of institutionalization, and some of the implications of these differences for his model (p. 82). Finally, he discusses distributive systems as wholes. Here he specifies a number of relationships, including the following:

that the degree of inequality in a distributive system will be directly proportional to the size of a society's surplus,[15] that rates of vertical mobility within distributive systems will vary directly with the rate of technological and social change, and that the degrees of class hostility in such systems will vary inversely with their rates of vertical mobility (pp. 86–87).

In the remainder of the book, Lenski applies his theory to a range of societies with different levels of technological development, ranging from hunting and gathering societies, through horticultural and agrarian societies, to industrial societies. In light of these findings, in the final chapter he makes a number of minor corrections to his model. For example, he finds it necessary to modify the relationship between technology and the political system to include the possibility that, while technology is necessary, it may not be a sufficient cause of political advance (or that it may simply be the generator of a "threshold effect"). He also finds it necessary to clearly distinguish between technology and economy because his application of the theory revealed that, in certain circumstances, the economy can vary independently of technology. Finally, he also adds two additional factors to his model — variations in ideology and variations in the personal attributes of leaders — because his application of the theory demonstrated that they are also influential in the shaping of distribution systems. Next, as a means for reinforcing the synthetic nature of his theory, he returns to the conservative and radical images of class inequality that he constructed at the beginning of the book and summarizes his theory's perspective with regard to each. He concludes that his theory shares conservatism's image of the nature of man, its position that inequality is inevitable, and its conception of the nature of classes. He also notes that his theory shares with the radical image its perspective on the nature of society and its viewpoint on the degree to which inequality generates conflict. Finally, he sees his perspective as different from the others with regard to the degree to which inequalities are maintained by coercion, the means by which rights and privileges are acquired, and the nature of the state and the law (pp. 441–43).

3. *Critique.* While a number of his critics give him high marks for the ambitious nature of his task (Dahrendorf 1966:714; Mayer 1966; Eulau 1967), there have also been a number of theoretical/ conceptual, methodological, and ideological criticisms directed against it as well. The most important of these center around the following issues: his use of the concept class, the level of abstraction in his theory, his use of the concept power, and his image of the future of advanced industrial society. Each of these will be discussed in turn.

A number of analysts of Lenski's theory have chided him for his use of the concept class (Reissman 1967; Giddens 1981; Grabb 1984). Because he, in a manner similar to Dahrendorf, applies the term to any group of persons who are similar to each other in terms of power, privilege, or prestige, his critics argue that the term becomes so general that it loses its traditional meaning as focusing on inequalities in the economic realm. In the words of one reviewer, "his framework makes a shambles of the concept class" (Reissman 1967:467).[16]

Others have noted that, perhaps because it represents an effort to develop a general theory that would apply to primitive as well as advanced societies, Lenski's theory is too abstract (Kahl 1967; Fallers 1966; Thernstrom 1966).[17] In the words of one reviewer: "its results are vitiated by a conceptual primitiveness that neglects some of the most important insights of modern social science" (Fallers 1966:718). Another analyst concludes that this problem renders the theory too abstract to test empirically (Kahl 1967), while still another remarks that, in his opinion, such problems result in Lenski's own evaluation of the theory refuting it (Dahrendorf 1966:717).

A third negative reaction to Lenski's theory concerns his use of the concept power. In a manner similar to Weber's use of the term, Lenski conceptualizes power in a generally pluralistic fashion (Grabb 1984:127). However, his critics observe that his multiple dimensions of power end up being applied in a manner very different from Weber's use of the term. According to these critics, Lenski's use of power tends to focus more on distributional issues, while Weber uses the term to focus on the relations between groups (Grabb 1984:127). Grabb concludes that, because of this, Lenski is more of a stratification theorist than Weber.

Finally, Lenski's critics have also focused on the ideological biases of his theory. These are expressed in the overall image of advanced capitalist society that his theory embraces. Here, Lenski is criticized for his theory's support for the status quo and, thus, for being less concerned with the negative implications of the increased power of the state and the growing presence of bureaucracy than Weber (Grabb 1984:129). He is also criticized for sharing with Dahrendorf the belief that the institutionalization of power will temper many of its negative implications for class inequality (Grabb 1984:129).[18]

Despite a number of important limitations, Lenski's work demonstrates (even more emphatically than does that of Dahrendorf) that it is possible to synthesize elements from both conservative and radical perspectives into a new theory that occupies a middle ground between the two older extremes. Grabb's (1984:130) assessment of Lenski's contribution concludes that "his multidimensional strategy suggests a rudimentary means for thinking about social inequality as a generalized phenomenon, a process that is critical for understanding class relations, but that arises and endures in numerous other forms as well."

SUMMARY AND CONCLUSIONS

The focus of attention in this chapter has been on two examples of conflict theories of class inequality, published between 1959 and 1966, that have had lasting impacts on the treatment of the subject in American sociology. Each of these theories reacted to the conservative biases of functionalist theory by constructing alternative perspectives that attempted to combine elements drawn from both functionalist and more radical perspectives, particularly the work of Max Weber, but, to a lesser extent, that of Karl Marx as well.

The first of these theories, that by Ralf Dahrendorf, seeks to develop a model of structural change based on class conflict. Its author insisted that defining classes based on the traditional Marxist notion of ownership/nonownership of productive property is now inappropriate and has based his definition on the possession/nonpossession of authority. He also rejected functionalism's social system as the unit of analysis, insisting that Weber's notion of imperatively coordinated association is more appropriate. He has expanded the use of the term "class" beyond the economic sector to include any conflict over authority within an ICA. He has insisted that, in contrast to Marx's time when class conflict was often violent and unpredictable, class conflicts are becoming institutionalized and disassociated from each other, thus lessening their violence and increasing the predictability of their outcomes. He has also argued that nonclass as well as class conflicts can play important roles as structural agents. Finally, he has claimed that, as a result of these influences, the rate of social change in modern, postcapitalist society is more likely to be evolutionary than revolutionary and has insisted that social inequalities continue to decrease in contemporary society. At the same time he argues that they serve important functions for society.

The second theory, that of Gerhard Lenski, also contains elements from both conservative and radical schools of thought. His theory was visualized as an open system that contains constant, dynamic, and structural elements. The constant elements in his theory are a complex image of man as social, but also self-serving, as possessing differing levels of ability and as being forced by scarcity to struggle for survival, and an image of society that is seen as complex, imperfect, and conflict-ridden. Based on these elements, the dynamic part of Lenski's theory postulates that class inequality is directly related to the amount of surplus a society's economy generates. His theory predicts conflicts among different groups over this surplus;

the major influence on the outcomes of these struggles is the relative power of the participants, which is asymmetrically distributed in society. Privilege (a measure of the amount of surplus received) and prestige are both seen as functions of relative power. The structure of social stratification in his model is conceptualized as complex and multidimensional; it contains three levels — individuals, classes, and class systems, each of which interacts with the others to influence the outcomes of the struggles over society's surplus. Finally, Lenski's theory also postulates a number of influences that mediate the operation of the major variables in the overall theory — in particular, the important role that political systems play in influencing the nature of class inequality in advanced industrial societies.

There have been several strategies employed in comparing the two theories. Some critics merely lump them together and offer blanket indictments of both. An example of this approach is Giddens (1981:73), who argues that both theories are fundamentally flawed because their (multivariate) conceptualizations of class make it impossible to decide which conflicts within society are the most relevant ones for social change. Other analysts stress their differences and compare them with regard to the extent to which they have accomplished their shared goal — developing a synthetic alternative to functionalism's one-sided characterization of class inequality in modern society. In this context, Grabb (1984:124) first credits Dahrendorf as the "first prominent attempt to move away from a doctrinaire structural-functional perspective" but then mirrors many of Dahrendorf's other critics' complaints that he makes many of the same mistakes that he accused functionalism of making. In contrast, Grabb observes that Lenski's approach, while sharing some of these same shortcomings, nonetheless moves far closer to a genuine middle ground position between the extremes of functionalism and conflict.[19]

While both these approaches to comparison are valid, pursuing the former path (i.e., that the two theories are more similar than different) leads to some interesting insights when the two theories are contrasted, as a pair, with the "parent" generation of class theories (i.e., functionalism and conflict [Marxist] theories).[20] First, these theories are similar to the functionalist perspective on class inequality in that they select similar (but by no means identical) aspects of Weber's viewpoints on modern capitalist society (for example, both the functionalist and these two theories have been accused of rejecting the more radical elements of Weber's perspective on class); they reject univariate definitions of class, based on economic criteria, for more broadly based definitions; they conceptualize an individual's class position as a composite of many different constituent elements that often do not overlap with each other (particularly in modern capitalist society); they postulate that class conflict has become increasingly institutionalized and regulated in modern capitalist society; they see the state as playing an increasingly important role in the process of conflict regulation in modern capitalist society; they postulate an evolutionary rather than a revolutionary model for social change; they point to a trend toward the lessening of social inequalities within modern capitalist society and postulate that this trend will continue into the future; and they essentially support the status quo of modern capitalist society. In contrast, the two theories are similar to radical conflict theory in that their models of society emphasize conflict rather than harmony; and they are dynamic theories (i.e., they stress change over stability as a more adequate characterization of society's normal state).

As this comparison suggests, while certainly not identical by any means with the functionalist theory of class inequality (nor with each other for that matter), the two theories, nonetheless, appear to have far more in common with functionalism than with its radical counterpart. This conclusion seems particularly ironic given that both these theories were offered as explicit reactions to the biases of functionalist theory that sought to overcome its shortcomings by incorporating features of the conflict model into their models. Even a casual perusal of their work will reveal that these theorists were, indeed, highly critical of both functionalist theory's image of society and its explanation for class inequality (not to mention its posturing toward the issue of social change). Given this fact, how is it possible that they could end up so similar to the very theory they were attacking? In order to address this question, it is necessary to examine these theorists' broader images of postcapitalist or industrial society. Evidence presented by both authors suggests that they share with the authors of the functionalist perspective the evolutionary liberal ideological orientation dominant during the period in which they constructed their theories. As noted above, this orientation holds that the current democratic capitalist political economy, while imperfect in many ways, can be effectively managed to avoid many of its negative consequences, and that, over the long run, these negative features will be meliorated (for these two theorists in particular, its extremes of class inequality).[21] One critic's characterization of Dahrendorf's normative orientation confirms this linkage: "Dahrendorf ultimately shares with these analysts [structural-functionalists and 'end of ideology' theorists] the same general optimism and faith in existing institutions that arose out of the prosperity and stability of the post–World War II period" (Grabb 1984:118). There is ample evidence in Lenski's discussion about industrial society that he shares this same (although perhaps a bit more cautious) outlook about the future.[22] The fact that their own theoretical orientations were similar to the dominant ideology of the early post–World War II period concerning the ultimate vitality of the political economy, in effect, served to limit these authors' perceptions of the need for change. When viewed in this manner, the apparent irony that these theories ended up more similar to the very theory they were attacking is more easily understood. A comparison between the biographies of these authors and that of Parsons, the major author of the functionalist perspective on class inequality, lends support for this conclusion. The fact that these authors shared with Parsons comfortable middle-class backgrounds, the advantages of higher and graduate educations at leading institutions, employment at prestigious academic institutions, and successful career trajectories is certainly compatible with the support for the political-economic status quo offered by their respective theories. However, it should also be noted that, in contrast to Parsons (whose youth was spent during the prosperity of the decade of the 1920s), the fact that these authors grew to adulthood during the Great Depression and each experienced difficulties during World War II is also compatible with the more cautious, and even critical, posturing toward the political economy that is present in their theories. As noted in the introduction to Part III, as collective awareness of America's growing political and economic crises increased during the decade of the 1960s, the dominant normative orientation began to change toward a viewpoint that was more critical toward society. Within such an environment, it should be expected that the perspective of the next generation of conflict scholars would be decidedly more radical than those of these first-generation scholars. The overview of "neo-Marxist" conflict perspectives on the subject in Chapter 7 will show that this was, indeed, the case.

NOTES

1. Gouldner (1970) claims that the functionalist theory also reflects the influence of Parsons' unique background as the son of upper-middle-class parents, who grew to maturity during the prosperity of the 1920s, who attended elite universities in both America and Europe, and who spent the Great Depression "insulated" from many of its day-to-day realities as a faculty member at Harvard University. No doubt, these influences were also operative in influencing the theory's character and form.

2. It is obvious from his earlier work that his exact phrase "some recent sociologists" refers to the functionalist perspective on society. A couple of sentences later in the paragraph he made this linkage more explicit.

3. With regard to this issue, Dahrendorf (1959:76) makes the following comparison: "*Class* is always a category for purposes of the analysis of the dynamics of social conflict and its structural roots, and as such it has to be separated strictly from *stratum* as a category for purposes of describing hierarchical systems."

4. The quotes around the term "industrial" are present to indicate that Dahrendorf (and many other contemporary authors) prefers that term to the earlier capitalist adjective. He notes that those preferring capitalist feel that using industrial accepts the status quo as "unobjectionable in a way in which those who

prefer to speak of capitalist societies have not" (Dahrendorf 1959:31). Dahrendorf does not agree and uses industrial, defending it as the more comprehensive of the two terms.

5. This particular modification challenges a key feature of orthodox Marxism's perspective on class because it destroys the link between class and private property and, thus, between the means and relations of production. Its adoption clearly places Dahrendorf outside the ranks of Marxists, despite the fact that he accepted several other important insights from Marx's work.

6. In taking this position, Dahrendorf stands with other "postindustrial society" theorists such as Galbraith (1958) and Bell (1960), who argue for the decreasing saliency of the capital-labor schism for modern society.

7. Wacquant (1985) employs the qualifying label "fundamentalist" to suggest that even Marx himself considered this model an oversimplified heuristic device. Thus, despite common misperceptions (including those of Dahrendorf), Wacquant claims that Marx saw the elements within the superstructure as having greater autonomy than this stylistic model suggests. See Carter (1988:Chap. 2) for additional discussion on this important issue within Marxism.

8. As a brief aside, with regard to this issue, Dahrendorf laments the lack of attention paid by the sociology of the late 1950s to the issue of the power of the state and its increasingly salient role within society. Others would later pick up on and explore this gap in information (Skocpol 1979; Block 1987).

9. Dahrendorf discusses the process through which quasi-groups are organized into interest-groups. According to him, there are a number of possible intervening variables that influence interest-group formation. These include "technical conditions of organization" (i.e., a group charter, personnel, etc.), "political conditions of organization" (i.e., freedom of coalition, the absence of police force, etc.), and "social conditions of organization" (i.e., means of communication among potential members, etc.).

10. Giddens (1981:73) links Dahrendorf's problem to the fact that his operationalization of class by means of authority relations deprives his theory of a causal model of why classes should be important as causal factors in social change. To Giddens, Dahrendorf's notion of class "rob[s] the notion of whatever there was that was distinctive in the traditional usage of the term."

11. This criticism is particularly interesting in that Dahrendorf himself criticized Parsons for his stress on norms and values to the exclusion of the factual substratum (Dahrendorf 1959:160).

12. Dahrendorf's more recent efforts, *Conflict After Class* (1967a) and *Life Chances* (1979), move even closer to the functionalist perspective by even further reducing the role of class in social change. In the former of these, he retains the original theory's focus on power and authority, but questions the extent to which interests remain socially structured, and focuses instead on the implications of individual contest for the continued vitality of society. The latter reaffirms Dahrendorf's contention in 1959 that there is a trend in postcapitalist society for inequalities to decrease, but expresses his fear that too much equality could lead to a decline in freedom and progress.

13. The information contained in this section is derived from a personal communication from Lenski dated August 1, 1986.

14. Lenski devotes a considerable amount of attention in this section on the dynamics of distribution systems to the institutionalization of force into legitimate power and the implications of this fact for how power is exercised and how regimes change, both evolutionarily and revolutionarily.

15. The author later modifies the nature of this relationship to be curvilinear to accommodate the fact that, for advanced industrial societies, political and economic inequalities appear to be less than they are in agrarian societies. He also

offers a number of explanations for why this tends to be the case that center around the role of increasing societal complexity and its impacts on the elite's ability to govern (pp. 313–14).

16. Some of these critics see this shift away from an economic basis for defining classes as destructive of establishing a causal model for explaining social change using class as the basic predictor (Giddens 1981).

17. In his defense, however, another reviewer observes that "Lenski's book is a model of theory construction that is highly instructive" (Eulau 1967:484).

18. Grabb (1984:130) does, however, make the point that Lenski remains more skeptical than Dahrendorf that these inequalities will eventually disappear.

19. Here, Grabb (1984:130) highlights Lenski's stress on the differential power to enforce rights as the common thread linking the various manifestations of inequality as a significant advance over Dahrendorf

20. This approach is bound to be controversial, particularly given the fact that the two clearly do differ in several ways. However, for heuristic purposes, such an exercise can offer insights, particularly when one goal for such a strategy is to form a benchmark for use in comparing these theories to later, more radical, theories on the subject.

21. This model of managed democratic capitalism was, in many respects, a uniquely American response to the Great Depression put together by Roosevelt and a Democratic Congress, based on the work of John Maynard Keynes, that stresses that capitalism is not a self-correcting economy, as classical economists such as Smith and Say postulated, but that it could be managed in such a way that both its "cycles" and many of its negative consequences could be controlled (Schlesinger 1958).

22. One of Lenski's predictions about the future of industrial societies is consistent with his theory's position with regard to this issue: "there is the possibility that new techniques of production . . . will create an era of abundance and relative equality for all" (p. 433) This prediction resonates well with Galbraith's perspective as presented in *The Affluent Society* (1958).

NEO-MARXIST PERSPECTIVES
ON CLASS INEQUALITY

As noted in Chapter 6, the decade of the 1960s was an important period for American social science in general and for sociology in particular; this period witnessed the first questioning of established consensus perspectives on social inequality and the eventual emergence of viable conflict alternatives to these perspectives. The introduction to Part III presented evidence indicating that events during this decade — such as the civil rights movement, the student protest over the war in Vietnam, the emergence of movements supporting other popular causes like women's liberation and the environment, and urban riots during the latter years of the decade — provided critical challenges to the perspectives dominant within American social science. These established perspectives, which were themselves reflections of events within American society during earlier post–World War II decades, had themselves only recently been articulated and institutionalized within the various disciplines. As a result of these challenges, however, new and, in some cases, radically different perspectives were put forward in an effort to understand and interpret the various societal crises of the period.

Within the subject matter area of interest here — class inequality in American sociology — two perspectives emerged to challenge functionalism's viewpoint on social inequality — one based primarily on the work of Max Weber (labeled "neo-Weberian"), and another, more radical perspective based on the work of Karl Marx (labeled "neo-Marxist"). This chapter provides an overview and critique of neo-Marxist perspectives on class inequality within American sociology.

THE EMERGENCE OF RADICAL ALTERNATIVES
WITHIN AMERICAN SOCIAL SCIENCE

In order to fully appreciate the emergence of these neo-Marxist theories, the focus of the discussion must be broadened somewhat to include American social science in general. There are several reasons why this is necessary. First, the various radical social science alternatives were responses to the same set of societal crises and the relative inabilities of extant perspectives within the social sciences to address them adequately. Second, the radical alternatives share, in orthodox Marxism, a much more narrow and, in some senses, more coherent theoretical perspective than those derived from other sources — including classical liberalism — by the various established social science theories (Attewell 1984). For this reason, the radical alternatives in each of the various disciplines offer similar analyses of the causes and consequences of the problems of the 1960s.[1] Third, combined with these factors, the relative marginality of radical authors within the more traditional academic disciplines also contributed to the interdisciplinary character of these theories.[2] For these reasons, then, the radical challenge to the more established perspectives within the social sciences was a generalized one and thus needs to be analyzed at a higher level of abstraction than at the level of a particular discipline.

The Radical Challenge

As was the case with the theories discussed earlier in the book, the radical perspectives on modern capitalist society that began to emerge during the decade of the 1960s must be seen as a complex reaction to both rapidly changing societal conditions and the relative inabilities of extant perspectives — both liberal and (earlier) radical — to sufficiently predict and explain these conditions. As noted above, in contrast to the first decade and a half following the end of World War II, the events of the 1960s created a crisis within the social sciences, because the theories that were dominant during those years seemed unable to predict or explain events such as student activism and growing unemployment and poverty. Responses from sociology and economics (the most central of the social science disciplines for this discussion) to these events will demonstrate this point.

Within sociology, the general response of the functionalist perspective, with its emphasis on social order and stability, was that the events of the 1960s were unanticipated, disruptive, and destabilizing. One popular explanation for the student movement, for example, was that it was largely the result of a shift in the values of students influenced by changes in their middle-class parents' approach to socialization (away from "repressive" toward more "permissive" practices), stimulated by the work of pediatrician Dr. Benjamin Spock (Ehrenreich 1989).[3] Within economics, on the other hand, established theories of unemployment (and poverty), consistent with their origins in a rapidly growing postwar U.S. economy, tended to exaggerate the roles of individualist (i.e., "human capital") factors and to minimize the role of growing "structural" unemployment (and resulting poverty) that began to characterize the American economy during this decade (compare Becker 1967; D. Gordon 1972).

Yet the radicals' rejection of established perspectives on the social issues of the decade did not mean that these theorists necessarily uncritically adopted orthodox Marxism as an alternative. As will be demonstrated later, many of these radical scholars were also convinced that, like the established theories, the Marxist orthodoxy was somewhat out-of-date and thus an inappropriate substitute for these theories. In response to this belief, these radical scholars also sought, in various ways, to modify the orthodox perspective in light of the unique problems of contemporary capitalist society.

The Nature of Contemporary Capitalist Society

One of the most significant early challenges to established perspectives within the social sciences (and, in some senses to orthodox Marxism as well) was Baran and Sweezy's *Monopoly Capital*, published in 1966.[4] The authors begin their argument by examining the explanations offered for contemporary capitalist industrial society by both neo-classical economic theory and orthodox Marxism. They fault neo-classical theory for its micro bias (i.e., its failure to develop a comprehensive theory of capitalist society) and for its assumptions regarding the self-regulating character of markets (Baran and Sweezy 1966:Chap. 3). While they offer several diverse explanations for these tendencies (such as the ideological biases of the theorists), they also claim that a major problem with these theories is the fact that they are unduly bound by the assumption of competitive markets derived from classical economic theory (or that assumption qualified by the addition of the notion of irregular business cycles).

In contrast to neoclassical theory, Baran and Sweezy praise orthodox Marxism for its "focus on the social order as a whole, not on the separate parts" and for "a methodology and a theory . . . which go far toward explaining how our society works and where it is going" (p. 3). However, they also criticize Marxist orthodoxy for its dependence on the same model of "competitive" capitalism that hinders neoclassical (and its predecessor, classical economic) theory. They argue that, in the United States from the 1880s forward, the competitive markets that characterize both these perspectives were gradually being replaced by "controlled" or "monopoly" markets, and that only by realizing this important *qualitative* shift within modern capitalism is an adequate understanding possible. Their characterization of this new form of capitalism is that

> monopoly capitalism is a self-contradictory system. It tends to generate even more surplus, but it fails to provide the investment and consumption outlets required for the absorption of a rising surplus and hence for a smooth working of the system. Since surplus which cannot be absorbed will not be produced, it follows that the normal state of the monopoly capitalist economy is stagnation (p. 108).

They then draw out a number of implications of monopoly capitalism for society as a whole. For example, they argue that the chronically high unemployment (and poverty) that was becoming characteristic of American society when they wrote is a result of the underutilization of productive capacities characteristic of monopoly capitalism. They also contend that the deterioration of relations between blacks and whites within the United States is another consequence of monopoly capitalism. Further, they see American militarism and imperialism abroad and domestic efforts at manipulating consumer desires through advertising as direct negative consequences of efforts to increase surplus absorption and thus avoid economic stagnation. Finally, they generalize these effects as follows: "monopoly capitalism, for all the productivity and wealth it has generated, has utterly failed to provide the foundations of a society capable of promoting the healthy and happy development of its members" (p. 285).

In this study, Baran and Sweezy offer a comprehensive critique of established perspectives within both liberal and Marxist social science, and they set forth an improved model for the analysis of contemporary capitalist society based on the notion of monopoly. As they admit, however, the model they have proposed is tentative and not comprehensive. In particular, while they devote attention to several of the salient consequences of monopoly capitalism, they ignore others. One of the most important of the consequences they neglect is the effect of monopoly capitalism on the class structure of modern capitalist society. As will be demonstrated below, this complex problem has continued to occupy neo-Marxist scholars since the publication of *Monopoly Capital*.

THE CLASS STRUCTURE OF
MODERN CAPITALIST SOCIETY

Perhaps the simplest way to begin the presentation and analysis of the neo-Marxist theories of social inequality is to say that the issue of the nature of the class structure of modern capitalist society is far more complicated today than it was during the times of both the major theorists of competitive capitalist society (Adam Smith and Karl Marx). While both these scholars believed that an increasingly complex division of labor was an inevitable consequence of modern capitalist society, neither of them was able to foresee just how complex this process would become.[5]

Modern analysts of the changes in the class structure of capitalist society that have taken place since the days of Smith and Marx have offered different interpretations (Schaeffer 1976). Traditional liberal theorists, on the one hand, have tended to stress the blurring of class boundaries and the declining saliency of class for the life chances of the citizens of modern capitalist society (see the chapters in Part II). Conflict theorists (both liberal and radical), on the other hand, begin with the assumption that the continuing development of capitalism has complicated the more simple class structures that both Smith and Marx depicted for the competitive capitalist society of their days, but stress, nonetheless, that class remains a salient influence on both the life chances of the citizens and on the constantly changing nature of society itself.

The Orthodox Marxist Perspective on Class

Given the fact that neo-Marxist perspectives on class use orthodox Marxism's class theory as their benchmark, it is necessary to briefly review Marx's observations on the subject of class in capitalist society. Marx, like Smith before him, begins his analysis with a materialist interpretation of society — that is, the mode of production of society is the single most important influence on all other aspects of the social organization of society, including other institutions such as the political structure, the family, education, as well as the forms of social consciousness within society (Wacquant 1985). Marx postulates that there are six basic modes of production — primitive communism, slavery, feudalism, capitalism, socialism, and communism. He argues that each of these (except the last) contains built-in contradictions, and that each society will inexorably move through each as these contradictions emerge and are eventually resolved. Finally the society will reach the final stage, communism, which contains no internal contradictions, and this stage becomes the setting for the full realization of human potentialities, Marx's ultimate goal.

Within each mode of production, men must, of necessity, enter into productive relations with each other in order to meet their subsistence needs. The nature of these "social" relationships is determined by the mode of production. Within capitalism, his major focus of attention, there are two positions within these productive relationships, and Marx uses the label "class" to characterize each —

one group owns the means of producing the means of subsistence (the business class or bourgeoisie); the other simply owns the capacity for labor (the working class or proletariat). Marx also identifies a third position, the producers of simple commodities (labeled small businessmen or the petite bourgeoisie). This group, however, because of its position within the productive process, is seen as tangential to the capitalist mode of production (Wright 1978), and Marx postulates that it will gradually disappear as capitalism matures, leaving "two great hostile classes," the bourgeoisie and the proletariat, whose interests are unavoidably contradictory.

Marx sees the conflict between these two classes as escalating within capitalist society as the bourgeoisie is forced by market pressures (an unavoidable consequence of the [competitive] capitalist mode of production) to lower the wages of the proletariat to levels insufficient for its survival. As its material conditions deteriorate, the proletariat (labeled in this instance a "class-in-itself" because its members share an objective position within the productive process) will begin to realize that its interests are contradictory to those of the bourgeoisie and it will (as a "class-for-itself," a group sharing both objective position and subjective awareness) begin to engage in a revolutionary struggle against the bourgeoisie.

The completion of this struggle will result in a radical, qualitative transformation of society as the capitalist mode of production (with all its institutional and ideological trappings) dies and socialism (with entirely different institutional and ideological baggage) is born. Yet, as noted above, this society is also doomed by its own set of internal contradictions, and thus it, too, will eventually be transformed into communist society, Marx's final stage of history.

From this brief sketch, it can be seen that Marx not only saw classes as a major structural feature of capitalist society, but he also saw the conflict dynamic between the classes of capitalist society as the method by which society changes from one mode of production to another. There are two aspects of his theory that seem particularly important for its application to the class structure of contemporary society. First, there is no evidence to date of a capitalist industrial society that has made the transformation from capitalism to socialism as predicted by the theory. Combined with the absence of such revolutionary action, studies have repeatedly shown that working class consciousness and militancy, particularly in the most advanced capitalist societies, remains muted. Second, the class structure of advanced capitalist society, rather than becoming increasingly bifurcated into two internally homogeneous classes with contradictory interests and a declining middle group in between, seems (to date at least) to have evolved somewhat differently. The proletariat has, by some accounts at least, become more heterogeneous, and the middle elements, with similarities to both the proletariat and the bourgeoisie, have not "withered" away as suggested by orthodox Marxist theory.[6] Neo-Marxist theorists of social inequality have addressed these issues.

Neo-Marxist Theories of Classes in Advanced Capitalist Society

Neo-Marxist scholars who have attempted to update Marx's perspective to the realities of contemporary capitalist society have centered their attention on the diverse effects on the class structure of the transition from competitive to monopoly capitalism. In particular, they have focused their attention on the proliferation of various new groups within the capitalist mode of production between the bourgeoisie and the proletariat. Ehrenreich and Ehrenreich (1979) are typical of this group of scholars.

They begin by noting that, despite the fact that the middle elements between capital and labor within the capitalist mode of production continue to grow in relative size, earlier neo-Marxist writers, in an effort to be consistent with Marxist orthodoxy, either ignored the problem or insisted that, like the petite bourgeoisie in orthodox Marxism, these elements would disappear as capitalism matured. They also make an observation about an important paradox in modern (American) capitalist society — that it is the *middle*, and not the *working,* class that exhibits an ideology favoring changes within the institutional arrangements of society. Yet they also note that both orthodox Marxism and subsequent radical scholarship have had little or nothing to say about the role of this class in the process of the transition of capitalist society.

This situation began to change during the decade of the 1960s, however, as neo-Marxist scholars began to pay more systematic attention to this group, and the Ehrenreichs claim that much progress has been made in deciding where to locate them within the class structure of modern capitalist society. While it is certainly true that neo-Marxist scholars have devoted a great deal of attention to this issue, their claim to the contrary, it is not as certain that much progress has been made. In fact, this literature can be characterized as much by its polemics as by its clarity of argument (Wright 1980:323).

The differences of opinion among neo-Marxist class scholars tend to center around the issues of just where to place these groups of individuals, what label to employ to describe them, and how to characterize the roles of such groups as forces for change within the revolutionary process. Because the work of Erik O. Wright has been so influential in research on these issues, the framework employed here to structure the discussion of previous research is derived from his work.[7] Wright (1980) has divided these efforts into four different strategies: some theorists claim that these new elements belong to a new working class; others believe that these new elements are members of the older petite bourgeoisie of Marxian orthodoxy; others have argued that these new elements constitute a new middle class; and finally, some believe that these new elements occupy contradictory positions between pairs of the major classes within the class structure of monopoly capitalist society. Wright has also recently (1985a) proposed a fifth approach that is a hybrid of several of the others. Each of these approaches will be reviewed below.

"New Working Class" Solutions

A number of neo-Marxist theorists solve the problem of explaining the differences between the class structure of competitive capitalist society depicted by orthodox Marxism and that of modern, monopoly capitalist society by insisting that, while transformations of the technical division of labor may have generated new divisions within classes, these have not in any way altered the overall class relations within the capitalist mode of production (Wright 1980:335). Because of this latter claim, the class structures outlined by this group of scholars remain the most consistent with that of the orthodox perspective.

A typical example of this perspective is the work of Charles Anderson.[8] He begins presentation of his perspective by insisting that "a Marxist model must begin with property as central to class definition" (Anderson 1974:124). By using property as his major criterion, Anderson identifies two classes within the capitalist mode of production, each characterized by distinctly different objective interests — those with property (capitalists) and those without (workers). He also identifies a third class — the petite capitalists — within the simple commodity mode of production.

He then adds an additional refinement to the classification scheme — functional status or position. This attribute is defined as whether or not the position's role is either directly necessary to the material and social well-being of the working class, or exploitative of or parasitical to the labor of others. Anderson insists that this is not really a separate and independent criterion, but sees it as merely an operational aid in defining subclasses within the basic dichotomous model. Then, using these two criteria (property ownership and functional status), Anderson divides the work force into the classes and their various subcategories.

His working class includes both the traditional working class of orthodox theory (i.e., craftsmen, operatives, and laborers) as well as several nontraditional groups such as production-related white-collar workers, most managers, service-producing workers (both white- and blue-collared), humanist intellectuals and artists, and the lumpenproletariat.

The capitalist class includes both the "propertied and often powerful rich" who exploit the workers as well as several additional subclasses including "servants of capital" (chauffeurs, maids, grounds keepers, private tutors, etc.), who live entirely off the surplus value of the working class and meet the personal needs of capitalists; financial personnel; some governmental officials and employees; and some upper-level managers.

Additionally, Anderson also identifies an "old" middle class composed of independent professionals, small businessmen, and family farmers. Yet he also excludes from membership in this group some physicians and lawyers whose functional status links them more directly to the capitalist class. These he moves into the "servants of capitalists" subclass.

Despite the modifications to the traditional Marxist class model that result from the addition of the technical division of labor as a secondary defining attribute in his scheme for modern capitalist society, Anderson, like other new working-class theorists, tends to minimize the effects of these additional complications on class conflict and change (Wright 1980:335). He remains confident that objectively defined class interests supersede those based on the technical division of labor in influencing conflict and change in society.

One major consequence of the strategy of new working-class theorists is that they tend to place social positions with fundamentally different class interests into a large, heterogeneous working class. Since the major value of the notion of class is its role as a basis for explaining class struggle in society, this strategy serves to weaken the structural basis for such groups to organize themselves into effectively organized social forces (Wright 1980:339).

"New Petite Bourgeoisie" Solutions

A second approach to the problem of the persistence and growth of the middle layers in modern monopoly capitalist society is the position that these groups constitute a new element within the petite bourgeoisie of orthodox Marxism. The most comprehensive version of this alternative is that of Nicos Poulantzas.[9]

The key to understanding Poulantzas' approach to this problem lies in his division of wage earners into productive (those who directly produce surplus value) and unproductive (those who do not directly produce surplus value) segments (Wright 1980:345). He argues that the maturation of capitalism produces a steady increase in the proportion of this latter group of wage earners.[10]

Yet he claims that this group poses a major classification problem for traditional Marxism. Because it shares with the proletariat the fact that its members do not own the means of production and are thus dependent on wage labor for their subsistence, the group should logically be placed in the proletariat. However, because the group differs from the proletariat in that it does not directly produce surplus value, and it exercises political or ideological domination over the members of the proletariat — characteristics more typical of the bourgeoisie — it cannot be unambiguously placed there. At the same time, it also differs from the traditional bourgeoisie because it neither owns the means of production nor directly expropriates surplus value from productive workers. Also, since the group does not own even limited means of production, it cannot be placed within the petite bourgeoisie either. Hence, Poulantzas claims that these unproductive wage earners cannot be placed in any of the classes of traditional Marxism using relationship to the means of production alone as a criterion of class placement (Wright 1980:345).

As a means for resolving this classification problem, Poulantzas examines orthodox Marxism's criteria for defining classes. He stresses that, for Marx, social classes exist only in the form of class struggle and practices, and notes that this fact has often been overlooked by his successors in the radical tradition. This leads Poulantzas to affirm that "position within the capitalist mode of production" is, by itself, no longer a sufficient basis for defining classes in modern monopoly capitalist society.[11] He asserts that two additional criteria that more explicitly reflect the changing dynamic character of class interactions are necessary to classify groups adequately into classes — the political and ideological relations of position incumbents (Poulantzas 1975:14). By combining the two criteria, Poulantzas concludes that most unproductive workers actually lie outside the capitalist mode of production and must therefore be classified as new members of the petite bourgeoisie since they have more in common with this group than with the other two classes. He justifies this placement as follows: "If certain groupings which at first seem to occupy different places in economic relations can be considered as belonging to the same class, it is because these places, although they are different, nevertheless have the same effects at the political and ideological level" (p. 205).

While Poulantzas' solution does preserve the homogeneity of the proletariat, it does so at the expense of several key elements within the Marxian legacy. First, the utility of his distinction between productive and unproductive labor has been questioned. Wright (1980:348) argues that both these segments of the labor force are exploited by the bourgeoisie and, because of this, they seem to have more in common than Poulantzas' scheme indicates (recall that Anderson [1974], after making a similar distinction, did not consider it to be sufficiently important to justify removing such wage earners from the proletariat). Second, combining this segment of the work force with the traditional petite bourgeoisie also is questionable. For one thing, they do not own property in the same sense as does the traditional bourgeoisie. For another, this group of wage earners participates in the capitalist mode of production, while the traditional petite bourgeoisie does not. In light of these key differences between the two groups, Poulantzas' claim that the two groups belong together because they share an ideological similarity seems somewhat specious (Wright 1980:349).

"New Middle Class" Solutions

Another solution to the problem of the appearance and expansion of newer elements between orthodox Marxism's bourgeoisie and proletariat in modern monopoly capitalist society contends that these elements are a part of neither the working class nor the petite bourgeoisie (even if newer parts of each). This perspective insists instead that they constitute a fundamentally different class in and of themselves. Perhaps the best known example of this strategy is the Ehrenreichs' (1979) concept of a "professional-managerial" class (PMC).

They begin with the statement that the accumulation and concentration of capital (i.e., the rise of monopoly capitalism) during the final decades of the nineteenth century has fundamentally reorganized the nature of working class life, both in the workplace and in the community. Three elements of this reorganization are stressed: the reorganization of the production process itself, the penetration of commodities into working class life, and the emergence of mass institutions for the social control of workers. The Ehrenreichs claim that these changes have resulted in the emergence of a new class, a "professional-managerial" class, that performs a necessary function within modern monopoly capitalist society that the traditional classes can no longer perform — that of the reproduction of capitalist culture and capitalist class relations (Ehrenreich and Ehrenreich 1979:12).

The Ehrenreichs also claim that, in order to define classes adequately within monopoly capitalist society, it is necessary both to enlarge traditional Marxism's single criterion of class definition (i.e., as positions within productive relations) to include roles in the reproduction of the class structure, and to specify a second major criterion — the sharing of a coherent social and cultural existence. According to these authors, when these criteria are applied to the middle elements in monopoly capitalist society, the result is a new class, the PMC, that is both separate from, and distinct from, the traditional classes of Marxian orthodoxy.

The authors justify this claim by demonstrating that, while the PMC shares similarities with each of the other classes, it also has interests that are distinct from them. For example, while it shares with the capitalist class the goal of the reproduction of capitalism, it also seeks to reform capitalism and to mediate the conflict between capital and labor — goals often antithetical to capital's interests. While it shares with workers a lack of ownership of the means of production and the fact that both are necessary to the productive process of capitalism, the PMC is also antagonistic toward workers because it has expropriated the skills and culture once indigenous to the working class. They also contend that the PMC cannot be equated with the traditional petite bourgeoisie because that class lies "outside the polarity of capital and labor," while the PMC lies inside this polarity (p. 18). Thus they conclude that the PMC is a new class in modern monopoly capitalist society, caught between capital and labor in a "complex web of conflicting and complementary class interests" (Wright 1980:353).

The Ehrenreichs then discuss the potential role of the PMC in class struggle and revolutionary change within monopoly capitalist society. They add support to their claim that the PMC is an independent class by noting both that, in the United States at least, it has traditionally been ideologically distinct from the working class (i.e., it has been more liberal) and that it has been more active politically. Despite these claims, however, the Ehrenreichs then return to the traditional Marxist dictum that the basic conflict within capitalist society remains between capital and all workers and view the antagonism between the PMC and workers as undercutting the potentials for revolutionary action on the part of the working class. In this light, they see as important goals for the PMC the understanding of its own class origins and overcoming the barriers that have isolated it from the working class.

Despite its rather innovative solution to the issue of what to do with the middle elements in monopoly capitalist society, the Ehrenreich's perspective has not been uncritically accepted by other radical scholars. Reaction to their scheme has tended to focus on three issues: the criteria employed in defining the PMC, the heterogeneity of the PMC, and its role in the dynamics of class conflict. Several scholars have criticized the Ehrenreichs for the criteria they employ to define the classes of monopoly capitalist society. Both Noble (1979) and Szymanski (1979) chide them for separating production and reproduction, arguing that Marx saw the two as inseparable determinants of class position. Schaeffer and Weinstein (1979:160) expand this critique to include not only the production-reproduction dichotomy, but also manual-mental and wage-salary variables, noting that these are insufficient bases for determining class in American society. Other critics focus on the heterogeneity of the PMC as defined by the Ehrenreichs (compare Cohen and Howard 1979; Wright 1979a; Aronowitz 1979), noting that the various elements that they lump together are simply too diverse to possess the common interests Marx insisted that classes must share (Albert and Hahnel 1979). These authors claim that the Ehrenreichs do not convince their readers that these middle elements are both sufficiently similar to each other and different enough from the other, more traditional class categories in the Marxist lexicon to constitute an independent class in the sense that Marx intended the term.

Finally, the Ehrenreichs have also been criticized for their analysis of the role of the PMC in class struggle and the revolutionary process. Despite the fact that they make an effort to demonstrate that the interests of the PMC are unique when compared to other classes and that their role in the struggle for a more just society is also different from those of the other classes, their critics find their defense inadequate (compare Cohen and Howard 1979; Wright 1979a; Aronowitz 1979). As noted above, the Ehrenreichs seem to want it both ways. They argue for the uniqueness of the interests of the PMC in monopoly capitalist society, but they also embrace the traditional Marxist notion that it is the proletariat that is the revolutionary class, even in monopoly capitalist society, and that the PMC must somehow become aware that their interests and those of the working class are at least similar if not identical before concerted action for change is likely to occur.

Solutions Involving "Contradictory Locations"

The fourth solution to this problem insists that the diverse middle elements that lie between the various pairs of classes in modern capitalist society cannot be characterized as classes at all, but must be seen as "contradictory locations" within the class relations of modern capitalist society.[12] This perspective is presented in the early writings of Wright (1978, 1979a, 1979b, 1980, 1985a).

Wright (1985a:34) begins his discussion by presenting four important assumptions about classes within the Marxian framework: that they are positions (not the individuals that occupy these positions), that classes can only be understood in terms of their relations with other positions, that there is an intrinsic antagonism between classes, and that this antagonism is located within productive relations themselves. These assumptions provide him with a conceptual framework from within which classes are to be defined and understood.

In operationalizing the criteria used to define classes in modern capitalist society, Wright also (like the other neo-Marxist updates discussed above) finds it necessary to modify orthodox Marxism's conceptualization of class as based solely on property ownership. His alternative strategy is to stress positions within what he calls the "social relations of production." He thus defines classes as "common positions within a special kind of contradictory social relationship, social relations of production" (Wright 1979a:20). To Wright (1979a:24), in the capitalist mode of production, these social relations can be broken down into three interdependent, hierarchical processes: social relations of control over money capital, social relations of control over physical capital, and social relations of authority. Each of these levels controls or limits the activities at the next level down (i.e., ownership of money capital sets limits on the control over physical capital, and those set limits on the control of authority, etc.).

In applying these criteria to modern capitalist society, at the most abstract level (the level of the pure capitalist mode of production), the interrelationship among the various processes defines only two major classes — owners and workers — with opposite positions on each of the processes (i.e., owners control investment decisions, which set limits on physical means of production, which set controls on labor — while workers lack control at each level). However, at a lower, less abstract level — the level many neo-Marxists label the "social formation" — other class positions appear for two reasons (Wright 1980:329–30). First, because some simple commodity production still occurs alongside capitalism, it is necessary to add a third class to represent this location — the petite bourgeoisie. Second, because, at this less abstract level, the three processes do not always perfectly coincide (i.e., the same position may not consistently possess [or be excluded from] ownership, physical control and authority), this creates positions with "contradictory locations" between pairs of the major classes. Given this lack of correspondence, these positions will have objective interests that do not coincide with those of any of the three major classes. Thus they cannot be combined with any of them as some of the earlier solutions have suggested. Despite this, however, because of the overlap between their interests and those of the classes they lie between, Wright is also not prepared to grant them independent status as a new class as did the Ehrenreichs (1979). He prefers the label "contradictory locations within class relations." It is important to note here that he does not consider these positions contradictory simply because they do not neatly fit into any one of the basic classes. He insists instead that they are contradictory because they simultaneously share class interests with two classes, but have interests identical with neither (Wright 1980:331).

For Wright, it is these positions that are the key to understanding the class positions of the middle elements of modern capitalist society. He identifies three of these as being particularly important, each lying between one of the sets of pairs of orthodox Marxist classes (see Figure 7.1). These are labeled "managers and supervisors," "small employers," and "semiautonomous employees." He then provides an overview of how their locations determine the unique sets of interests that set them off from the class categories.

Wright's model has not gone unchallenged by radical authors. He, himself (Wright 1985a), isolates four conceptual problems with

FIGURE 7.1 — Wright's "Contradictory Locations" Model

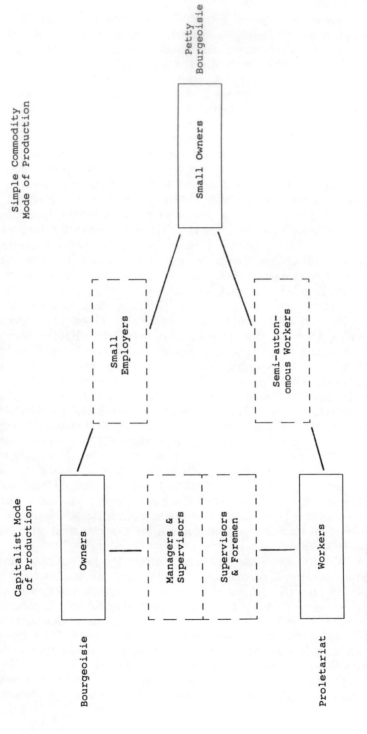

Source: Wright (1985a:48).

this scheme: the "contradictoriness" of contradictory locations, the status of autonomy, the absence of an analysis of postcapitalist societies, and the displacement of exploitation by domination in the concept class. I will examine each of these briefly below.

Holmwood and Stewart (1983:235) criticize Wright and other modern stratification theorists who use the notion of "contradiction" for using the concept as a means for rescuing the "categories of a deficient theory by the addition of different theoretical principles which operate alongside the pre-existing theory." In other words, to them, the application of the notion of contradiction impedes the further theoretical development necessary to expand the theory's explanatory power.

Others have taken Wright to task for his use of autonomy as an additional criterion for the determination of class (Wright 1985a:55). This is particularly the case for his category "semiautonomous" workers. Just how much autonomy do these workers have in modern capitalism and can this be used to differentiate them from both workers and petite bourgeoisie?

A third common reaction to Wright's contradictory locations scheme is the issue of its applicability to postcapitalist society (Wright 1985a:55). His, like other, attempts to update the orthodox perspective does not provide a great deal of insight into postcapitalist class structures.

Finally, Wright has also been criticized for shifting his attention away from exploitation as a major criterion for defining classes to domination. He admits, for example, that for his category of managers in particular, the contradictory locations scheme has substituted domination for exploitation. By this substitution, then, he has moved closer to the neo-Weberian perspective discussed in Chapter 6, particularly to that of Dahrendorf (1959).[13]

Wright has reacted to these criticisms, particularly to the last, by offering a basic redirection of the contradictory locations scheme, moving more explicitly back toward exploitation as a basic criterion of class membership and struggle. This latest scheme will be discussed below.

A Solution Restoring Exploitation
to a Central Position

Wright's *Classes* (1985a), represents a reorientation of his thinking toward both classes in general and the issue of how to deal with the middle elements within modern capitalism in particular. In response to the accusation that his earlier perspective (Wright 1979b) relied too heavily upon domination within productive relations as a key supplementary attribute to property ownership for defining classes, Wright's latest perspective stresses the importance of exploitation as a determinant.

The theoretical inspiration for this newest perspective is derived from a leading rational-choice Marxist, John Roemer, who has identified as a key problem confronting Marxists today the question of how workers are exploited (Roemer 1982). He answers this question through the application of game theory, defining exploitation as a situation in which a group of actors has a *conditionally feasible alternative* under which its members would be better off. Within capitalism, then, workers are exploited because they would be better off (and owners correspondingly worse off) if they were to withdraw from the game with their per capita share of society's productive resources.

The key to understanding the linkage between this rational choice model and Wright's latest model of classes is that Roemer sees such exploitation within capitalism as being grounded in property relations: "Capitalist exploitation is the appropriation of the labor of one class by another class, realized *because of their differential ownership of or access to the nonhuman means of production*" (Roemer 1982:268 [italics added]). This model, because it is based on exploitation, necessarily challenges any definition of class (such as Wright's earlier model) based on domination within production, since Roemer views domination as subordinate to exploitation, and thus as an unacceptable criterion for such a definition (Rose and Marshall 1986). Despite his earlier rejection of Roemer's argument, in his latest scheme Wright (1985a) accepts this argument, and stresses various forms of "effective control" of productive assets as the criterion for class definition.

Based on this criterion, Wright defines three relations of exploitation within modern capitalist society, and employs these to differentiate his classes. The first is the major means of exploitation within capitalism — ownership of the means of production. Applying this criterion both separates the owning classes (the bourgeoisie, small employers, and the petite bourgeoisie) from the various wage-earner classes and (at least partially) differentiates among them (see Figure 7.2).

The remaining (wage-earner) classes are then identified by their positions on two subordinate relations of exploitation also character-istic of modern capitalist society — organizational and skill/credential assets. The former refer to the fact that organization — "conditions of coordinated cooperation among producers in a complex division of labor" — is an asset that is a basis for exploitation (Wright 1985a:79), while the latter deal with the potential role that the possession of special training and certification can play in exploi-tation in modern capitalist society. For each of these sets of assets, Wright then defines three positions — dominant, contradictory, and

FIGURE 7.2 — Wright's "Exploitation" Model

		Assets in the Means of Production			
		Owners of means of production	**Non-Owners [wage labourers]**		
Owns sufficient capital to hire workers and not work		1 Bourgeoisie	4 Expert Managers	7 Semi-Credentialed Workers	10 Uncredentialed Managers	+
Owns sufficient capital to hire workers but must work		2 Small Employers	5 Expert Supervisors	8 Semi-Credentialed Supervisors	11 Uncredentialed Supervisors	>0	Organization assets
Owns sufficient capital to work for self but not to hire workers		3 Petty Bourgeoisie	6 Expert Nonmanagers	9 Semi-Credentialed Workers	12 Proletarians	-
			+	>0	-	
			Skill/credential assets			

Source: Wright (1985a:88).

subordinate. Cross-classifying these two sets of assets results in nine additional groups of positions (see Figure 7.2).

In contrast to his earlier scheme, where he labeled his groups "contradictory locations," Wright now labels these new groups "classes" in their own right. Despite this terminological switch, however, he still holds fast to the claim that these middle classes still occupy contradictory locations, only this time "within exploitation relations" (Wright 1985a:87). This is interesting in light of the criticisms that have been made of this strategy (compare Holmwood and Stewart 1983) and his own admission that the concept can be confusing (Wright 1985a:52–53). One important difference in his usage of the concept, this time, is his insistence that the contradictory locations of the latest scheme are contradictions within the capitalist mode of production; in the earlier scheme they were contradictions *between* modes of production (Wright 1985a:53).

The notion of the contradictory character of the middle classes in his latest scheme remains a central ingredient in his theory of social change and the roles of classes within the process of social change. Here, he breaks with Marxian orthodoxy's claim that the proletariat is the unique or even central rival to the capitalist class. He suggests in particular that two of the middle classes — managers and state bureaucrats — are potential alternative sources for change that capitalism has been able, through its high productivity, to buy off in the past. He speculates that, should capitalism be unable to maintain sufficient profits to provide these groups with remunerative benefits and career opportunities, they could become leading forces for change, in effect replacing the proletariat. He also notes that, because the interests of these classes are sufficiently different from the proletariat, their revolutionary solution to the problems of contemporary capitalism is not necessarily the same as that of the proletariat, although he does see their mutual interests as more similar to each other than to those of the owning classes (Wright 1985a:126).

Perhaps in anticipation of his critics, Wright, himself, has suggested four problems with the new scheme. First, with regard to his use of organization as a dimension of organizational assets, he admits that managers' and bureaucrats' claims to social surplus based on these assets are difficult to separate from their claims based on skills and credentials (Wright 1985a:93). He also compares this alternative to the notion of positional exploitation that stresses the strategic importance of a job within the organization. Yet he rejects both of these alternatives in favor of his original measure (organization), because the latter captures better the fact that managers do relate to workers and that this particular interaction is exploitative.

He also comments on his second organizational assets variable, (skills/credential assets), noting that ownership of skill assets may not be a sufficient basis of class relations. He concludes that perhaps this criterion should be reserved to distinguish internal divisions within classes, rather than classes themselves.[14]

His third issue deals with the interaction among forms of exploitation. His model assumes that different forms of exploitation interact in an additive manner (i.e., that they do not reinforce each other). This strategy is taken because to do otherwise would make the model much more conceptually complex. Yet he admits that the potential for interaction exists at the empirical level.

Finally, Wright also notes that he has ignored nonproductive sources of exploitation in his model such as religion, control over military violence, sexism, and racism. He notes that, while these other sources of exploitation are important, exploitation based on property relations remains central to theories of social change and to subsistence.

Although the new scheme is certainly more conceptually sophisticated than the original (Rose and Marshall 1986), one of its critics claims that it attempts to overcome the shortcomings of the original scheme more by definitional fiat than by making genuine theoretical advances (Burris 1988). For example, despite Wright's return to exploitation as the key defining attribute of classes in the new scheme, Burris (1988:62) makes the point that neither organizational nor skills/credentials assets are easily distinguishable from the domination/authority variable of the earlier scheme.[15] Related to this point, other critics have accused the model of being more Weberian than Marxist in its nature. Both Mann (1986) and Rose and Marshall (1986) note that the new model seems to reject the structural and economistic model of class formation typical of neo-Marxist scholarship. Rose and Marshall reinforce their claim by characterizing Wright's discussion of various problems involved in describing the class structure of modern capitalist society as a presentation of commonly shared notions within the Weberian perspective as though they were "novel" observations. These remarks suggest that both critics would agree with Parkin's (1979) assertion that most neo-Marxists are moving closer to Weber's perspective on classes in modern capitalist society.[16]

Nor does Wright seem to have adequately dealt with the second major criticism of the first scheme — his use of the notion "contradictory locations" as labels for the three new positions in his earlier scheme. This label was chosen for these positions because it emphasized that the objective interests of these new locations are "internally inconsistent" because they partially reflect the different, and mutually antagonistic, interests of the pairs of classes with which they are associated, and the fact that they were defined at the secondary level. Wright now claims that switching to his new bases for differentiating the nonowning classes (exploitation based on organizational and skills/credentials assets) makes the material interests of the new positions more clear, and their status as qualitatively distinct positions more defensible (Wright 1985b:91). This assertion remains subject to interpretation, however.

There are also several criticisms of Wright's application of Roemer's work to support his new perspective. Mann (1986) observes that Roemer's withdrawal rule seems to be based on the notion that everyone should get the same economic returns and that this is unrealistic. Rose and Marshall (1986) suggest that Wright's modifications of Roemer's perspective are so great that they undermine the value of his work and question the necessity of including Roemer at all in constructing a theory stressing exploitation as a major mechanism for control. Both critics also note that Wright has done little to accommodate women in his new model.[17] And Mann (1986) thinks that Wright has not paid enough attention to the differences between managers in the public and private sector and the potentially different political roles they would be expected to play in class conflict.[18]

Other more narrowly methodological criticisms of Wright's latest model have also been made. Some have criticized the arbitrary nature of Wright's number for distinguishing among the various owner categories (Rose and Marshall 1986). Others criticize Wright for the nature of his divisions within the organizational and skills/assets variables (Meiksins 1988; Rose and Marshall 1986). Wright has also not provided sufficient insights into just how the various classes defined by the interrelationship between these two dimensions can be interrelated with each other.[19]

The radical ideological foundation of Wright's perspective is also a potential point for criticism. More mainstream scholars tend to reject his scheme because it questions the ultimate vitality of capitalist society. In contrast, many of his fellow Marxists also criticize his scheme's underlying ideology, but for different reasons — they see the scheme as capitulating in many ways to a more liberal image of the class structure and society that supports the status quo (Resnick and Wolff 1987; Kamolnick 1988).[20] Debate among scholars about this issue demonstrates the growing ideological diversity (and, to some extent, tolerance) that is present within the discipline concerning the issue of class inequality.

Despite these criticisms, however, Wright's work is certain to remain a major focus for discussions among both neo-Marxists and Weberian scholars concerning the issues of class formation and class conflict in modern capitalist society. Because this particular scheme is employed in a multinational data set on class structure and class consciousness constructed by Wright and his associates (Wright 1985b), the means by which Wright operationalizes this latest class scheme is discussed in an appendix to this chapter.

SUMMARY AND CONCLUSIONS

This chapter has presented an overview and critique of neo-Marxist research on the conceptualization and measurement of class within American social science during the past 20 years. This resurgence of radical interest in modern capitalist society that began during the decade of the 1960s should be interpreted as a reaction to both the dramatic events of that period, international and domestic, and the failure of established liberal social science theories to offer adequate explanations for the events of that decade in American history. Yet these scholars did not uncritically substitute orthodox Marxism for these liberal theories, because they discovered that it, too, had shortcomings. A commonly accepted reason for the inapplicability of both these theories is the fact that each was the by-product of competitive capitalist society and that, certainly by the post–World War II period, American society had matured into a monopoly capitalist society that offered somewhat different challenges to scholars attempting to understand its class structure and dynamics (Baran and Sweezy 1966).

In this light, a major challenge to neo-Marxist class scholars is the proliferation of new groups in addition to the traditional classes of Marxist orthodoxy that have resulted from the maturation of capitalism. The chapter divided efforts to classify these new groups into several different approaches based on where each places these new groups and how they define their unique roles in the class struggle. The first, labeled the "new working class" solution, places most, if not all, of these new groups within the traditional proletariat based on the fact that they share with this class a common position on the traditional Marxist criterion of class placement, the ownership of productive assets. While scholars using this approach do often apply additional criteria, such as the functional status of positions, to define subclasses within the proletariat, they nonetheless believe that the objective position of these groups in terms of property ownership remains the major determinant of class position, and, thus, class interests. Critics argue that the result of this strategy is a very heterogeneous group with diminished potential for collective organization and action.

A second attempt to resolve this problem is labeled the "new petite bourgeoisie" solution. Here, while property ownership remains the primary criterion for class placement, two additional variables are deemed necessary to define class positions — the political and ideological relations of position incumbents. Applying these expanded criteria, the new groups are excluded from the bourgeoisie because they do not own the means of production. Yet, despite their common position with the proletariat on the property variable, they are seen as different from that group because of their positions of domination in ideological and political relations. The solution to this dilemma taken by these theorists is to argue that they are new elements of the petite bourgeoisie because they share political and ideological interests with this class. Critics have argued that a major problem with this solution is the fact that the two groups differ in at least two senses — they occupy positions within different modes of production, and the new petite bourgeoisie does not own property whereas the old elements of this class are defined primarily in terms of this criterion.

A third approach to the problem is labeled the "new middle class" solution. This strategy also begins with the traditional criterion of position within productive relations as the major determinant of class membership, but adds an additional requirement — the sharing of a coherent social and cultural existence. When these criteria are applied to the classes of modern capitalist society, these authors argue that the new groups cannot be combined with any of the traditional classes because their interests are distinct from each of the others. The solution is to label these groups a new class in their own right and to argue that the key problem is to forge ties between this class and the proletariat. Critics, however, note that these authors artificially separate the production and reproduction roles of classes and fail to sufficiently justify the placing of heterogeneous groups within the same class position.

A fourth approach is labeled the "contradictory locations" approach. This strategy stresses the role of social relations of production in defining classes in modern capitalist society. Different social relations are defined by means of three criteria: control over money capital; control over physical capital; and authority. Applying these criteria results in three positions in which there is agreement among the three criteria — the bourgeoisie, the proletariat, and the petite bourgeoisie — and three positions in which they contradict — managers and supervisors, small employers, and semiautonomous workers. The first three are labeled "classes," but the latter three are labeled "contradictory" locations, because their interests do not correspond closely with any of the traditional classes. There are two criticisms of this perspective. First, some have argued that the use of the notion contradictory locations impedes the growth of theory in this area by avoiding addressing the shortcomings of extant Marxist theory. Others have accused this perspective of moving away from Marxist toward Weberian perspectives on class in stressing domination as a means for differentiating positions.

Subsequent research within this tradition has moved away from domination as a secondary-level defining attribute by stressing two means of exploitation (to supplement the primary criterion of ownership of the means of production) as defining criteria for class positions: possession of organization and skills assets. Application of the first of these yields three ownership classes and application of the second and third results in nine additional wage-earner classes. The use of the label "class" for the wage-earner groups mutes some of the criticisms lodged against the earlier scheme, but Wright still insists that these positions are contradictory in character because they contain a mixture of the various criteria employed. In particular, the potential roles of some of these classes in activities designed to modify the existing societal structure are also stressed. This solution has also been questioned. Specifically, the ambiguities among the various wage-earning categories have been criticized as well as the use of the organizational and skills/credentials assets as a basis for defining classes.

As seems obvious from the information presented in this chapter, research by neo-Marxists on the class structure of modern capitalist society has increased dramatically in both volume and sophistication during the past 20 years. Despite the fact that many of the issues raised by these researchers remain unresolved, there is no question that the discipline has benefitted from the debates within this tradition of research. Several indications of the value for the discipline of this research are that neo-Marxist perspectives have begun to appear within the literature of the discipline, scholars are beginning to examine the underlying assumptions of both liberal and radical theories, and, as the efforts reviewed in this chapter demonstrate, attempts are being made to integrate the two traditions, taking advantage of the benefits offered by each.[21] Speculation concerning some of the potential offered by such efforts will be presented in the final chapter.

APPENDIX: OPERATIONALIZING WRIGHT'S CLASS SCHEME

Wright uses three variables to differentiate among the various classes in his scheme: assets in the means of production, organizational assets, and skills/talent assets. The first of these both separates the various owner classes from the wage-earner classes and differentiates among the owner classes. One aspect of this asset, self-employment, separates owners from wage earners. A second aspect, the number of employees, separates the various owner classes from each other as follows: bourgeoisie — 10 or more employees; small employers — 2 to 10 employees; and petite bourgeoisie — 0 to 1 employees (Wright 1985a:150).

The wage-earner classes are then differentiated from each other based on the remaining two bases for class exploitation — organizational assets and skills/talent. The organizational asset variable is operationalized based on a "managerial location typology" that is a composite of several variables (see Table 7.1). The first is

TABLE 7.1
Operationalizing Wright's Exploitation Model

Assets in the means of production

	Self employed	*Number of employees*
Bourgeoisie	Yes	10 or more
Small Employers	Yes	2-10
Petty Bourgeoisie	Yes	0-1*
Wage-earner	No	

*Conceptually, the petite bourgeoisie should be restricted to owners of the means of production who have no employees. However, because of an unintended ambiguity in the questionnaire design, an unknown proportion of respondents who state that they have one employee really had none (i.e. they considered themselves an employee), and thus we have defined petty bourgeoisie as having no more than one employee.

Assets in organization control

	Directly involved in making policy decisions for the organization	*Supervisor with real authority over subordinates*
Managers	Yes	Yes
Supervisors	No	Yes
Non-management	No	No

Note: The actual criteria used were somewhat more complex than indicated here, since a variety of other criteria were used to deal with certain kinds of problematic cases (e.g., a respondent who claims to make policy decisions directly and yet does not have real authority over subordinates).

Assets in scarce skills/talent

	Occupation	*Education credential*	*Job autonomy*
Experts	Professionals Professors Managers	B.A. or more*	
Marginal	School teachers Craftworkers Managers Technicians	less than B.A.	
	Sales	B.A. or more	Autonomous
	Clerical	B.A. or more	Autonomous
Uncredentialled	Sales	less than B.A. or	Non-autonomous
	Clerical	less than B.A. or	Non-autonomous
	Manual non-crafts		

*In Sweden the criterion adopted here was a High School degree or more because of the differences in the timing of the expansion of university education in the two countries and the nature of the real training involved in a high school degree in Sweden.

Source: Adapted from Wright (1985a:150).

decision-making, coded as follows: does not participate in decisions; provides advice, but does not directly participate; and participates directly in decisions. The second is an authority variable, coded as follows: does not supervise or does, but has only one subordinate; supervises, but does not have either task or sanctioning authority; supervises and has task, but not sanctioning authority; and supervises with tasks and sanctioning authority. The third variable is whether or not the person is a manager in a formal organizational hierarchy. As noted in Table 7.1, this larger managerial location typology is collapsed into three values: manager, supervisor, and nonmanagement.

The second variable differentiating wage earners is skills/talent. This variable is operationalized using three variables — occupational position, education, and job autonomy. Table 7.1 presents the combinations of these variables that result in three values: experts, semicredentialed, and uncredentialed. These two variables are then cross-classified to generate the classes that were shown in Figure 7.2.

NOTES

1. Despite the fact that these radical responses are based on orthodox Marxism, it is important to note that they are not simply rote applications of orthodox Marxism to the events of the 1960s. They are also responses to the difficulties in applying that theory, based on mid-nineteenth century English capitalist society, to the unique problems of contemporary capitalist societies.

2. Attewell (1984) provides an informative discussion of the effects of academic marginality upon the theoretical efforts of these scholars. His discussion also offers an explanation for why these theories were more similar in their form and structure to the theories they challenged than was earlier radical scholarship.

3. See Keniston (1968) and Feuer (1909) for more comprehensive explanations for the source of activism among American college students during this period in its history. Ehrenreich (1989) stresses the challenge that the student movement presented for middle-class intellectuals, and chastises Feuer's analysis as being shortsighted.

4. In contrast to earlier chapters, this chapter will not provide an overview of the biographies of all the theorists discussed. This does not mean that biographical influences are unimportant for these theories; there are simply too many theorists involved in the development of this perspective. An exception to this rule will be made for the most prominent of the neo-Marxist theorists on the subject of class inequality, Erik O. Wright.

5. It is perhaps unfair to characterize the two as agreeing on this point. Certainly Smith believed that the division of labor was not only necessary but ultimately beneficial to increased productivity and to the generation of social surplus (Clarke 1982). Marx's viewpoint on the subject is somewhat more complicated. While he did believe that a division of the production process was more productive, he also assumed that the labor force would become more homogeneous during the course of capitalist development as tasks formerly performed by skilled craftsmen were increasingly automated in order to reduce the costs of production.

    6. Braverman (1974) both reviews the perspective of Marxian orthodoxy on the issue of the "deskilling" of work in capitalist society and demonstrates how this argument applies to modern, monopoly capitalist society.

    7. Wright was born in 1947; his parents were middle-class college professors. He was a college student during the 1960s at Harvard University and was a participant in the student movement during this period. He was a graduate student at the University of California during the early 1970s and belonged to the "Union of Marxist Social Scientists." He then joined the faculty of the University of Wisconsin and was tenured there and now holds the rank of Professor of Sociology. He has had a number of large research grants to support his research activities. He also muses that, while he is sure that his success has impacted his work over the years, he is not sure just how so (Wright 1985a:3).

    8. Wright (1980) offers several scholars as his examples of this perspective — including Loren (1977) and Cutler et al. (1977). I have chosen Anderson's work because he was one of the first among American sociologists to attempt to apply Marx to modern capitalist society. His perspective is quite similar to those discussed by Wright (1980).

    9. Wright (1980) notes that there are three different versions of this strategy — to stress skills and credentials as a form of property, to stress the distinction between productive and unproductive labor, and to consider all wage earners whose income is greater than the value of their labor power — as means for defining the "new" petite bourgeoisie. The example I present represents the second, and most popular, of these approaches. While Wright's (1980) overview of this approach does list a number of American scholars, I chose to discuss the work of a European scholar because his perspective is the best-developed example of this approach. See Wright's (1980) discussion for examples of American scholars using this alternative.

    10. Nicholas (1967:39–40) believes that capitalism itself creates what he calls a "surplus" class for two reasons: they are required to service and maintain capitalism, and they are necessary to consume the ever-growing surplus. He also claims that Marx's own theoretical model leads to the unavoidable conclusion that the middle class is a consequence of the rise of surplus in the maturation of capitalism despite his claim that this group would disappear during this process.

    11. Poulantzas (1975:14) also makes the point that Marx, himself, insisted that political and ideological relations are an important supplement to the economic variable in defining classes despite the fact that he has often been interpreted otherwise by subsequent analysts.

    12. In a later work (Wright 1985a) on the subject, Wright engages in an informative discussion of just how the notion of contradictory locations emerged (and changed) during the course of his work.

    13. If this is true, and it appears to be so, a statement made in Frank Parkin's (1979:25) rather polemical analysis and critique of Marxism seems to take on added significance: "Inside every neo-Marxist there is a Weberian struggling to get out."

    14. Wright's claim that skills/credentials are a basis for exploitation does seem weaker than his similar claim regarding organizational assets. It remains unclear just how such exploitation is organized and manifested in the social relations of production.

    15. Grimes (1989:459) observes that, in contrast to Wright's approach, Albert and Hahnel (1981:137–38) employ the term "redistribution" and differentiate between types of exchange relationships and exploitation. The latter refers to direct exchange relationships between parties with different bargaining powers, while the former refers to advantages of one group over another that are not the result of direct confrontation. They claim that this new concept enables them to "focus on

objectively unequal relationships when there is no immediate interface between the parties themselves."

16. Grimes (1989:459) points out that, while some of Wright's critics see his efforts to remain loyal to the fundamentals of Marxism as creating a sort of conceptual straitjacket from which he cannot escape (Burris 1988:45), others see his latest attempt at integrating the ideas of Marx and Weber to good advantage (Mann 1986:838).

17. Wright (1989) has subsequently addressed the place of women in the class structure. He notes that his original goal was to deal with the middle class within a Marxist framework. Class theories involving women and families are what he labels "mediated class relations" and add a far more complicated dimension to either class or gender alone.

18. Other critics have focused on the arbitrary nature of his divisions in the organizational skills/assets variables and the difficulties inherent in interrelating these two dimensions with traditional capitalist exploitation (Meiksins 1988; Burris 1988; Stinchcombe 1988). Wright has also been criticized for his relative lack of attention to the interrelationship between class location and class formation (Meiksins 1988; Brenner 1988). Wright (1988) has responded to these critics by clarifying and defending his choices.

19. Many of the criticisms noted above come from within conventional (i.e., non-Marxist) social science scholarship. Wright's work has also attracted commentary and criticism from neo-Marxist scholars. Many of these latter scholars (e.g., Resnick and Wolf [1987] and Kamolnick [1988]) go so far as to accuse Wright of literally "misinterpreting" Marx's basic epistemology in his efforts to use the tools of conventional ("bourgeois") sociology to update orthodox Marxism's perspective on class to advanced capitalist society. An example of the type of criticism typical of this group is Carchedi's (1987:128–29) claim that Wright's very methodology forces him to focus on individuals, not classes, and that this strategy is totally inconsistent with a Marxist analysis of social phenomena. Gouldner (1980, 1985) discusses the theoretical diversity among Marxists. See Vaillancourt (1986) for an overview and critique of the range of different epistemological, theoretical, and methodological strategies that Marxists employ in their research.

20. Attewell's (1984) analysis of the evolution of radical political economics within American social science points out that academic Marxists face constant pressure to be scientific and to conform their methodology to dominant conceptions of science and scholarship. He also shows how many contemporary radical scholars have begun to use essentially bourgeois tools to demonstrate the inferiority of dominant perspectives within the discipline and to press for paradigm modification.

21. A recent example of this trend toward greater interaction between conventional and Marxist scholarship is an article by Michael Burawoy that appeared as the lead article in the December 1990 issue of the *American Sociological Review*. The focus of the article is an assessment of the claim by many within the conventional academy that Marxism is not a science. The author examines the evolution of Marxist thought employing a model of the evolution of scientific thought derived from Lakatos (1978). Buroway argues that, in a manner similar to conventional science, Marxist thought also conforms to the model of a progressive scientific research program.

IV

SUMMARY AND CONCLUSIONS

8

SUMMARY AND CONCLUSIONS

This study has traced the careers of major theories of class inequality within twentieth-century American sociology, stressing the linkages between the nature of these theories, salient characteristics of the larger societal and disciplinary settings, and their author's biographies. This final chapter first provides an overview of the findings of the study and then uses these to address a final issue — speculation about the directions in which contemporary perspectives on class inequality within the discipline are headed.

OVERVIEW OF FINDINGS

Chapter 1 began by reviewing two existing studies on the subject of class inequality within the discipline — those by Charles Page (*Class and American Sociology* [1940]) and Milton Gordon (*Social Class in American Sociology* [1963]) — observing that, among other things, the period of coverage provided by these studies ended with the late 1950s. The study proposed an update of these studies both temporally, to the present (the early 1990s), and substantively, in light of contemporary perspectives on the organization of meta-theoretical perspectives within the discipline. A framework for the study was then developed based on the work of the scientific historian Thomas Kuhn (1970) and subsequent efforts to apply his perspective to sociology. It was concluded that, while sociology probably lacks paradigms in the sense in which Kuhn defined the term, within the discipline, nonetheless, there are reasonably well-organized perspectives that persist over time. The label "schools of thought" was chosen for these perspectives, and I argued that they are distinctive in several significant ways: each is value-laden or ideological; each has fundamentally different images of the natures of man and society; and these images lead each to different understandings of the nature

FIGURE 8.1 — A Schematic Diagram of Ideologies, Theoretical Antecedents, Schools of Thought, and Major Theorists of Class Inequality in Twentieth-Century American Sociology

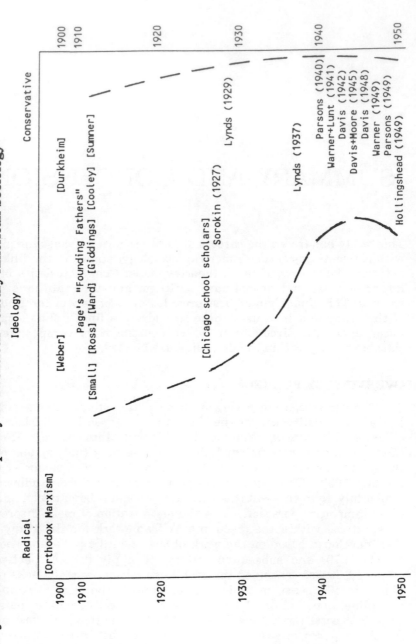

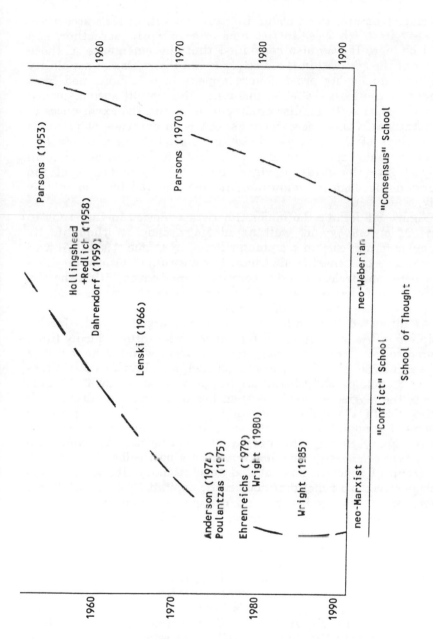

School of Thought

"Consensus" School   "Conflict" School

neo-Weberian   neo-Marxist

of social structure, the various institutions within that structure, the ways in which these institutions interact with each other, and social change. It was also concluded that the emergence of these schools of thought within the discipline and their relative popularity over time among its practitioners appear to be conditioned by a number of contextual effects, including the overall sociohistorical and ideological settings, disciplinary factors, and the experiences of their authors within these settings. Since an overview of previous applications of this framework to the discipline as a whole had already revealed its potential promise as a tool for structuring an analysis into the study of class inequality by members of the American sociological community, it was adopted for use in this study.

Figure 8.1 locates the major theorists reviewed in the study in terms of chronology as well as ideology/school of thought. Its particular format combines a similar figure by Grabb (1984:115) with observations by Lenski (1966:Chap. 1) concerning the interrelationships between ideologies and theoretical perspectives within the discipline. The following paragraphs summarize the major findings using this figure as a point of reference.

As discussed in Chapter 2, sociology emerged as a distinctive discipline in the last quarter of the nineteenth century, during times of rapid social change. Its emergence was facilitated by the fact that the perspectives of older, more established, social science disciplines such as economics and political science proved too narrow in focus to address the myriad of problems then facing society. The discipline's origins lie in the reform movement known as the Progressive Movement, and its early roots were both sacred and secular in nature. Early during the period of its origins, the American intellectual community was dominated by a particular ideology that one group of scholars has labeled "evolutionary liberalism"; this ideology stresses a belief that democratic capitalist society, while not perfect, is essentially benign and can be reformed and improved through planned social intervention. During this early period in its history, the discipline borrowed theoretical and methodological tools from other, more established, disciplines.

The review of research conducted on the perspectives of the founding fathers of the discipline by Page and Gordon revealed that, while class inequality was not a dominant interest of scholars within this early period in the discipline's history, there was, nonetheless, attention devoted to the subject. Further, it was observed that there was also variety in the ways in which these scholars dealt with the subject (Figure 8.1 attempts to visually portray the ideological diversity of these theorists). Despite the attention that scholars of the period devoted to the issue of class inequality, however, the chapter concluded that, for most of these early sociologists, the effects of class were largely superseded by those of community during the first 30 years in the discipline's history.

Part II of the book reviewed the emergence and eventual theoretical hegemony of a consensus school perspective on class inequality labeled "functionalism." The setting within which this perspective emerged was a diverse one. It was first used in research during the decade of the 1920s, a period of peace and great material prosperity for most Americans, dominated by a version of the "evolutionary liberal" ideology that was more supportive of the status quo than was the case earlier in the discipline's history. The materials in Chapter 3 revealed that Robert and Helen Lynd were the first to apply elements of the perspective in their study of "Middletown." Their study revealed that, despite the material abundance of the mid-1920s, class inequality was a significant feature of life in this American community. The chapter observed that this finding was, in many ways, divergent from both the dominant ideology of the period and the theoretical perspective that they initially employed to guide their research.

Subsequent applications of various versions of the functionalist perspective in the study of class inequality in American community life were conducted by the Lynds and by W. Lloyd Warner during the 1930s, a period of economic decline and social chaos, during which the tenets of the dominant ideology were increasingly challenged by more radical perspectives based on different assumptions about society. The Lynds' restudy of "Middletown" revealed even greater class inequalities and demonstrated the markedly different consequences of the Depression for the different classes in Middletown. In contrast, Lloyd Warner's study of "Yankee City," conducted during this same period, found a much more harmonious class structure with far fewer negative consequences. Elements of the perspective were once again applied during the 1940s, again a time of relative prosperity and renewed faith in the American political economy. Here, both Warner and August Hollingshead used the perspective to study the same community. While both found class inequalities, they differed in their interpretation of the impacts of these inequalities. Warner's interpretation of the role of "social classes" was more consistent with the emerging functionalist perspective of early twentieth-century social anthropology in that he stressed their functional role in providing motivation for the members of the population. Hollingshead, in contrast, demonstrated how differences in "social class" had positive consequences for those adolescents higher up in the class structure of the community and negative consequences for those lower down in that same structure. Hollingshead continued his focus on the negative consequences of class inequality in his study of the interrelationships between social class and mental illness in New Haven, Connecticut, during the 1950s. There, he and

his coauthor Frederick Redlich documented the negative mental
health consequences of social class position. Despite the diversity in
the particular applications of the perspective by these early scholars
(these differences are reflected in their relative positions in Figure
8.1) and the different interpretations they provided for the impacts of
class inequality, the chapter demonstrated that scholars were applying elements of the functionalist perspective in research on class
inequalities in American community settings before it was first
presented as a formal theory during the decade of the 1940s.

Chapter 3 also detailed the manners in which this first generation of scholars conceptualized and measured class. It noted that the
earliest studies derived measures that were based on respondents'
perception of the class structure of the (smaller) community, while
later efforts developed more objective, multivariate indicators in an
effort to provide indexes of class inequality applicable to/in larger
community settings.

Chapter 4 explored the process through which the functionalist
theory of inequality was formalized within the literature of the
discipline. As noted there, this process began during the decade of
the 1930s, when the American political economy with its accompanying justificatory ideology was under great stress as the result of
a worldwide Depression, and continued during the early 1940s, when
democracy itself was under challenge from fascist regimes during
World War II. The chapter presented evidence that the theory was, in
many ways, a reaction to these challenges, as its major architect,
Talcott Parsons, sought to construct an integrated social science
perspective that defended democratic capitalism from the challenges
of his day, particularly those of the only other macro theory of society
available at the time, that of Marx. It was noted that Parsons' theory,
in light of the apparent failure of the economy to provide the integration necessary to hold society together, substituted cultural values
instead. As presented in this chapter, his theory views society as a
system of institutions organized around functional requirements,
whose overall integration is based on the consensus of its members.
In contrast to Marx's theory, it stresses stability over change, evolution over revolution, and the ultimate viability of democratic capitalism over its collapse and transformation.

Within the context of this general perspective, Parsons and his
students Kingsley Davis and Wilbert Moore subsequently addressed
the issue of class inequality in several essays published beginning in
1940. Consistent with the overall theory, the functionalist theory
viewed society's class structure not as essentially disintegrative, but
as integrative. To these theorists, "social stratification" — the hierarchical ranking of different positions based on their relative statuses
in society — was an unconsciously evolved device to make sure that
the most able individuals are matched with the most important

positions within society. In other words, according to the theory, an individual is motivated to achieve based on the social approval (operationalized as the relative status accorded his or her occupational position by society) he or she receives, and the net result is the best match of individuals and positions, which, not coincidentally, is seen as ultimately functional for society as a whole. This achievement-based model was defended as integrative because it is viewed as grounded in the society's shared moral code and is thereby legitimated; it is also subject to negotiation and change over time.

Because of the theory's support for the extant system of class inequality in society, it was criticized for its conservative biases and its unrealistic model of society. As discussed in Chapter 4, one of the several reasons why this perspective became the dominant viewpoint on class inequality within the discipline for the next 20 or so years was that it mirrored so well the U.S. position of dominance in the post–World War II world, the relative prosperity and expanded opportunities for many Americans that resulted, and the atmosphere of optimism about the present and hope for the future that pervaded the society during this unique period in its history. The positioning of its major architects in Figure 8.1 attempts to visually portray the fact that, as this perspective became dominant within the discipline, there was an accompanying shift toward a more conservative position with regard to the subject of class inequality. The chapter concluded with the observation that, because the perspective's major scholars were not applying the perspective in social research, they didn't offer detailed information concerning the manners in which class could be operationalized and measured.

Chapter 5 discussed and analyzed efforts within the discipline to conceptualize and measure various forms of class inequality beginning during the late 1940s. These measures were shown to be the result of several trends both within American society as a whole and within the discipline during this time period. Societal level influences included the rapid urbanization (and suburbanization) of society that began during the early 1950s, and the growing integration of its parts into a national whole. The materials reviewed in the chapter revealed that this trend rendered many of sociology's earlier approaches obsolete, and scholars rapidly had to adapt their theories, methods, and the overall image of the discipline to a new and constantly changing national reality. The discipline's reaction to these new challenges was the acceptance of the functionalist perspective as its dominant perspective; the institutionalization of the image of the sociologist-as-scientist as the dominant role model for its practitioners; the adoption of survey research as the dominant research design; and the assumption of an expanding role in providing inputs to policymakers at the national level. As discussed in Chapter 5, the result was that researchers interested in class inequality during this period in the nation's history increasingly turned their attention to measuring class within the confines of survey research, focused at the national level.

Mirroring functionalism's choice of occupation as the most salient dimension of an individual's position in society, the major approaches discussed in the chapter sought some means for developing a scale for use in research that ranked occupations into a hierarchy. There were two major approaches taken in this task: the first focused its attention on respondents' rankings of the relative prestige of occupations; the second, on the relative socioeconomic status of occupations. The chapter concluded that the relative popularity of these approaches within the discipline had (and has) less to do with their relative technical sophistication (which was shown to be flawed in various ways), than with their compatibility with functionalist theory's unique perspective on class inequality, its resonance with the overall societal context, and its resulting popularity within the discipline.

The chapters in Part III detailed the emergence of various conflict alternatives to the functionalist theory of class inequality that have appeared in the literature since the late 1950s. A review of the overall societal context within which these theories were constructed revealed that the decade of the 1960s was an important turning point in American history. Sometime during the late 1950s and early 1960s, the country reached its peak as the world's leading political and economic power. While the decade of the 1950s was one of expanding opportunity and declining inequalities for many Americans, by the early 1960s, these trends were either halted or reversed and various groups that had not shared (or were no longer sharing) in the prosperity of the early post–World War II years were becoming increasingly vocal about their disadvantaged positions. By the latter part of that decade, an increasingly unpopular war in Vietnam was inhibiting governmental efforts to address the problems of the disadvantaged and undermining its image both domestically and internationally. During the decade of the 1970s, a fiscal crisis began in earnest as increased energy prices, growing domestic expenditures, and escalating world-system maintenance commitments clashed with an economy whose pace of growth had begun to slow because of declining productivity and increasing competition from Western Europe and Japan.

As a response to these events, over the course of this period, the collective mood in the United States became increasingly pessimistic as faith in both the political system and the institutions of society (particularly the economy) began to decline. The materials noted that, within the intellectual community, a number of important books were published that challenged the collective wisdom of the 1950s on a number of subjects. For sociology, this decade marked the beginning of a long period of introspection, as the dominant theory, and its methodological and institutional trappings, were examined and criticized and alternative perspectives were proposed.

Chapter 6 examined the first challenges to the functionalist perspective on class inequality. As shown there, each of these scholars began by criticizing the theory for its conservative ideology, for its implicit consensus image of social harmony, for its viewpoint on the nature and roles of classes in society, and for its failure to deal adequately with the issue of social change. These scholars then contrasted this image with those implicit in more radical scholarship, and they constructed theories of class inequality that sought to correct the biases of both the older traditions by combining elements derived from each into a new synthetic perspective that was based around a model of society that explicitly stressed conflict as the normal state of affairs. These first challenges to functionalism's theory of class inequality were labeled "neo-Weberian," because their major theoretical inspiration came from the work of Max Weber.

As presented in the chapter, Ralf Dahrendorf's (1959) theory took as its unit of analysis Weber's "imperatively coordinated association" (ICA), postulating that conflict within such groups over the distribution of authority is an endemic feature of life in what he called postcapitalist society. He defines classes as locations within ICAs that occupy different positions with regard to the possession or nonpossession of authority; class conflict is viewed as conflict over the distribution of authority within ICAs; and social change is seen as any alteration in the pattern of the distribution of authority within ICAs. The chapter concluded that, given that individuals belong to multiple ICAs and their positions within them don't necessarily overlap, the potential for polarized conflict is muted in Dahrendorf's theory. The author, himself, emphasizes this point even further when he postulates that, because class conflict is institutionalized and regulated within postcapitalist society, there is a bias toward evolutionary rather than revolutionary change.

The second "neo-Weberian" theory of class inequality reviewed in the chapter was that of Gerhard Lenski (1966). His theory's major focus is on the question of how a society's resources are distributed. Lenski argues that inequality in the distribution of resources tends to increase as a society's surplus increases, and the major variable that determines the amount of surplus available is the society's level of technological development. Within a given society, Lenski's theory postulates that differential power determines both the distribution of these surpluses (privilege) and the prestige they bestow on its possessors. The theory defines classes as groups with similar amounts of power, privilege, and prestige, and class systems as competing systems of classes based on different principles of distribution. Because of the complex nature of the class structure in his theory,

Lenski postulates that class conflict is typically more fragmented than focused, when compared with radical theories on the subject. Further, the materials in the chapter showed that Lenski also contends that, because power tends to become institutionalized in advanced industrial society, many of the negative consequences of class inequality are mediated by the political institution.

Following its presentation of these theories, Chapter 6 then contrasted them with both functionalist and Marxist theories of class inequality and concluded that, while they are different from both, they are far more similar to the former theory than to the latter. This finding was initially viewed as somewhat ironic given that each theorist had sought to distance himself from the functionalist theory. The explanation offered by the chapter for the similarities between their theories and the functionalist theory was that these authors, to a great extent, shared with the functionalists similar backgrounds within early post–World War II Western capitalist society, and, as a result, their theoretical orientations were based on a similar faith in the overall vitality of capitalist society.

The materials in Chapter 7 dealt with a second group of conflict theories of class inequality — "neo-Marxist" theories. In contrast to the "neo-Weberian" theorists discussed in Chapter 6, who explicitly sought (even if they did not reach) a middle ground between the two extremes of functionalism and Marxism, this chapter revealed that these theorists focused more narrowly on the task of updating Marx's perspective, based on the capitalist society of the mid-nineteenth century, to the realities of late-twentieth-century capitalist society. This orientation did not necessarily mean that these theories didn't make use of other perspectives — they did, particularly those of Weber. What it meant was that they remained more consistent with Marx's original formulation than other conflict-based theories.

The chapter began with a discussion of the reemergence of radical social science in the United States, beginning in the 1960s, using Baran and Sweezy's *Monopoly Capital* (1966), a radical critique of both classical liberal and Marxist theories of capitalist society, as an example. It then turned to a discussion of research within the Marxist tradition on the subject of class inequality within capitalist society. This discussion began with an overview of the work of Marx himself on the subject and concluded that any attempt to update his perspective to the realities of contemporary capitalist society has to address two key issues — the continued heterogeneous nature of the class systems of modern capitalist society, particularly the growth and continued vitality of the middle classes, and the lack of working-class militancy. It was observed that most theorists who addressed these issues have acknowledged the impact of the transformation from "competitive" to "monopoly" capitalism as an important determinant of the different nature of the class structure of modern capitalist society when compared to that of Marx's time. According to the materials developed in Chapter 7, the questions these modern theorists typically addressed included: where to place these new classes within the class structure of modern capitalist society, what to call them, and how to describe their roles as forces for change within the society. The chapter then reviewed various approaches to responding to these questions, concluding with an overview of the innovative work of Erik O. Wright. This author, in contrast to Marx, who postulated only one "relation of exploitation" between classes (i.e., the ownership of productive property), a two-class model of society, and working-class militancy, argues that, within modern capitalist society, there are three such "relations of exploitation," one major and two subordinate: ownership of productive property (the major); organizational exploitation (subordinate); and skills/credentials exploitation (subordinate). Cross-classifying these exploitation bases, Wright derives a scheme for describing the class structure of advanced capitalist society that contains a total of 12 classes. The chapter also points out that Wright views other groups in addition to workers, particularly managers and state bureaucrats, as potential alternative sources for militancy and social change. The chapter concluded by summarizing the reactions of critics to his model, observing that he has been criticized by both radical and liberal class theorists — by the former for moving too far away from Marxist orthodoxy, and by the latter for remaining too closely confined by its conceptual straightjacket.

MODERN THEORIES OF CLASS INEQUALITY: DIVERGENCE OR CONVERGENCE?

Keeping in mind the findings of the study, one final issue remains to be addressed: where are modern American perspectives on class inequality headed? Are the various perspectives becoming less alike, or are they converging toward some sort of grand synthesis as Lenski suggested in 1966? The materials reviewed in this study demonstrate that the answer to this question depends heavily upon the period in the discipline's history about which it is asked. The freehand lines in Figure 8.1 represent an attempt to summarize visually the parameters of the discipline's treatment of the subject in terms of the major dimensions of this study — the ideologies and schools of thought of the major theorists. As portrayed there, American scholarship on class inequality during the early years of the discipline's history was ideologically diffuse, covering much of the continuum that Lenski (1966) defined as encompassing Western thought on the subject historically (a trend toward divergence).

Beginning during the decade of the 1930s, the discipline's parameters on the subject narrowed as the functionalist perspective

was first applied in U.S. community settings, was then formalized by
Talcott Parsons and his students, and finally became hegemonic
within the discipline. As demonstrated in Part III, this perspective
was constructed as a defense of the status quo of early twentieth-
century and, later, post–World War II capitalist society and, thus,
explicitly rejected more radical perspectives on the subject, particularly that of Marx. As the consensus school of thought became
increasingly hegemonic within sociology, the discipline's treatment
of class inequality became increasingly status quo oriented and more
narrow in focus. This is depicted in Figure 8.1 by the shift to the right
in the freehand lines as well as by the narrowing of the distance
between them (a trend toward convergence).

Beginning during the decade of the 1960s, a number of scholars
began to react against the ideological biases and narrow focus of
functionalist theory. Both Ralf Dahrendorf (1959) and Gerhard
Lenski (1966), after contrasting the functionalist theory with more
radical perspectives in order to demonstrate the biases of both, sought
to synthesize elements of two traditions into a middle ground between
the two extremes. The fact that their own theoretical orientations
prevented their perspectives from moving sufficiently far away from
the functionalist perspective to suit some of their critics should not
detract from what their efforts did accomplish for the discipline.
First, their research provided an important stimulus to a reawakening of interest in the issues surrounding class inequality in
American society. Second, their explicit adoption of a conflict model
of society opened the door for the discipline's consideration of more
radical perspectives on the subject, and this served to widen the
parameters of the debate within the discipline once more (a trend
toward divergence). Not only this, but the widespread acceptance of
many of their indictments of the functionalist perspective began an
overall shift within the discipline toward the left ideologically in the
debate over the issue of class inequality. One result of this ideological
shift was that, by the 1970s "structural functionalism has been
largely supplanted as a serious alternative to Marx in the current
literature on social inequality" (Grabb 1984:116).[1] This shift in the
discipline's focus is visually portrayed by the freehand lines in
Figure 8.1.

With the decline of the functionalist viewpoint on class inequality, and the shift to the left on the ideological spectrum that resulted,
current debate on the subject within American sociology is now
increasingly confined to various conflict school perspectives on the
subject. This suggests additional convergence, but there is still sufficient diversity within the various subschools of conflict theory (i.e.,
neo-Weberian and neo-Marxist) that the debate both within and
between these subschools remains lively. The question remains,
based on the information provided by my overview of research on the

subject within the discipline, can anything further be said about the current state of affairs with regard to the convergence-divergence issue?

My interpretation of the evidence suggests that the answer to this question is yes. With the demise of the functionalist perspective on class inequality, the divergence that began with the challenges that Dahrendorf and Lenski made to functionalism and the resulting opening up of the discipline's parameters to the perspectives of modern radical scholars reached its peak and has reversed itself; there is now evidence of a growing convergence between neo-Marxist and neo-Weberian scholars on the issue of class inequality. While much of contemporary research by neo-Weberians is by scholars outside American sociology (i.e., Parkin [1972, 1979] and Giddens [1981]), and, thus, beyond the parameters of this study,[2] it does seems clear that, among neo-Marxist scholars within the country (Erik O. Wright in particular), movement away from orthodox Marxism's more polarized viewpoint on class toward a synthetic position that incorporates key elements of Weber's perspective on the subject has begun. The fact that Wright's movement toward a synthesis between the ideas of Marx and Weber has been applauded by scholars more sympathetic to Weber's viewpoint, but widely condemned by many of his fellow neo-Marxists, is a testament to the ideological character of the debate that surrounds the issue of class inequality within American sociology. In fact, as discussed in Chapter 7, some of the furor over his incorporation of Weber's notion of authority as a secondary variable defining class position in his first class scheme led to his moving back in his second scheme toward a set of criteria more consistent with the exploitation posturing of orthodox Marxism. However, as also noted in that chapter, one of his critics has observed that this movement back toward Marxian orthodoxy was accomplished more by definitional fiat than by an actual change of position. While this evidence of convergence is by no means conclusive, it is suggestive of the potential direction in which the debate concerning class inequality is moving in late twentieth-century American sociology.

In conclusion, whether or not my interpretation of a convergence between or among the various perspectives is accurate, it seems clear that interest in class inequality is, once again, moving up in the discipline's hierarchy of subjects that require attention, and, therefore, that the issues discussed in this study will continue to be of concern to the American sociological (and social science) community. I believe that a strategy that stresses the embeddedness of relative levels of disciplinary interest in the subject within larger sociohistorical, ideological, disciplinary, and biographical settings facilitates a more complete understanding of its career as a topic of interest within the discipline.

NOTES

1. While Grabb's (1984) conclusion applies to theoretical debates within the discipline concerning the issue of class inequality, it is interesting that researchers continue to apply those measures of relative class (status or socioeconomic status) inequality that depend heavily on the functionalist perspective for their theoretical rationale. There are a couple of potential explanations for this practice. The first is that contemporary researchers continue to embrace parts of the functionalist perspective on class inequality while rejecting others. For example, many researchers continue to visualize the class structure present in American society as comprised of a large number of classes arranged in a hierarchy. At the same time, these researchers are increasingly likely to question the functionalist assumption that the nature of the interrelationships among these classes is necessarily harmonious. A second potential explanation for the continued use of these measures is that they are more likely than neo-Marxist alternatives either to be explicitly included in extant data sets or the variables necessary to calculate them are more likely to present there. It will be interesting to see what effect the wider availability of these latter measures will have on researcher preferences in the future.

2. In retrospect, my initial decision to limit the book's attention to U.S. perspectives on class inequality had different impacts on the various theories discussed in the book. While the theoretical inspiration for the perspectives discussed in Parts I and II were certainly of European origin, the unique U.S. setting and the tremendous growth of the discipline in the United States resulted in the development of U.S. perspectives on class inequality in relative isolation from contemporary European scholarship during the periods in question. For the later post–World War II period — the time of the development of the conflict perspectives discussed in Part III — the growing similarities among all advanced capitalist societies, the increasing theoretical sophistication of European scholarship on class inequality, and its wider availability to U.S. audiences, made it more difficult to exclude at least some European scholarship from the book. For these reasons, I made the decision to include explicit discussion of the perspectives of two European scholars, Dahrendorf and Poulantzas, whose impacts on U.S. scholarship were too important to ignore. At the same time, I decided to exclude others, most notably Parkin and Giddens, whose direct influence on U.S. perspectives on social inequality has not been as great to date. Despite my decision, there is evidence that the influence of these latter scholars on U.S. perspectives is growing (Grabb, 1984).

REFERENCES

Abrahamson, Mark, Ephraim Mizrucki, and Carlton Hornung. *Stratification and Mobility*. New York: Macmillan, 1976.

Albert, Michael, and Robin Hahnel. "A Ticket to Ride: More Locations on the Class Map." In *Between Labor and Capital*, ed. P. Walker. Boston: South End Press, 1979.

____. *Marxism and Socialist Theory*. Boston: South End Press, 1981.

Alexander, Jeffrey. *Twenty Lectures: Sociological Theory Since World War II*. New York: Columbia University Press, 1987.

____. "Parsons' 'Structure' in American Sociology." *Theoretical Sociology* 6 (Spring 1988): 96–102.

Alford, Robert, and Roger Friedland. *Powers of Theory*. Cambridge: Cambridge University Press, 1985.

Allen, Frederick. *Only Yesterday*. New York: Harper and Brothers, 1931.

____. *Since Yesterday: The Nineteen-Thirties in America*. New York: Bantam Books, 1940.

Anderson, Charles. *The Political Economy of Social Class*. Englewood Cliffs, N.J.: Prentice-Hall, 1974.

Aronowitz, Stanley. "The Professional-Managerial Class or Middle Strata." In *Between Labor and Capital*, ed. P. Walker. Boston: South End Press, 1979.

Attewell, Paul A. *Radical Political Economy Since the Sixties*. New Brunswick, N.J.: Rutgers University Press, 1984.

Bain, Reid. "Trends in American Sociological Theory." In *Trends in American Sociology*, ed. S. Chapin. New York: Harper and Brothers, 1929.

Bannister, Robert C. *Sociology and Scientism: The American Quest for Objectivity, 1880–1940*. Chapel Hill: University of North Carolina Press, 1987.

Baran, Paul A., and Paul M. Sweezy. *Monopoly Capital*. New York: Monthly Review Press, 1966.

Becker, Gary. *Human Capital and the Personal Distribution of Income*. Ann Arbor: University of Michigan Press, 1967.

Bell, Daniel. *The End of Ideology*. New York: Free Press, 1960.

Bendix, Rinehart, and Seymour Lipset. *Class, Status and Power*. 2d. ed. New York: Free Press, 1966.

Berle, A., and G. Means. *The Modern Corporation and Private Property*. New York: Macmillan, 1934.

Bernard, Jesse. "The History and Prospects of Sociology in the United States." In *Trends in American Sociology,* ed. S. Chapin. New York: Harper and Brothers, 1929.

Bernard, Thomas. *The Consensus-Conflict Debate: Forms and Content in Social Theories.* New York: Columbia University Press, 1983.

Blau, Peter, and Otis Duncan. *The American Occupational Structure.* New York: John Wiley, 1967.

Block, Fred. *Revising State Theory.* Philadelphia: Temple University Press, 1987.

Blumberg, Paul. *Inequality in an Age of Decline.* New York: Oxford University Press, 1980.

Boskoff, Alvin. *The Mosaic of Sociological Theory.* New York: Crowell, 1972.

Bourricaud, Francois. *The Sociology of Talcott Parsons.* Chicago: University of Chicago Press, 1981.

Boyd, Monica, and Hugh McRoberts. "Women, Men, and Socioeconomic Indices: An Assessment." In *Measures of Socioeconomic Status: Current Issues,* ed. Mary Powers. Boulder, Colo.: Westview Press, 1982.

Braverman, Harry. *Labor and Monopoly Capital: The Degradation of Work in the Twentieth Century.* New York: Monthly Review Press, 1974.

Brenner, Johanna. "Work Relations and the Formation of Class Consciousness." *Critical Sociology* 15 (1988): 83–89.

Bryant, C. "Kuhn, Paradigms and Sociology." *British Journal of Sociology* 26 (1975): 354–59.

Burawoy, Michael. "Marxism as Science: Historical Challenges and Theoretical Growth." *American Sociological Review* 55 (1990): 775–93.

Burris, Val. "New Directions in Class Analysis." *Critical Sociology* 15 (1988): 57–66.

Caplow, Theodore. *The Sociology of Work.* Minneapolis: University of Minnesota Press, 1950.

Carchedi, G. "Class Politics, Class Consciousness, and the New Middle Class." *The Insurgent Sociologist* (1987): 111–30.

Carlton, Eric. *Ideology and the Social Order.* Boston: Routledge and Kegan Paul, 1977.

Carson, Rachel. *Silent Spring.* Boston: Houghton-Mifflin, 1962.

Carter, Alan. *Marx: A Radical Critique.* Brighton: Wheatsheaf Books, 1988.

Chinoy, Ely. "Review of W. L. Warner and P. Lunt, *Social Class in America,*" *Canadian Journal of Economics and Political Science* 14 (1950): 256–62.

____. "Review of Milton Gordon, *Social Class in American Sociology.*" *American Sociological Review* 24 (February 1959): 115–16.

Clarke, Simon. *Marx, Marginalism and Modern Sociology.* London: Macmillan, 1982.

Cohen, Jean, and Dick Howard. "Why Classes?" In *Between Labor and Capital,* ed. P. Walker. Boston: South End Press, 1979.

Cohen, Joshua, and Joel Rogers. *On Democracy: Toward a Transformation of American Society.* New York: Penguin Books, 1983.

Cohen, Percy. *Modern Sociological Theory.* New York: Basic Books, 1968.

Coser, Lewis. "American Trends." In *A History of Sociological Analysis,* ed. T. Bottomore and R. Nisbet. New York: Basic Books, 1978.

Counts, George. "The Social Status of Occupations: A Problem in Vocational Guidance." *School Review* 33 (1925): 16–27.

Crowder, N. David. "A Critique of Duncan's Stratification Research." *Sociology* 8 (1974): 19–45.

Cutler, A., B. Hindess, P. Hirst, and A. Hussain. *Marx's Capital and Capitalism Today,* Vol. 1. London: Routledge and Kegan Paul, 1977.

Dahl, Robert A. *Dilemmas of Pluralist Democracy*. New Haven, Conn.: Yale University Press, 1982.

Dahrendorf, Ralf. "Toward a Theory of Social Conflict." *Journal of Conflict Resolution* II (1958): 170–83.

____. *Class and Class Conflict in Industrial Society*. Stanford, Calif.: Stanford University Press, 1959.

____. "Review of Gerhard E. Lenski, *Power and Privilege*." *American Sociological Review* 31 (October 1966): 714–18.

____. *Conflict After Class: New Perspectives on the Theory of Social and Political Conflict*. London: Longmans, Green, 1967a.

____. *Society and Democracy in Germany*. Westport, Conn.: Greenwood Press, 1967b.

____. *Life Chances*. London: Weidenfeld and Nicholson, 1979.

____. *Europe's Economy in Crisis*. New York: Holmes and Meier, 1982.

Davie, Maurice. "The Pattern of Urban Growth." In *Studies in the Science of Society*, ed. George Murdock. New Haven, Conn.: Yale University Press, 1937.

Davis, Kingsley. "A Conceptual Analysis of Stratification." *American Sociological Review* 7 (1942): 309–21.

____. "Review of W. L. Warner and P. Lunt, *The Status System of a Modern Community*." *American Journal of Sociology* 48 (January 1943): 511–13.

____. *Human Society*. New York: Macmillan, 1948.

Davis, Kingsley, and Wilbert Moore. "Some Principles of Stratification." *American Sociological Review* 10 (1945): 242–49.

De Waal Malefijt, Annemarie. *Images of Man: A History of Anthropological Thought*. New York: Alfred Knopf, 1974.

Doyle, Alan, and Wolfgang Opitz. "A Reappraisal of Socioeconomic Status Measurement: An Analysis Comparing the Nam/Powers SES and the Duncan SEI." Paper presented at the annual meetings of the Southwestern Sociological Association, Houston, 1985.

Duncan, Otis. "A Socioeconomic Index for All Occupations." In *Occupations and Social Structure*, ed. A. Reiss. Glencoe, Ill.: Free Press, 1961.

Durkheim, Emile. *The Division of Labor in Society*. New York: Macmillan, 1933.

Eckberg, Douglas, and Lester Hill. "The Paradigm Concept and Sociology: A Critical Review." *American Sociological Review* 44 (December 1979): 925–37.

Edwards, Alba. "Social-Economic Groups of the United States." *Quarterly Journal of the American Statistical Association*, 15 (1917): 643–61.

____. "A Social-Economic Grouping of the Gainful Workers of the United States." *Journal of the American Statistical Association* 28 (1933): 377–87.

____. *A Social-Economic Grouping of Gainfully Employed Workers of the United States, 1930*. Washington, D.C.: U.S. Government Printing Office, 1938.

____. *Comparative Occupational Statistics for the United States, 1870 to 1940*. Washington, D.C.: U.S. Government Printing Office, 1943.

Ehrenreich, Barbara. *Fear of Falling*. New York: Pantheon Books, 1989.

Ehrenreich, Barbara, and John Ehrenreich. "The Professional-Managerial Class." In *Between Labor and Capital*, ed. P. Walker. Boston: South End Press, 1979.

Eisenstadt, S. N. *The Form of Sociology: Paradigms and Crises*. New York: John Wiley, 1976.

Eulau, Heinz. "Review of Gerhard E. Lenski, *Power and Privilege*." *American Political Science Review* 61 (June 1967): 482–85.

Fallers, Lloyd. "Review of Gerhard E. Lenski, *Power and Privilege*." *American Sociological Review* 31 (October 1966): 718–19.

Faris, Robert. "Review of A. B. Hollingshead, *Elmtown's Youth*." *American Journal of Sociology* 56 (1950): 93–96.

Featherman, David, and Philip Hauser. "Prestige or Socioeconomic Scales in the Study of Occupational Achievement." *Sociological Methods and Research* 4 (1976): 402–22.

Featherman, David, and Gillian Stevens. "A Revised Socioeconomic Index of Occupational Status: Application in the Analysis of Sex Differences in Attainment." In *Measures of Socioeconomic Status: Current Issues*, ed. Mary Powers. Boulder, Colo.: Westview Press, 1982.

Feuer, Lewis. *The Conflict of Generations*. New York: Basic Books, 1969.

Ford, H. "The Pretensions of Sociology." *American Journal of Sociology* 15 (July 1909): 96–104.

Ford, Kathleen, and Judith Gehret. "Occupational Status Scores from the 1980 Census Public Use Samples." Mimeographed paper, Department of Population Dynamics, Johns Hopkins University, n.d.

Friedan, Betty. *The Feminine Mystique*. New York: Dell, 1963.

Friedrichs, Robert. *A Sociology of Sociology*. New York: Free Press, 1970.

Galbraith, John K. *The Affluent Society*. New York: New American Library, 1958.

Giddens, Anthony. *The Class Structure of Advanced Societies*, 2d ed. London: Hutchinson, 1981.

Goldschmidt, Walter. "Social Class in America — A Critical Review." *American Anthropologist* 52 (1950): 483–98.

Gordon, David. *Theories of Poverty and Underemployment*. Lexington, Mass.: D.C. Heath, 1972.

Gordon, Milton. *Social Class in American Sociology*. New York: McGraw-Hill, 1963.

Gouldner, Alvin. *The Coming Crisis in Western Sociology*. New York: Basic Books, 1970.

____. *The Two Marxisms*. New York: Seabury Press, 1980.

____. *Against Fragmentation*. New York: Oxford University Press, 1985.

Grabb, Edward. *Social Inequality: Classical and Contemporary Theories*. Toronto: Holt, Rinehart and Winston of Canada, 1984.

Grandjean, B., and F. Bean. "The Davis-Moore Theory and Perceptions of Stratification: Some Relevant Evidence." *Social Forces* 54 (1975): 166–80.

Grimes, Michael D. "The Functionalist Perspective on Social Inequality: Some Neglected Theoretical and Conceptual Roots." *Sociological Inquiry* 58 (Spring 1988a): 182–93.

____. "'External' vs. 'Social Constructionist' Models in the Sociology of Knowledge: Alternative or Complementary Approaches?" *Sociological Inquiry* 58 (Winter 1988b): 344–60.

____. "Class and Attitudes toward Structural Inequalities: An Empirical Comparison of Key Variables in Neo- and Post-Marxist Scholarship." *Sociological Quarterly* 30 (1989): 441–63.

Gusfield, Joseph, and Michael Schwartz. "The Meaning of Occupational Prestige: Reconsideration of The NORC Scale." *American Sociological Review* 28 (1963): 265–71.

Hall, Oswald. "Review of W. L. Warner, *Social Class in America*." *American Journal of Sociology* 56 (1951): 369.

Harrington, Michael. *The Other America: Poverty in the United States*. New York: Penguin Books, 1962.

____. *The New American Poverty*. New York: Holt, Rinehart and Winston, 1984.

Haug, Marie. "An Assessment of Inequality Measures." In *Issues in Social Inequality*, ed. G. Thielbar and S. Feldman. Boston: Little, Brown, 1972.

Haug, Marie, and Marvin Suchman. "The Indiscriminant State of Social Class Measurement." *Social Forces* 49 (1971): 549–62.

Hauser, Philip, and David Featherman. *The Process of Stratification: Trends and Analyses.* New York: Academic Press, 1977.

Hays, H. R. *From Ape to Angel.* New York: Alfred Knopf, 1965.

Hinkle, Roscoe. *Founding Theory of American Sociology, 1881–1915.* Boston: Routledge and Kegan Paul, 1980.

Hinkle, Roscoe, and Gisela Hinkle. *The Development of Modern Sociology.* Garden City, N.Y.: Doubleday, 1954.

Hodge, Robert, Paul Siegel, and Peter Rossi. "Occupational Prestige in the United States, 1925–1963." *American Journal of Sociology* 70 (1964): 286–302.

Hofstadter, Richard. *The Age of Reform.* New York: Alfred Knopf, 1955.

Hollingshead, August. "Trends in Community Development." Ph.D. diss. University of Nebraska, 1935.

———. *Elmtown's Youth.* New York: John Wiley, 1949.

Hollingshead, August, and Frederick Redlich. *Social Class and Mental Illness.* New York: John Wiley, 1958.

Holmwood, J., and A. Stewart. "The Role of Contradictions in Modern Theories of Social Stratification." *Sociology* 7 (May 1983): 234–54.

Holton, Gerald. "On the Role of Themata in Scientific Thought," *Science* 188 (1975): 328–34.

Horan, Patrick. "Is Status Attainment Research Atheoretical?" *American Sociological Review* 43 (August 1978): 534–41.

Horowitz, Irving. *C. Wright Mills: An American Utopian.* New York: Free Press, 1983.

Horton, John. "Order and Conflict Theories of Social Problems." *American Journal of Sociology* 70 (May 1966): 701–13.

Huaco, George. "A Logical Analysis of the Davis-Moore Theory of Stratification." *American Sociological Review* 28 (October 1963): 801–4.

———. "The Functionalist Theory of Stratification: Two Decades of Controversy." *Inquiry* 9 (1966): 215–40.

———. "Ideology and General Theory: The Case of Sociological Functionalism." *Comparative Journal of Society and History* 28 (January 1986): 34–54.

Hunt, Douglas. "Review of Robert and Helen Lynd, *Middletown.*" *The Annals* 146 (November 1929): 271–72.

Johnson, Paul. *Modern Times: The World from the Twenties to the Eighties.* New York: Harper and Row, 1983.

Jones, Robert. "The New History of Sociology." *Annual Review of Sociology* 9 (1983): 447–69.

Kahl, Joseph. "Review of Gerhard E. Lenski, *Power and Privilege.*" *Sociological Review* 15 (March 1967): 82–84.

Kamolnick, Paul. *Classes: A Marxist Critique.* New York: General Hall, 1988.

Keniston, Kenneth. *Young Radicals.* New York: Harcourt, Brace and Jovanovich, 1968.

Kennedy, Paul. *The Rise and Fall of the Great Powers.* London: Unwin Hyman, 1988.

Kerbo, Harold. *Social Stratification and Inequality.* New York: McGraw-Hill, 1983.

Kinloch, Graham. *Ideology and Contemporary Sociological Theory.* Englewood Cliffs, N.J.: Prentice-Hall, 1981.

Kornhauser, Ruth. "The Warner Approach to Social Stratification." In *Class, Status, and Power,* ed. R. Bendix and S. Lipset. New York: Free Press, 1953.

Kriesberg, Louis. "The Bases of Occupational Prestige." *American Sociological Review* 27 (1962): 236–44.

____. *Social Inequality*. Englewood Cliffs, N.J.: Prentice-Hall, 1979.

Kuhn, Thomas. *The Structure of Scientific Revolutions*, 2d ed. Chicago: University of Chicago Press, 1970.

____. "Second Thoughts on Paradigms." In *The Structure of Scientific Theories*, ed. F. Suppe. Urbana: University of Illinois Press, 1974.

Kuklick, Henrika. "A 'Scientific Revolution': Sociological Theory in the United States, 1930–1945." *Sociological Inquiry* 43 (1972): 3–22.

Kuper, Adam. *Anthropologists and Anthropology*. London: Allen Lane, 1973.

Lakatos, Imre. *The Methodology of Scientific Research Programmes*. Cambridge: Cambridge University Press, 1978.

Langham, Ian. *The Building of British Social Anthropology*. Boston: D. Reidel, 1981.

Lee, Albert M. *Sociology for Whom?* New York: Oxford University Press, 1978.

Lenski, Gerhard. *Power and Privilege*. New York: McGraw-Hill, 1966.

Lewis, Michael. *The Culture of Inequality*. Amherst: University of Massachusetts Press, 1978.

Lipset, Seymour. "Social Stratification and Social-Class Analysis." In *Consensus and Conflict: Essays in Political Sociology*, ed. S. M. Lipset. New York: Transaction Books, 1985.

Lipset, Seymour, and Rinehart Bendix. "Social Status and Social Structure: A Reexamination of Data and Interpretations: I." *British Journal of Sociology* 2 (June 1951): 150–68.

Lockwood, David. "Some Remarks on 'The Social System.'" *British Journal of Sociology* 7 (June 1956): 134–46.

Lodahl, J., and G. Gordon. "The Structure of Scientific Fields and the Functioning of University Graduate Departments." *American Sociological Review* 37 (1972): 57–72.

Lopreato, Joseph, and Lionel Lewis. "An Analysis of Variables in the Functional Theory of Stratification." *Sociological Quarterly* 4 (1963): 312–20.

Loren, Charles. *Classes in the United States*. Davis, Calif.: Cardinal Publishers, 1977.

Lynd, Robert. *Knowledge for What?* Princeton, N.J.: Princeton University Press, 1940.

____. "Review of August B. Hollingshead, *Elmtown's Youth*." *American Sociological Review* 14 (1949): 560–1.

Lynd, Robert, and Helen Lynd. *Middletown: A Study in Modern American Culture*. New York: Harcourt, Brace and World, 1929.

____. *Middletown in Transition: A Study in Cultural Conflicts*. New York: Harcourt, Brace, 1937.

Madge, John. *The Origins of Scientific Sociology*. New York: Free Press, 1962.

Manchester, William. *The Glory and the Dream*. Boston: Little, Brown, 1974.

Maney, Ann. "Review of A. Hollingshead and F. Redlich, *Social Class and Mental Illness*." *Social Forces* 38 (March 1960): 271–73.

Mann, Michael. "Classes, Swedes and Yanks." *Contemporary Sociology* 15 (November 1986): 837–39.

Masterman, M. "The Nature of a Paradigm." In *Criticism and the Growth of Knowledge*, ed. I. Lakatos and A. Musgrave. Cambridge: Cambridge University Press, 1970.

Matras, Judah. *Social Inequality, Stratification, and Mobility*. Englewood Cliffs, N.J.: Prentice-Hall, 1975.

Matthews, Fred. *Quest for an American Sociology: Robert Park and the Chicago School*. Montreal: McGill University Press, 1977.

Mayer, Kurt B. "Review of Gerhard E. Lenski, *Power and Privilege*." *Social Forces* 45 (October 1966): 283–84.

Mazur, Allan. "The Littlest Science." *American Sociologist* 3 (August 1968): 195–200.

Meiksins, Peter. "A Critique of Wright's Theory of Contradictory Class Locations." *Critical Sociology* 15 (1988): 73–82.

Miller, S. and E. Mishler. "Social Class, Mental Illness, and American Psychiatry." *Milbank Memorial Fund Quarterly* 37 (April 1959): 174–99.

Mills, C. Wright. "Review of W. Warner and P. Lunt, *The Social Life of a Modern Community*." *American Sociological Review* 7 (1942): 263–71.

———. *The Power Elite.* New York: Oxford University Press, 1956.

———. *The Sociological Imagination.* New York: Oxford University Press, 1959.

Mullins, Nicholas. *Theories and Theory Groups in Contemporary American Sociology.* New York: Harper and Row, 1973.

Myers, Jerome. "Note on the Homogeneity of Census Tracts." *Social Forces* 32 (May 1954): 364–66.

Nader, Ralph. *Unsafe at Any Speed.* New York: Grossman, 1966.

Nam, Charles, and Mary Powers. *The Socioeconomic Approach to Status Measurement.* Houston: Cap and Gown Press, 1983.

Nam, Charles, and Walter Terrie. "Measurement of Socioeconomic Status from United States Census Data." In *Measures of Socioeconomic Status: Current Issues,* ed. Mary Powers. Boulder, Colo.: Westview Press, 1982.

Nicholas, Martin. "Proletariat and Middle Class in Marx: Hegelian Choreography and the Capitalist Dialectic." *Studies on the Left* 7 (January/February 1967): 22–47.

Noble, David. "The PMC: A Critique." In *Between Labor and Capital,* ed. P. Walker. Boston: South End Press, 1979.

North, Cecil, and Paul Hatt. "Jobs and Occupations: A Popular Evaluation." *Opinion News* 9 (1947): 3–13.

Oberschall, Anthony. *The Establishment of Empirical Sociology.* New York: Harper and Row, 1972.

O'Connor, James. *The Fiscal Crisis of the State.* New York: St. Martin's Press, 1973.

Page, Charles. *Class and American Sociology: From Ward to Ross.* New York: Dial Press, 1940.

Parkin, Frank. *Class Inequality and Political Order.* London: Paladin, 1972.

———. "Social Stratification." In *A History of Sociological Analysis,* ed. T. Bottomore and R. Nisbet. New York: Basic Books, 1978.

———. *Marxism and Class Theory: A Bourgeois Critique.* London: Tavistock, 1979.

Parsons, Talcott. *The Structure of Social Action.* New York: McGraw-Hill, 1937.

———. "An Analytical Approach to the Theory of Social Stratification." *American Journal of Sociology* 45 (1940): 841–62.

———. *Essays in Sociological Theory.* Glencoe, Ill.: Free Press, 1949.

———. *The Social System.* Glencoe, Ill.: Free Press, 1951.

———. "A Revised Analytical Approach to the Theory of Social Stratification." In *Class, Status and Power,* ed. R. Bendix and S. Lipset. New York: Free Press, 1953.

———. *Societies: Evolutionary and Comparative Perspectives.* Englewood Cliffs, N.J.: Prentice-Hall, 1966.

———. "On Building Social System Theory: A Personal History." *Daedalus* 99 (1970a): 826–81.

———. "Equality and Inequality in Modern Society or Social Stratification Revisited." *Sociological Quarterly* 40 (Spring 1970b): 13–72.

Pease, John, William Form, and Joan Rytina. "Ideological Currents in American Stratification Literature." *American Sociologist* 5 (May 1970): 127–37.

Pfautz, Harold, and Otis Duncan. "A Critical Evaluation of Warner's Work in Community Stratification." *American Sociological Review* 15 (1950): 205–15.

Polenberg, Richard. *One Nation Divisible*. New York: Penguin, 1980.

Poulantzas, Nicos. *Classes in Contemporary Capitalism*. London: New Left Books, 1975.

Powers, Mary, ed. *Measures of Socioeconomic Status: Current Issues*. Boulder, Colo.: Westview Press, 1982.

Powers, Mary, and Joan Holmberg. "Occupational Status Scores: Changes Introduced by the Inclusion of Women." *Demography* 15 (1978): 183–204.

Reiss, Albert. *Occupations and Social Status*. Glencoe, Ill.: Free Press, 1961.

———. "Sociology: The Field." *International Encyclopedia of the Social Sciences* 15 (1967): 1–23.

Reissman, Leonard. *Class in American Society*. Glencoe, Ill.: Free Press, 1959.

———. "Review of Gerhard E. Lenski, *Power and Privilege*." *Political Science Quarterly* 82 (September 1967): 466–67.

Report of the National Advisory Commission on Civil Disorders. New York: Bantam Books, 1968.

Reser, Richard. "Review of A. B. Hollingshead, *Elmtown's Youth*." *Social Forces* 28 (1949): 211–12.

Resnick, Stephen, and Richard Wolff. *Knowledge and Class*. Chicago: University of Chicago Press, 1987.

Ritzer, George. "Sociology: A Multiple Paradigm Science." *American Sociologist* 10 (August 1975): 156–67.

———. *Sociology: A Multiple Paradigm Science*. Boston: Allyn and Bacon, 1980.

———. *Sociological Theory*. New York: Alfred Knopf, 1983.

Rivers, William H. R. *Social Organization*. New York: Alfred Knopf, 1924.

Rocher, G. *Talcott Parsons and American Sociology*. New York: Barnes and Noble, 1975.

Roemer, John. "New Directions in the Marxian Theory of Exploitation and Class." *Politics and Society* 3 (1982): 253–88.

Rose, David, and Gordon Marshall. "Constructing the (W)Right Classes," *Sociology* 20 (August 1986): 440–55.

Rossides, Daniel. *The American Class System*. Boston: Houghton-Mifflin, 1976.

Sargent, Lyman. *Contemporary Political Ideologies*, 5th ed. Homewood, Ill.: Dorsey Press, 1981.

Savage, Steven. *The Theories of Talcott Parsons*. New York: St. Martin's Press, 1980.

Schaeffer, Robert. "A Critique of the 'New Class' Theorists: Towards a Theory of Working Class in America." *Social Praxis* 4 (1–2, 1976–77): 75–99.

Schaeffer, Robert, and James Weinstein. "Between the Lines." In *Between Labor and Capital*, ed. P. Walker. Boston: South End Press, 1979.

Schlesinger, Arthur, Jr. *The Crisis of the Old Order, 1919–1933*. Boston: Houghton-Mifflin, 1957.

———. *The Coming of the New Deal*. Boston: Houghton-Mifflin, 1958.

Schwendinger, Herman, and Julia Schwendinger. *The Sociologists of the Chair*. New York: Basic Books, 1974.

Shaw, Clifford. *Delinquency Areas*. Chicago: University of Chicago Press, 1929.

Sherman, Howard. *Foundations of Radical Political Economy*. Armonk, N.Y.: M. E. Sharpe, 1983.

Siegel, Paul. "Prestige in the American Occupational Structure." Ph.D. diss. University of Chicago, 1971.

Simpson, Richard. "A Modification of the Functional Theory of Stratification." *Social Forces* 35 (1956): 130–39.

Sjoberg, Gideon. "Review of Milton Gordon, *Social Class in American Sociology*." *American Journal of Sociology* 64 (May 1959): 647–48.

Skocpol, Theda. *States and Social Revolutions*. New York: Cambridge University Press, 1979.

Small, Albion. "The Subject Matter of Sociology." *American Journal of Sociology* 10 (November 1904): 281–98.

____. "Fifty Years of Sociology in the United States." *American Journal of Sociology* 21 (1916): 721–864.

Smith, Don. "Review of Milton Gordon, *Social Class in American Sociology*." *Social Forces* 37 (May 1959): 371–72.

Smith, Mapheus. "Proposal for Making a Scale of Occupational Status." *Sociology and Social Research* 20 (1935): 40–49.

____. "An Empirical Scale of Prestige Status of Occupations." *American Sociological Review* 7 (1943): 185–92.

Sorokin, Pitirim. *Social Mobility*. New York: Harper and Brothers, 1927.

____. "Review of Charles Page, *Class and American Sociology*." *American Sociological Review* 5 (August 1940): 662.

Steel, Ronald. *Pax Americana*. New York: Viking Press, 1967.

Stevens, Gillian, and Joo Cho. "Socioeconomic Indexes and the New 1980 Census Occupational Classification Scheme." *Social Science Research* 14 (1985): 142–68.

Stinchcombe, Arthur. "Some Empirical Consequences of the Davis-Moore Theory of Stratification." *American Sociological Review* 28 (October 1963): 805–8.

____. "Education, Exploitation, and Class Consciousness." *Critical Sociology* 15 (1988): 67–71.

Svalstoga, Kaare. *Social Differentiation*. New York: David McKay, 1965.

Szymanski, Albert. "A Critique and Extension of the Professional-Managerial Class." In *Between Labor and Capital*, ed. P. Walker. Boston: South End Press, 1979.

Tausky, Curt. "Parsons on Stratification: An Analysis and Critique." *Sociological Quarterly* 6 (1965): 128–38.

Thernstrom, Stephan. "Review of Gerhard E. Lenski, *Power and Privilege*." *American Sociological Review* 31 (October 1966): 719–20.

Tiryakian, Edward. "The Significance of Schools in the Development of Sociology." In *Contemporary Issues in Theory and Research*, ed. W. Snizek, E. Fuhrman, and M. Miller. Westport, Conn.: Greenwood Press, 1979.

Trieman, Donald. *Occupational Prestige in Comparative Perspective*. New York: Academic Press, 1977.

Tumin, Melvin. "Some Principles of Stratification: A Critical Analysis." *American Sociological Review* 18 (August 1953): 387–93.

____. "Competing Status Systems." In *Labor Commitment and Social Change in Developing Areas*, ed. A. Feldman and W. Moore. New York: Social Science Research Council, 1960.

Turner, Jonathan. "From Utopia to Where?: A Strategy for Reformulating the Dahrendorf Conflict Model." *Social Forces* 52 (1973): 236–44.

____. *The Structure of Sociological Theory*. Homewood, Ill.: Dorsey Press, 1982.

Vaillancourt, Pauline. *When Marxists Do Research*. New York: Greenwood Press, 1986.

van den Berghe, Pierre. "Dialectic and Functionalism: Toward a Theoretical Synthesis." *American Journal of Sociology* 28 (1963): 695–705.

Vanfossen, Beth. *The Structure of Social Inequality*. Boston: Little, Brown, 1979.

Vidich, Arthur, and Stanford Lyman. *American Sociology: Worldly Rejections of Religion and Their Directions*. New Haven, Conn.: Yale University Press, 1985.

Vincent, George. "The Development of Sociology." *American Journal of Sociology* 10 (September 1904): 145–60.

Wacquant, Loic. "Heuristic Models in Marxian Theory." *Social Forces* 64 (1985): 17–45.

Wallerstein, Immanuel. *The Modern World System.* New York: Academic Press, 1976.

Warner, W. Lloyd. *A Black Civilization: A Study of an Australian Tribe.* New York: Harper and Row, 1937.

____. *Social Class in America.* Chicago: Social Science Research Associates, 1949a.

____. *Democracy in Jonesville.* New York: Harper and Row, 1949b.

Warner, W. Lloyd, and Paul Lunt. *The Social Life of a Modern Community.* New Haven, Conn.: Yale University Press, 1941.

Weber, Max. *The Theory of Social and Economic Organization.* Trans. A. M. Henderson and T. Parsons. New York: Free Press, 1947.

Weingart, Peter. "Beyond Parsons? A Critique of Ralf Dahrendorf's Conflict Theory." *Social Forces* 48 (1969): 151–65.

Wesolowski, Wlodzimierz. "Some Notes on the Functional Theory of Stratification." In *Class, Status and Power,* ed. R. Bendix and S. Lipset. 2d ed. New York: Free Press, 1966.

Westheus, Kenneth. "Class and Organization as Paradigms in Social Science." *American Sociologist* 11 (February 1976): 38–49.

Wilson, William J. *The Declining Significance of Race.* Chicago: University of Chicago Press, 1978.

____. *The Truly Disadvantaged.* Chicago: University of Chicago Press, 1987.

Wright, Erik O. *Class, Crisis and the State.* London: New Left Books, 1978.

____. "Intellectuals and the Class Structure of Capitalist Society." In *Between Labor and Capital,* ed. P. Walker. Boston: South End Press, 1979a.

____. *Class Structure and Income Determination.* New York: Academic Press, 1979b.

____. "Varieties of Marxist Conceptions of Class Structure." *Politics and Society* 9 (1980): 333–70.

____. *Classes.* London: Verso, 1985a.

____. *The Comparative Study of Class Structure and Class Consciousness: Public Use Codebook.* Ann Arbor, Mich.: Survey Research Center, 1985b.

____. "Exploitation, Identity, and Class Structure: A Reply to My Critics." *Critical Sociology* 15 (1988): 91–110.

____. "Women in the Class System." *Politics and Society* 17 (1989): 35–66.

Wright, Erik O., and Bill Martin. "The Transformation of the American Class Structure, 1960–1980." *American Journal of Sociology* 93 (July 1987): 1–29.

Wrong, Dennis. "The Functional Theory of Stratification: Some Neglected Considerations." *American Sociological Review* 24 (1959): 772–82.

Zorbaugh, Harvey. *The Gold Coast and the Slum.* Chicago: University of Chicago Press, 1929.

INDEX

ABOUT THE AUTHOR

MICHAEL D. GRIMES has held faculty positions at both the University of Houston and Louisiana State University, where he currently holds the rank of Associate Professor in the Department of Sociology. His research interests lie within the general area of societal inequality. Grimes has published a number of articles on various facets of this subject within sociological and other social science media including the *American Sociological Review, Social Forces, Sociological Inquiry,* and *The Sociological Quarterly.*